CREATING Keepsakes
SCRAPBOOK MAGAZINE

A TREASURY OF FAVORITES

Award-Winning
SCRAPBOOK PAGES

Presenting Over 800 Inspiring Scrapbook Pages and Tips
from Winners of the *Creating Keepsakes*
Scrapbook Hall of Fame for 2003, 2002, and 2001

PRODUCED EXCLUSIVELY FOR LEISURE ARTS

Creating Keepsakes

Founding Editor	Lisa Bearnson
Co-founder	Don Lambson
Editor-in-Chief	Tracy White
Special Projects Editor	Leslie Miller
Copy Editor	Kim Sandoval
Editorial Assistants	Joannie McBride, Fred Brewer
Administrative Assistant	Michelle Bradshaw
Art Director	Brian Tippetts
Designer	Joleen Hughes
Production Designers	Just Scan Me!, Exposure Graphics
Publisher	Mark Seastrand
Media Relations	Alicia Bremer, 801/364-2030
Web Site Manager	Emily Johnson
Assistant Web Site Editor	Sarah Thatcher
Production Manager	Gary Whitehead
Business Sales Manager	Tara Green
Business Sales Assistants	Jacque Jensen, Melanie Cain
Advertising Sales Manager	Becky Lowder
Advertising Sales, West Coast	Debbie Hanni, 801/583-1043
Advertising Sales, West Central	Barbara Tanner, 801/942-6080
Advertising Sales, East Central	Jenny Grothe, 801/377-1428
Advertising Sales, East Coast	RaNay Winter, 801/796-7037
Wholesale Accounts	800/815-3538
	Donna Hair, stores A–G, and outside of U.S., ext. 235
	Victoria James, stores H–R, ext. 226
	Kristin Schaefer, stores S–Z (except "Scr"), ext. 250
	Sherrie Burt, stores starting with "Scr," ext. 244
	Kim Robison, distributor accounts, ext. 251

PRIMEDIA
Consumer Magazine & Internet Group

Vice President, Group Publisher	David O'Neil
Circulation Director	Lisa Harris
Associate Circulation Director	Darcy Cruwys
Circulation Manager	Sara Gunn
Promotions Manager	Stephanie Michas
Business Manager	Laurie Halvorsen

PRIMEDIA, Inc.

Chairman	Dean Nelson
President & CEO	Kelly Conlin
Vice-Chairman	Beverly C. Chell

PRIMEDIA Consumer Media and Magazine Group

President & CEO	David G. Ferm
Chief Operating Officer	Daniel E. Aks
EVP, Consumer Marketing/Circulation	Steve Aster
SVP, Chief Financial Officer	David P. Kirchhoff
SVP, Mfg., Production & Distribution	Kevin Mullan
SVP, Finance	Kevin Neary
SVP, Chief Information Officer	Debra C. Robinson
SVP, Consumer Marketing	Bobbi Gutman
SVP, Human Resources	Kenneth P. Slivken
VP, Manufacturing	Gregory Catsaros
VP, Business Development	Jasja de Smedt
VP, Direct Response & Classified Advertising	Carolyn N. Everson
VP, Single Copy Sales	Thomas L. Fogarty
VP, Manufacturing Budgets & Operations	Lilia Golia
VP, Database / e-Commerce	Suti Prakash

PRIMEDIA Outdoor Recreation and Enthusiast Group

SVP, Group Publishing Director	Brent Diamond
VP, Comptroller	Stephen H. Bender
VP, Marketing and Internet Operations	Dave Evans
VP, Human Resources	Kathleen P. Malinowski

SUBSCRIPTIONS

To subscribe to *Creating Keepsakes* magazine or to change the address of your current subscription, call or write:

Phone: 888/247-5282
International: 760/745-2809
Fax: 760/745-7200

Subscriber Services
Creating Keepsakes
P.O. Box 469007
Escondido, CA 92046-9007

Some back issues of *Creating Keepsakes* magazine are available for $5 each, payable in advance.

CORPORATE OFFICES

Creating Keepsakes is located at 14901 Heritagecrest Way, Bluffdale, UT 84065. Phone: 801/984-2070. Fax: 801/984-2080. Home page: *www.creatingkeepsakes.com*.

Award-Winning Scrapbook Pages
Hardcover ISBN# 1-57486-407-6
Softcover ISBN# 1-57486-423-8
Library of Congress Control Number 2004102015

Published by Leisure Arts, Inc., 5701 Ranch Drive, Little Rock, Arkansas 72223, 501-868-8800. *www.leisurearts.com*. Printed in the United States of America.
Vice President and Editor-in-Chief: Sandra Graham Case
Executive Director of Publications: Cheryl Nodine Gunnells
Senior Publications Director: Susan White Sullivan
Director of Designer Relations: Debra Nettles
Licensed Product Coordinator: Lisa Truxton Curton
Special Projects Director: Susan Frantz Wiles
Special Projects Designer: Lisa Laney-Hodges
Associate Editors: Steven M. Cooper, Susan McManus Johnson, and Kimberly L. Ross
Senior Art Operations Director: Jeff Curtis
Art Imaging Director: Mark Hawkins
Imaging Technicians: Stephanie Johnson and Mark Potter
Publishing Systems Administrator: Becky Riddle
Publishing Systems Assistants: Clint Hanson, John Rose, and Chris Wertenberger
Senior Director of Public Relations and Retail Marketing: Stephen Wilson

Publisher: Rick Barton
Vice President, Finance: Tom Siebenmorgen
Director of Corporate Planning and Development: Laticia Mull Dittrich
Vice President, Retail Marketing: Bob Humphrey
Vice President, Sales: Ray Shelgosh
Vice President, National Accounts: Pam Stebbins
Director of Sales and Services: Margaret Reinold
Vice President, Operations: Jim Dittrich
Comptroller, Operations: Rob Thieme
Retail Customer Service Manager: Stan Raynor
Print Production Manager: Fred F. Pruss

AWARD-WINNING SCRAPBOOK PAGES

20

99

133

106

The Scrapbook Hall of Fame
CLASS OF 2001

276

277

be inspired to create your own keepsakes

SINCE I JOINED *Creating Keepsakes* magazine a little more than seven years ago, I've seen a lot of changes. Scrapbooking has grown from a largely regional pastime to the fastest growing hobby in America. It's no wonder. There are as many reasons to scrapbook as there are scrapbookers. Over and over, people tell me they love scrapbooking because it preserves their memories for future generations, it's a creative outlet, and it's fun.

I see hundreds of scrapbook pages every month. They remind me why I'm passionate about this hobby. For every scrapbook page I see, I know there's a scrapbook artist who has a story to tell. To honor the creators of these inspiring pages, we organized the

Creating Keepsakes Hall of Fame, inducting 25 new members each year. These artists consistently inspire us with their talented design ability, striking photography and heartfelt journaling.

In the pages of this book, we've gathered layouts from Hall of Fame inductees from the past three years. I think you'll find something you can learn from each one of these talented women. Look for ways you can transform their design ideas, techniques and journaling themes into your own scrapbook pages. With their inspiring ideas fresh in your mind, you'll be well on your way to creating your own masterpieces. ❤

Tracy

ALISON BEACHEM, 2003

TAUNYA DISMOND, 2002

With inspiring ideas fresh in your mind, you'll be well on your way to creating your own masterpieces.

JULIE TURNER, 2001

IDEAS TO NOTE: Kelly included stickers from a London souvenir book, torn pieces of a souvenir bag, an English pound note, a Westminster Abbey brochure, postcards and souvenir tickets on her layout. Kelly used the British pound note as a pocket to display the ticket stub and travel map.

"London Tags"

Supplies *Vellum:* Memory Lane; *Tags:* Avery; *Fiber:* On the Surface; *Rubber stamp:* Hero Arts; *Stamping ink:* VersaColor, Tsukineko; Fresco, Stampa Rosa; Ancient Page, Clearsnap, Inc.; *Clips:* Clipiola; *Other:* Archival Mist.

"I love square and rectangle punches.

They're perfect for cutting out parts of

photos to emphasize little details."

KELLY ANDERSON • TEMPE, AZ

"I love collecting unique images and ephemera for my scrapbook pages," shares Kelly. "Adding mementos and souvenirs adds so much interest and reflects the memories." Kelly's husband, Tony, likes to lend a hand, too. "Tony has developed an eye for all the little treasures I like to collect for my scrapbook projects," she says. "I love that he supports my passion for art."

"Paris"

Supplies *Alphabet rubber stamps:* PSX Design; *Stamping ink:* Source unknown; *Tag:* American Tag Co.; *Fiber:* On the Surface; *Brass tag:* Stampers Anonymous; *Rubber stamps:* Stampers Anonymous ("Paris" and "Remember"); *Photo corners:* Boston International; *Rectangle frame and brads:* Memory Lane Paper Co.; *Paris notecard:* Mudlark Papers, Inc.; *Other:* Chipboard, foam core, container lids, charms, envelope buttons, silver wax, domino piece, transparency sheet, postage cards, brochures, map, ticket stub and travel ephemera.

"Scottish Tartans"

Supplies *Page accents:* Fresh Cuts, EK Success; *Tags:* American Tag Co.; *Wood and Celtic knot buttons:* JoAnn's Stores; *Hemp:* Westrim Crafts; *Chalk:* Craf-T Products; *Colored pencils:* Memory Pencils, EK Success; *Other:* Fabric, postcards and Archival Mist.

IDEA TO NOTE: Kelly sewed plaid fabric onto the small tags to emphasize the variety of Scottish tartans.

"Gardens of Versailles"

Supplies *Wood letter:* Walnut Hollow; *Colored pencils:* Memory Pencils, EK Success; *Pen:* Zig Millennium, EK Success; *Punch:* Family Treasures; *Square frame:* Ink It!; *Fleur-de-lys studs:* Memory Lane Paper Co.; *Gold-leaf flakes:* Amy's Magic Foil Flakes; *Flowers and ribbon:* Elegant Accents.

IDEA TO NOTE: Kelly placed flower accents behind the sheer ribbon.

CREATING A GOLD-LEAFED TITLE

Gold-leafing is perfect for dressing up a title. Here, gold-leaf flakes in a variety of hues add a touch of class to wood letters. This look is easy to create with minimal supplies. Here's how:

TIP*:
Before you begin, sprinkle the gold-leaf flakes into a plastic sandwich container. They'll be easier to work with and won't create a mess.

FOLLOW THESE STEPS:

◆ Dab Duo adhesive on each letter and allow to dry (about 5–10 minutes).

◆ Press foil flakes onto your finger and dab over each letter.

MATERIALS:

☐ Wood letters (Walnut Hollow)

☐ Gold-leaf flakes

☐ Duo Embellishing Adhesive (USArtQuest)

—*by Kelly Anderson*

"Napoleonic Paris"

Supplies *Specialty papers:* Memory Lane Paper Co.; Mudlark Papers, Inc.; *Alphabet rubber stamps:* Hero Arts, PSX Design; *Stamping ink:* ColorBox, Clearsnap, Inc.; *Frames and studs:* Memory Lane Paper Co.; *Gold embossing powder:* PSX Design; *Paper clip:* Clipiola; *Colored pencils:* Memory Pencils, EK Success; *Photo corners:* Boston International; *Other:* Archival Mist and mini-antique postcards.

"Classic London"

Supplies *Wood letters:* Walnut Hollow; *Frame:* Source unknown; *Gold-leafing pen:* Krylon; *Square punch:* Marvy Uchida; *Other:* Black foam core, gold mat board and postcards.

THE MANY WAYS TO
SKATE
BOARD

You are such a funny boy
skateboarding. You tell me you are
'almost' skateboarding. You won't
stand up on it... too wobbly. You do
stand up but you bend down and hold
onto the front of it. These are
pictures of you and all your many
ways of skateboarding. You are
very cautious but once you get the
confidence in something, you are very
daring. Spring 2002

ACCORDING TO
DALLON

"Skateboard"

Supplies *Patterned paper:* Patchwork
Paper Designs;
Alphabet rubber stamps:
Hero Arts, PSX Design; *Computer
font:* Unknown, downloaded from
www.twopeasinabucket.com;
Stamping ink: Tsukineko;
Other: Charm.

"My favorite products are charms. Available in

so many sizes and themes, they're perfect for

adding a little detail to a layout."

ALISON BEACHEM • SAN DIEGO, CA

When it comes to scrapbooking, Alison finds inspiration everywhere,

from magazines and web sites to clothing and catalogs. Her favorite

technique? Paper tearing. "I use tearing on almost every page,"

shares Alison. "If a design idea doesn't come to me, I start by tearing one

of the papers I've chosen, then I work the layout around that design."

"Funny Boy"

Supplies *Patterned paper:* Carolee's Creations; *Fibers:* Adornments, EK Success; *Computer font:* 2Peas Fairy Princess, downloaded from *www.twopeasinabucket.com*; *Square eyelet:* Making Memories; *Perle cotton:* DMC.

"Wild Child"

Supplies *Handmade paper:* Graphics; *Alphabet rubber stamps:* The Missing Link; *Computer font:* 2Peas Sleigh Ride, downloaded from *www.twopeasinabucket.com*; *Stamping ink:* Tsukineko; *Embroidery floss:* DMC.

"Boogie Boards and Castles with Moats"

Supplies *Typewriter-key cutouts:* Limited Edition; *Computer font:* 2Peas Tuxedo, downloaded from *www.twopeasinabucket.com*; *Alphabet rubber stamps:* The Missing Link; *Spritzer and pens:* The Color Workshop; *Eyelets:* Making Memories.

"Play Ball"

Supplies *Mesh paper:* Magenta; *Alphabet rubber stamps:* PSX Design; *Charms:* Embellish It!; *Computer font:* Unknown, downloaded from *www.two-peasinabucket.com*; *Perle cotton:* DMC; *Brads:* American Tag Co.; *Other:* Twine.

USING TEXTURED PAPER

Textured paper comes in so many colors and, well … textures! Its subtle look can add visual interest to a layout without detracting from the photos or the story you want to tell. Try these ideas for incorporating texture into your layouts:

- Tear a strip of paper and adhere it under a photo. It's one of the easiest ways to incorporate texture into your design.
- Depending on the texture of the paper, you can run it through your printer and print a title or your journaling directly on it. If the paper is thin, adhere it to a sheet of cardstock, then send it through the printer.
- Use a large block of textured paper on your layout as an accent. Add stitching or eyelets to the edges to give the piece more definition.
- Create your own textured paper. Choose a few of your favorite colors of cardstock and spray both sides of each sheet with water (or run both sides under the faucet). Crumple the paper into a tight ball, then flatten it out. With your iron on low heat, press the paper until all of the water is removed. You can use the finished paper any way you choose.

With textured paper, the creative options are endless. Grab a sheet of paper and start experimenting!

—*by Alison Beachem*

"Tuck"

Supplies *Embossed paper:* Papers by Jennifer; *Letter stickers:* Sonnets, Creative Imaginations; *Computer font:* 2Peas Flea Market by Sharon Soneff, downloaded from *www.twopeasinabucket.com*; *3-D lacquer:* Crystal Lacquer; *Metal photo corners:* Making Memories; *Embroidery floss:* DMC.

faye morrow bell

2003

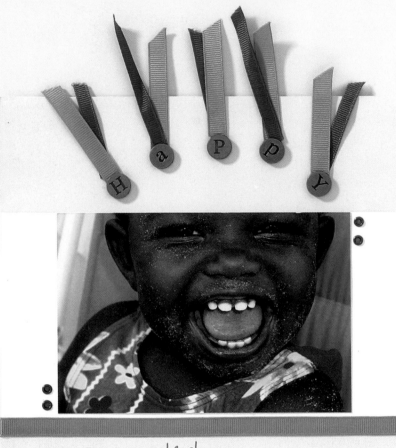

"Happy"

Supplies *Computer fonts:* Garamouche, Impress Rubber Stamps; 2Peas Cookie Dough, downloaded from *www.twopeasinabucket.com*; Ordner, Spellbound and Texas Hero, downloaded from the Internet; *Eyelet letters:* Making Memories; *Ribbon:* C.M. Offray & Son; *Eyelets:* Magic Scraps.

IDEA TO NOTE: The ribbons extend beyond the top of the cardstock, enhancing the sense of joy and exuberance.

We went to Tyler's beach today,
we walked among the dunes.
We filled our PAILS with seashells
that held such happy tunes.
We watched the SEAGULLS and cooled our toes
in frothy waves of blue.
We went to Tyler's beach today...
what a pleasant thing to do!

"My favorite product is anything that's silver and metal. I naturally gravitate toward cool color palettes, and silver is the perfect enhancement for the greens and grays I use so often."

FAYE MORROW BELL • CHARLOTTE, NC

Faye is a visual person, so it's no surprise she's inspired by product packaging and advertising. She's also energized by learning about other artists' studios. "I have books about studios and save magazine articles that feature artists in their work spaces," explains Faye. "I get a real charge out of 'imagining the possibilities.'"

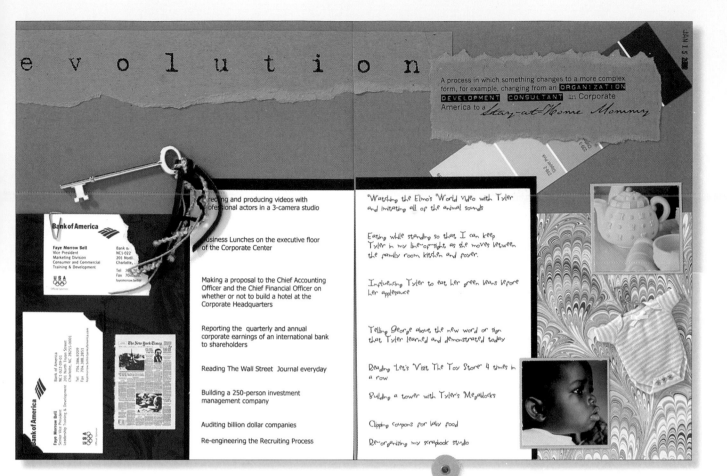

"Evolution"

Supplies *Patterned paper:* Frances Meyer; *Computer fonts:* Batik, Ordner Normal, Texas Hero, Yippy Skippy, News Gothic and Tahoma, downloaded from the Internet; *Skeleton key:* Hillman; *Sticker:* Jolee's Boutique, Sticko; *Newspaper accent:* Joshua's Lifestyle Collectibles; *Stamping ink:* Superior; *Photo corners:* Canson; *Other:* Business card, fibers, paint chips, paper clip and date stamp.

IDEAS TO NOTE: This layout compares Faye's daily activities as a senior vice president at an international financial institution to her activities as a stay-at-home mom. The activities are paired so you can read an activity on the left side of the page, then read the corresponding activity on the right-hand page.

USING FONTS EFFECTIVELY

I've always been intrigued with words and lettering. My dining room wallpaper is patterned with the viticultural profiles of wines in a script font. And our family's names are stenciled in black in a sans serif font in our living room.

I look for fonts and lettering techniques that will enhance my layout but not dominate the focal point. I want all of the design elements to work together to create a pleasing layout. Like scrapbooking in general, the great thing about font selection is that there are few rights and wrongs. It's more a matter of appropriateness. Following are a few things to consider when selecting fonts:

❶ **Consider the mood and feel of the layout.** Fonts communicate both on a conscious and an unconscious level. Read and compare the two sentences below:

I am happy.

I am happy.

At a conscious level, both of these sentences are true. But on an unconscious level, does one sentence *feel* more believable than the other?

❷ **Consider whether the font will be used for content or graphic lettering.** Content lettering refers to the title and journaling. The purpose of content lettering is to communicate information. Always select a font that is easy to read for your content.

Graphic lettering refers to text items other than titles and journaling, such as quotes, definitions and word blocks. Its purpose it to accent your artwork, just as you would with stickers, punches or eyelets.

❸ **Limit the number of different fonts you use on a layout.** I try to use no more than two or three fonts on one layout. Your lettering is an element of your artwork, but it shouldn't dominate the design.

Remember that selecting fonts is more art than science. So have fun!

—*Faye Morrow Bell*

"Elmo"

Supplies *Patterned paper:* Hot Off The Press; *Computer font:* Garamouche, Impress Rubber Stamps; *Eyelet letters:* Making Memories.

IDEAS TO NOTE: Faye inked the edges of each mat with a brown Zig Writer, then sandpapered all the edges and corners. She stained the tag with walnut ink.

"Carnival"

Supplies *Computer fonts:* Antique Type, Jungle Juice and Graverplate, downloaded from the Internet; *Feather:* FiberCraft; *Craft wire:* Darice; *Eyelets:* Making Memories; *Corner rounder:* Creative Memories; *Pen:* Zig Writer, EK Success; *Walnut ink:* Postmodern Design; *Other:* Chinese coin, tag, hemp cord and sandpaper.

When the Sesame Street segment, ELMO'S WORLD, is broadcast…it becomes just that in our house…"Elmo's World"! Tyler loves ELMO and time stands still for her as she hangs on to his every word! Aunt Kendra gave Tyler the "Thought of the Day Elmo" for Christmas. When you press ELMO'S right hand, he sings the theme song. When you press his left hand, he discusses his 'thought of the day' (which changes every 24 hours). Elmo's favorite topics include bananas, bugs, hair, hats, balls and fish! In addition to a couple of other plush ELMOS, Tyler also has Elmo books, videotapes and ELMO socks.

CARNIVAL

PHILLIPSBURG - SINT MAARTEN - DUTCH WEST INDIES

Jump-Up Parade

What a treat! Our fifth anniversary wedding trip to St. Martin/St. Maarten coincided with the annual Carnival celebration in Phillipsburg. Carnival begins just after Easter and lasts 17 days and nights. The celebration is wonderful display of the French, Dutch and West Indian cultures found on the island.

Each evening, there is a "jump-up" parade along Front Street (the main street) in Phillipsburg. The four-mile long parade includes floats, live bands and brightly costumed dancers. The streets are filled with the sounds of calypso, soco and other steel band sounds. And not to be missed is Carnival Village with more than 100 food booths featuring conch, johnny cakes and other island specialties.

Spring 2000

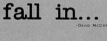

"Toys"

Supplies *Patterned paper:* Anna Griffin; *Computer fonts:* Texas Hero and Graverplate, downloaded from the Internet; *Rubber stamp and stamping ink:* Stampin' Up!; *Ribbon:* C.M. Offray & Son; *Square punch:* Marvy Uchida; *Charm:* The Card Connection; *Photo corners:* Canson.

IDEA TO NOTE: Faye stamped the bookmark with an inkpad, inked the edges with a pen, and mounted it using pop dots.

Books fall open --- You fall in...
-DAVID McCORD

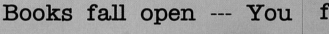

How A Baby Grows
Baby Angels
Pretty Brown Face
Mr. Brown Can Moo, Can You?
Sometimes I Like to Curl Up in a Ball
Let's Visit the Toy Store
Let's Visit the Pet Store
The Cheerios Play Book
The Ear Book
The Eye Book
The Big Book of Beautiful Babies
The Counting Book
God Bless
Ten, Nine, Eight
My Name is Elmo
Colors
Grover
What I See in the City
Harold and the Purple Crayon

And my how Tyler has fallen! Like most toddlers, you love books and reading. A few of your favorite titles are shown here. But you're also very interested in the letters of the alphabet and how the letters come together to create words. I introduced you first to the letter "A". You identified it on your own in Wal-Mart at 16 months old! At nineteen months, you recognize and identify the letters 'A, B, C, O, T, Y and S'. You love to get the newspaper in the morning and "read" it to me. That means scanning it with your eyes and fingers and saying aloud the 7 letters that you recognize. You also read letters in magazines, on television, billboards and anywhere else you see them!

"Books Fall Open"

Supplies *Computer fonts:* Texas Hero, Graverplate and Typist, downloaded from the Internet; Arial, Microsoft Word: *Rubber stamps:* Stampin' Up, Inkadinkadoo; *Stamping ink:* VersaMark, Tsukineko; *Stickers:* Jolee's Boutique, Sticko; *Bead chain:* Hillman; *Corner rounder:* Creative Memories; *Newspaper accents:* Joshua's Lifestyle Collectibles; *Pen:* Zig Writer, EK Success; *Pop dots:* All Night Media; *Other:* Fiber.

"Dream"

Supplies *Textured paper:* Books by Hand; *Mesh:* Magenta; *Rubber bands and Scrabble tiles:* Ink It!; *Rubber stamps:* PSX Design; *Stamping ink:* Marvy Uchida; *Fibers:* On the Surface; *Brads:* American Tag Co.

"I couldn't scrapbook without my computer. With the flexibility I gain from scanning and altering my photos and the time I save formatting my computer journaling, I can get much more done in much less time."

JENNIFER BESTER • READING, MA

Jennifer has been scrapbooking for more than three years, but it wasn't until she found an online scrapbook community that she really found her groove. "By sharing layouts and pictures with friends across the country," says Jennifer, "I've learned more about myself and how and what I want to scrapbook." Jennifer's greatest inspiration, however, comes from her daughter. Shares Jennifer, "Every time I think of something I wish I could ask my mother, I'm moved to create another layout for my daughter."

"Boo!"

Supplies *Patterned paper:* Crafter's Workshop; *Handmade paper and mesh:* Magenta; *Vellum:* Paper Source; *Computer font:* Garamouche, Impress Rubber Stamps; *Rubber stamps:* PSX Design; *Stamping ink:* Tsukineko; *Brads:* American Tag Co.

IDEA TO NOTE: Jennifer designed the fish to match her daughter's swimsuit.

"Two Little Fishies"

Supplies *Computer font:* Tweed, downloaded from the Internet; *Fish accents:* Jennifer's own designs; *Fibers:* On the Surface; *Eyelets:* Impress Rubber Stamps.

"Gotta Run"

Supplies *Computer fonts:* Typist (title) and Rubberstamp (journaling), downloaded from the Internet; *Other:* Metal label holder.

IDEA TO NOTE: Jennifer created the photo with a process called Polaroid Transfer. Using a Daylab machine, she took a Polaroid picture of a slide. Then, before the Polaroid had fully developed, she transferred the image onto a wet piece of watercolor paper.

DIGITALLY ALTERING PHOTOS

Although I like to keep my scrapbook pages on the simple side, I do strive to create different moods on my pages. Sometimes I'm in the mood for a sleek, modern look. Other times, a memory warrants a layout with a softer feeling. When my photos don't fit with my creative inclinations, I use my scanner to help me achieve the look I'm shooting for. Here's how:

◆ When I want to place the focus on one or two photos but still want to include other favorite shots, I leave my favorite photo in the 4" x 6" size, then scan a few others and print them out in a significantly smaller size. This works for me because I don't have to crop the originals and can save them for another layout.

◆ Using a slide/transparency adapter, I scan an actual strip of negatives to create the look of a contact sheet used by professional photographers. In black and white, the negative strip lends an artistic feel to my layouts. In a sepia tone, the strip creates an old-fashioned look that's perfect for heritage or collage-style layouts.

Whether using photo-editing software to create the edges and borders that work so well for those soft, romantic pages, or playing around with colors and tones to create a more graphic look, I've found hundreds of ways to alter the look of my photos—and my layouts—with my scanner. It's one tool that's worth checking out!

—by Jennifer Bester

jenni bowlin

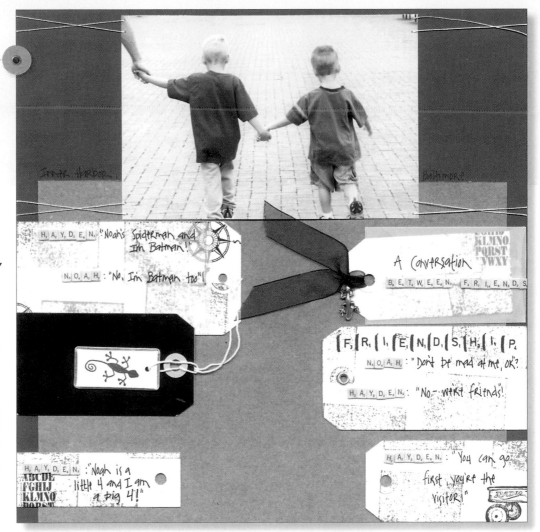

IDEA TO NOTE: Jenni created the tags' background by randomly marking the inkpad directly onto the tags.

"A Conversation Between Friends"

Supplies *Handmade paper:* Artistic Scrapper; *Rubber stamps:* Limited Edition (alphabet), PSX Design (Radio Flyer), Magenta (lizard), Stampotique Originals ("Friendship"), Stampabilities (compass); *Stamping ink:* Nick Bantock; *Alphabet tiles:* Limited Edition; *Metal-rimmed tags:* Making Memories; *Ribbon:* Europa; *Vellum holder:* Anima Designs; *Other:* Charm and embroidery floss.

"My second love is interior design. Many of my color combinations come straight from the pages of interior design magazines."

JENNI BOWLIN • MT. JULIET, TN

"I've always had an 'old' heart," shares Jenni. "I'm the one in the family who gets the old photos and memorabilia." Jenni's love of the past also inspires her scrapbooking style. She loves to incorporate nostalgic findings into her scrapbook designs—whether it's a torn piece of a baby gown, old button cards or vintage jewelry. Says Jenni, "Scrapbooking is a way for me to give these things new life."

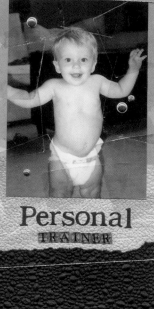

"Words of Wisdom"

Supplies *Handmade paper:* Plaza Art; *Patterned paper:* The Paper Patch; *Rubber stamps:* Raindrops on Roses (mesh), Stampers Anonymous (diamond), PSX Design (Radio Flyer), Magenta (sun); *Stamping ink:* Nick Bantock; *Walnut ink:* Postmodern Design; *Ribbon:* Art Chix; *Metal:* Art Emboss; *Metal stamps:* Pittsburgh; *Other:* Beads, stick and wire.

"Personal Trainer"

Supplies *Handmade paper:* Plaza Art; *Computer font:* Teletype, Printmaster; Hampton Arts ("Personal"); *Rubber stamps:* PSX Design (crackle), The Moon Rose ("Journal"), A Stamp in the Hand (dip pen); *Foil:* Reynolds Craft Foil; *Shrink plastic:* Stampendous!; *Brads:* American Tag Co.; *Mica:* US ArtQuest.

IDEA TO NOTE: To create the tiles, Jenni stamped the alphabet onto clear shrink plastic and shrunk it.

PERSONALIZING METAL ACCENTS

Scrapbookers love metal. And with a little effort and the right tools, you can take this versatile product a step further by personalizing it with titles, captions, dates and more. Gather the supplies listed here, then follow the steps below:

MATERIALS YOU'LL NEED:
- ☐ Lightweight metal (24 gauge)
- ☐ Metal stamp set (available at hardware stores and some scrapbook stores)
- ☐ Solvent-based inkpad
- ☐ Hammer
- ☐ Self-healing mat

❶ Choose the size, shape and color of your metal.

❷ Ink the stamp with a solvent-based inkpad (like Staz-On). This will make your impressions stand out so they can be read easily.

❸ Place the metal piece on a self-healing mat and set your first stamp in place. Hit the top of the stamp using moderate force with your hammer. If the impression isn't deep enough, put your stamp back into place (it should easily slide into the impression) and hit again.

❹ Repeat Steps 2 and 3 for each letter in your title or caption.

TIPS:
- ◆ If you forget to ink your stamps before impressing, you can add color afterward by using an inkpad and a pointed cotton swab. Or try Rub 'n Buff metallic wax for a "messy" effect.
- ◆ Lightweight metal can be punched, cut or wrapped, so you have several options when attaching it to your layout. Try punching a small hole on each side of a metal strip and attaching it to your page with mini-brads or eyelets. Or try wrapping a strip around a premade tag or journaling box. The possibilities are endless!
- ◆ If your metal is too shiny for your project, rub it with sandpaper before impressing to take off the sheen.

—by Jenni Bowlin

"Future Seamstress"

Supplies *Handmade paper:* Artistic Scrapper; *Mesh:* Magenta; *Rubber stamps:* Paper Impressions (border), Stampington & Co. (baby buttons), Plaid (flower); *Walnut ink:* Postmodern Design; *Ribbon:* Europa; *Buttons:* Manto Fev; *Calligraphy pen, nib and ink.* Watson Guptill; *Mica:* US ArtQuest; *Other:* Antique hatpin, tape measure, trim and book page.

"Blue-Eyed Boy"

Supplies *Patterned paper and frame:* Anna Griffin; *Alphabet rubber stamps:* A Stamp in the Hand; *Stamping ink:* Stampa Rosa; *Star nailhead:* ScrapWorks; *Ribbon:* Europa; *Typewriter keys:* FoofaLa; *Mica:* US ArtQuest; *Other:* Vintage doily, buttons, monogram, tags and trim.

"A Day in the Life"

Supplies *Handmade paper:* Plaza Art; *Rubber stamps:* Raindrops on Roses (mesh), Stampin' Up! (heart), Inkadinkadoo (locket), Fred B. Mullet (sponge), Limited Edition (gate key), Pittsburgh (mini alphabet); *Computer font:* Times New Roman, WordPerfect; *Stamping ink:* Memories; *Ribbon:* Europa; *Eyelets:* Creative Imaginations; *Craft wire:* Artistic Wire Ltd.

PHOTO BY ALAN CLARK

Figure 1. Use letter stamps and computer fonts to create overlapping titles. *Page by Faye Morrow Bell.* **Supplies** *Pen:* Zig Scroll & Brush, EK Success; *Metal charm with words:* Scraps Ahoy; *Rubber stamps:* Stampers Anonymous; *Stamping ink:* Stampin' Up!; *Photo corner:* Canson; *Silver bead:* Westrim Crafts; *Eyelets:* Magic Scraps; *Jute:* Darice; *Date stamp:* Office Depot; *Computer fonts:* Carpenter TW, FontHaus; GF Ordner Normal and Mom's Typewriter, downloaded from the Internet; *Other:* Dictionary page.

Stamp on Top of a Title

A great way to add interest to a title is to stamp on top of your computer journaling. For the layout in Figure 1, I aligned and printed the words "My Studio" in a cursive computer font. Next, I used a simple alphabet stamp to stamp the word "Atelier" (French for "studio") over it with white ink. I staggered the stamped letters, but maintained baseline balance (meaning your eye sees a straight line when you look at the stamped word, despite the variation in the letter placement).

The color contrast combined with letter placement gives the title texture and movement. I found it a great option for this lengthy title.

—*Faye Morrow Bell, Charlotte, NC*

IDEAS TO NOTE: To create the title, Dawn stamped and embossed sea glass. She also embossed the metal corners with UTEE mixed with copper powder to blend with the reds in the layout.

SIT UP STRAIGHT
WE'RE ALMOST THROUGH
HOLD YOUR HEAD UP HIGH
THE SUN IS BRIGHT, A FEW MORE SHOTS
PLEASE DON'T LET OUT A SIGH.
ONE MORE ROLL
LET'S CHANGE THE LENS
AND MOVE BY THIS BIG TREE
DON'T LOOK DOWN, JUST STRIKE A POSE
AND FLASH YOUR SMILE AT ME.
I KNOW IT'S HARD TO KEEP THIS UP
YOUR FACE IS GETTING SORE
BUT PATIENCE, SON,
IT'S WORTH THE TIME
HOLD STILL FOR
ONE MORE

"Just One More"

Supplies *Patterned paper:* Magenta; *Handmade paper:* Creativepapersonline.com; *Alphabet rubber stamps:* PSX Design; *Computer font:* CK Chemistry, "Fresh Fonts" CD, *Creating Keepsakes; Embossing ink:* Stamp-n Stuff, Stampendous!; *Embossing powder:* UTEE, Suze Weinberg; *Paper yarn:* Twistel, Making Memories; *Sea glass:* Gayle's Glass; *Chalk:* Craf-T Products; *Transparency:* 3M; *Poem:* Dawn's own work; *Other:* Date stamp and burlap.

"My favorite tools are my embossing gun and stamping inks. They allow me to alter pre-made materials so they blend well with the colors on my layout."

DAWN BROOKEY • LA CRESCENTA, CA

Dawn's artistic mother introduced her to scrapbooking two years ago. "She offered to buy me art supplies so I could return to the drawing and painting I did when I was younger," shares Dawn. "Instead, I asked her to buy scrapbook supplies so I could creatively display the boxes of photographs I'd taken of my family." • Dawn loves embellishments and challenges herself to use supplies in fresh, creative ways. "What I love most about this craft is that it's constantly evolving," explains Dawn. "My passion for scrapbooking will never wane as long as I have boxes of pictures and new supplies to entice me."

IDEA TO NOTE: Dawn embossed the metal tags with orange ink and UTEE to match the layout.

"How Many Licks?"

Supplies *Specialty paper:* Creativepapersonline.com; *Computer font:* Fontdinerdotcom, downloaded from the Internet; *Stamping ink:* ColorBox, Clearsnap, Inc.; *Embossing ink:* Stamp-n Stuff, Stampendous!; *Embossing powder:* UTEE, Suze Weinberg; *Vellum tags:* Making Memories; *Orange glass:* Artistic Enhancements; *Fibers:* Rubba Dub Dub (yellow), Artistic Enhancements (orange); *Page pebble:* Making Memories; *Poem:* Dawn's own work; *Other:* Eyelet, lollipop wrapper and stick.

SPOTLIGHTING SMALL ELEMENTS

I love to spotlight certain features in photographs with small elements like Page Pebbles (from the Making Memories Details line) and watch crystals. Their clear color and three-dimensional shape add texture, which draws the eye, but they don't stand out so much that they break up the photographs.

In my "Blueberries" layout, for example, I used a watch crystal to focus on my daughter's hand reaching for the berries on the tree (see page 27). In this large photograph, the eye might first be drawn to her face because her hand is hidden in the bushes. The watch crystal calls attention to the action of picking the berries, which is an integral part of the layout.

I used a Page Pebble in a similar way on my "How Many Licks?" page. Because the lollipop is so important to the story, I high-lighted it with a Page Pebble. It brings attention to the candy without over-whelming the photo.

Whenever you want to draw attention to a small feature in a photograph, look for small elements such as watch crystals, Page Pebbles, Conchos and even frames to add a big punch.

—by Dawn Brookey

"Blue Berries"

Supplies *Computer fonts:* CK Extra, "Fresh Fonts" CD, *Creating Keepsakes*; Schmutz Corroded and Carpenter, downloaded from *www.scrapvillage.com*; *Skeletonized leaves:* All Night Media; *Mesh:* Magenta; *Fibers:* On the Surface; *Vellum tags:* Making Memories; *Circle punch:* Fiskars; *Watch crystal:* Deluxe; *Poem:* Dawn's own work; *Other:* Brads.

IDEAS TO NOTE: The front of the layout is cut between the photo and the title to open up and expose the inside. The layout is held closed by fibers wrapped around two brads.

IDEAS TO NOTE:
Dawn stamped the title block on a piece of mica, then embossed and adhered it to another piece of mica using pop dots for a layered effect. She also inserted the Conchos backward so the prongs resemble shark teeth.

"Bite"

Supplies *Handmade paper:* Creativepapers-online.com; *Alphabet rubber stamps:* PSX Design; *Stamping ink:* Memories; *Embossing powder:* Stamp-n Stuff, Stampendous!; *Silver thread:* Darice; *Mica:* US ArtQuest; *Metal prongs:* Conchos (adhered backward), ScrapWorks; *Pop dots:* All Night Media.

When you are **happy**, your smile sings a song.
Our day runs so smoothly, no thing can go wrong.
When you are **frightened**, you reach out your arms.
You seek only comfort, withholding all charms.
When you are **social**, with friends by your side
You still take your brother along for the ride.
When you are **worried**, you wrinkle your face
It's hard to console you, we just give you space.
When you are **angry**, one eye gets real small
That smile fades to grimace, you're no fun at all.
When you are **vocal**, there's so much to say
It's trying to keep interruptions at bay.
When you are **bossy**, you just take control
You work well to get us to all seek your goal.
When you are **gentle**, your touch is so slight
Your voice is a whisper as still as the night.
When you are **loving**, a glow fills your face
You snuggle and dole out the tightest embrace.
When you are **with me**, just tagging along
I look for your smile to sing me a song.
                                    ~Mommy

IDEAS TO NOTE:
Dawn stamped and embossed the title on a piece of mica. She cut the blue patterned paper, matted it on a piece of blue hand-made paper, then adhered it to a full-size sheet of the blue patterned paper so the patterns align.

"Sing Me a Song"

Supplies *Patterned papers:* 7 Gypsies (music notes), Glad Tidings (blue swirl); *Vellum:* Paper Adventures; *Handmade paper:* Source unknown; *Computer font:* Sonyanna ScriptSSi, downloaded from the Internet; *Alphabet rubber stamps:* PSX Design; *Stamping ink:* Memories (black), ColorBox (teal), Clearsnap, Inc.; *Embossing powder:* Stamp-n Stuff, Stampendous!; *Poem:* Dawn's own work; *Mica:* US ArtQuest; *Chalk:* Craf-T Products; *Other:* Brads, nailhead and tulle.

"Circa 1993"

Supplies *Patterned papers:* 7 Gypsies (script), Autumn Leaves ("The voyage of your dreams"); *Computer font:* CK Newsprint, "Fresh Fonts" CD, *Creating Keepsakes; Mesh:* Magenta; *Tag:* Club Scrap; *Rubber stamps:* JudiKins (travel collage), Stampers Anonymous (alphabet, numeric, collage frame), Club Scrap (build collage); *Page accents:* Fresh Cuts, EK Success; *Ribbon:* C.M. Offray & Son; *Stamping ink:* Memories (black), ColorBox (blue and gray), Clearsnap, Inc.; VersaMark, Tsukineko; *Embossing powder:* UTEE, Suze Weinberg; Stamp-n Stuff (copper), Stampendous!; *Eyelets:* Making Memories.

"Chocolate Cake"
Supplies *Charms:* Making Memories; *Pen:* Zig Millennium, EK Success.

CHOCOLATE
cake
And you loved every bite! It was yummy and messy and you got it ALL over the place... just like you were supposed to at your very FIRST BIRTHDAY!!!

HAPPY BIRTHDAY TO YOU!

JANuARY 21 2002

IDEA TO NOTE: This page is part of a series of first birthday pages. Each page uses the same color scheme.

"My favorite tools are my digital camera, my

X-acto knife, my thesaurus, and my Zig pens."

ALI EDWARDS • CRESWELL, OR

Ali started scrapbooking with the intent of organizing the photos from her son's first year of life. "Scrapbooking enables me to combine my love of design with my passion for preserving those priceless day-to-day memories," shares Ali. Her inspiration comes from the natural environment just outside her door—the vivid colors in her garden inspire her to create unique color combinations. She's also inspired by her son's developing personality. Says Ali, "He's experiencing so many things for the first time each day; it reminds me to look at everything from a fresh perspective."

"Everyday Joy"

Supplies *Vellum:* Paper Adventures; *Letter stickers:* Liz King, Sticko; Mrs. Grossman's; *Computer font:* Problem Secretary, downloaded from the Internet; *Tag:* Ali's own design; *Pen:* Zig Millennium, EK Success.

"The Mini"

Supplies *Computer font:* Girls Are Weird, downloaded from the Internet; *Pen:* Zig Millennium, EK Success; *Car accents:* Source unknown.

"Grandpa Gary"

Supplies *Patterned paper:* Source unknown; *Glass alphabet stickers:* Making Memories; *Button:* Mom's Collection; *Pen:* Zig Millennium, EK Success; *Punch:* EK Success.

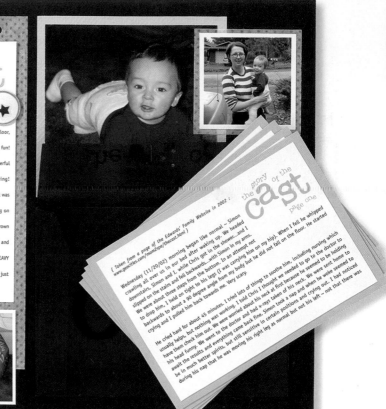

The story of the cast

You weathered this "minor" bump in the road so well ~ it didn't stop you from scooting around on the floor, playing with your toys, or having fun! Your positive attitude and wonderful smile greeted us every morning! Sometimes you would get tired {it was especially tough for you sleeping on your back all the time ~ you had grown to like sleeping on your tummy} and grumpy...and man was that cast HEAVY & DIRTY! But you made it through just fine...what a TROOPER!!!

The story of the cast — page one

[Taken from a page of the Edwards' Family Website in 2002 : www.geocities.com/momiype/thecast.html]

Wednesday (11/20/02) morning began like normal ~ Simon crawling all over us in our bed after waking up. We headed downstairs, Simon and I, while Chris got in the shower...and I slipped on the stairs and fell backwards...with Simon in my arms. We were about three steps from the bottom. In an attempt not to drop him, I held on tight to his legs {I was carrying him on my hip}. When I fell he whipped backwards to about a 90 degree angle from my body but he did not fall on the floor. He started crying and I pulled him back towards me. Very scary.

He cried hard for about 45 minutes. I tried lots of things to soothe him, including nursing which usually helps, but nothing was working. I told Chris I thought we needed to go to the doctor to have them check him out. We were worried about his neck at first because he seemed to be holding his head funny. We went to the doctor and had x-rays taken of his neck. We were sent home to await the results and everything came back fine. Simon took a nap and when he woke seemed to be in much better spirits, but still sensitive in certain positions and crying out. I had noticed during his nap that he was moving his right leg as normal but not his left – not that there was

IDEA TO NOTE: The vellum envelope contains four pieces of cardstock that detail the story of how her son broke his leg.

"The Cast"

Supplies *Computer fonts:* Problem Secretary (title) and ITC Officina Sans Book (journaling), downloaded from the Internet; *Star sticker:* me & my BIG ideas; *Circle tag:* Avery; *Button:* Mom's Collection; *Vellum envelope:* Thibierge & Comar Papetiers, Cromatica.

USING COLOR EFFECTIVELY

One of the most fundamental elements on a scrapbook page, color evokes emotion and lends interest, as well as cohesion, to a layout. One of my favorite ways to use color is to frame a photo or journaling block with thin strips of a bright, primary color, then repeat the same color elsewhere on the layout. I'm particularly fond of reds, oranges and yellows—they brighten up pages, giving them a little extra zing.

Don't be afraid to step outside of your comfort zone and experiment with unique color combinations. It's one medium that's perfect for play!

—by Ali Edwards

EVERY CHILD IS AN

Artist

the problem is how to remain an artist once he grows up.
Picasso

IDEA TO NOTE: Ali cut her own letters and paired them with letter stickers to create her title.

"Artist"

Supplies *Letter stickers:* Liz King, Sticko; Mrs. Grossman's; *Flower eyelet charm:* Making Memories; *Pen:* Zig Millennium, EK Success.

Summer is a treasure trove of *magic moments*

Figure 1. Use metal-rimmed tags to frame small accents on your page. *Page by Nichol Magouirk for Creative Imaginations.* **Supplies** *Textured cardstock:* Bazzill Basics; *Vellum and dot-lets:* Doodlebug Designs; *Vellum stickers:* Shotz Thoughtz, Creative Imaginations; *Circle punch:* EK Success; *Tags:* American Tag; *Circle tags and page pebbles:* Making Memories; *Glass beads:* JudiKins; *Other:* Watch crystal.

Stitched Frame Accents

I really enjoy the look created by cutting the center from metal-rimmed tags and using them to "frame" different elements on layouts. I came up with a creative way to attach the frames to your layouts. Here's how:

❶ Cut the inside from a metal-rimmed tag using an X-acto knife. Leave just the metal frame.

❷ Punch a shape to fit the tag from patterned paper, cardstock or a photo. Place it behind the appropriate frame.

❸ Set your sewing machine to the widest setting for a zigzag stitch.

❹ Carefully line up the sewing machine needle above the frame and paper. Begin stitching over the frame. The needle should go back and forth on either side of the frame. Turn the page as needed to stitch around the entire frame.

❺ Once the frame is stitched to the layout, you can add embellishments such as vellum stickers, watch crystals filled with beads, metal letter charms, letter stickers or more.

To create the circle accents on my summer layout (Figure 1), I punched various sizes of circles from the Swimming Pool Shotz, adhered vellum Shotz Thoughtz stickers to two of the circle tag frames, then stitched them on using the technique described above. I added watch crystals filled with clear beads to the centers of the two remaining frames.

—Nichol Magouirk
for Creative Imaginations

September 2002
Lynn Valley

I guess you can call it a Canadian
thing. Wherever you find rocks
you are sure to see these rock
sculptures dotting the landscape.
Inukshuk, the Inuit word for the
rock sculptures, that were once
used to mark routes in the tree
baron north.

One rock perched on top another
sure it looks easy   until you try it.
Daddy was very determined to
make his inukshuk as large as he
could.

"Inukshuk"

Supplies *Patterned paper:* Scrip Scrap;
Computer fonts: 2Peas Gift and 2Peas
Chicken Shack, downloaded from
www.twopeasinabucket.com.

"My favorite scrapbooking tool is my camera.

I want my photos to take center stage and the rest

of the page to highlight the photos. Sometimes

they're the only embellishments I need."

TRACY KYLE • COQUITLAM, BRITISH COLUMBIA

Rarely a day goes by that Tracy doesn't work on her scrapbooks. Whether it's taking photos,
searching for inspiration, finding the "perfect" paper or putting a page together, she
makes time every day to do something. "I'm a slow scrapbooker and can spend days on a
layout," confesses Tracy. "I keep everything out on my table and move elements around
each time I walk by. Only when I'm completely happy do I stick everything down."

"Patience"

Supplies *Patterned paper:* Rocky Mountain Scrapbook Company; *Alphabet rubber stamps:* Wordsworth; *Computer fonts:* 2Peas Nevermind, downloaded from *www.twopeasinabucket.com*; *Metal tags:* Making Memories; *Stamping ink:* ColorBox, Clearsnap, Inc.

"Laughter"

Supplies *Patterned paper:* Magenta; *Vellum:* Close To My Heart; *Rubber stamp:* Impress Rubber Stamps; *Computer font:* 2Peas Flea Market by Sharon Soneff, downloaded from *www.twopeasinabucket.com*; *Stamping ink:* ColorBox, Clearsnap, Inc.

Isabella · 4 years · 2002

Tracy · 4 years · 1973

Everyone always tells me how much we look alike. I have heard it time and time again, yet, I never really saw it myself. Well, you are fair skinned like I am, but really that was it. Then one day I came across a picture of myself at the age of four, the same age you are now. All of a sudden, I could see it: the eyes, the chin, the cheeks, the smile . . . yes, we do look similar, very similar. Now I can see that we are truly woven from the same thread.

Woven

of the   same

thread

"Woven of the Same Thread"

Supplies *Patterned papers:* Rebecca Sower (green), EK Success; Rocky Mountain Scrapbook Company (blue); *Stickers:* Magenta; *Computer fonts:* Gigi, downloaded from the Internet; 2Peas Think Small, downloaded from *www.twopeasinabucket.com*; Garamouche, Impress Rubber Stamps; *Pen:* Zig Writer, EK Success; *Chalk:* Craf-T Products; *Pop dots:* All Night Media.

EYE-CATCHING TITLES

A title is an important element on any layout. You can give it the attention it deserves with a few easy techniques:

◆ Span your title over a two-page spread. It will tie the pages together and create a dramatic look.

◆ Experiment with different fonts, paying attention to the mood each font evokes. You can even combine fonts to create a unique look.

◆ Find interesting ways to present your title on the page. Try using rubber stamps or cut-out letters printed on cardstock. You can also change the orientation of your title so it's vertical on the page.

When it comes to creating titles, your options are only limited by your creativity!

—by Tracy Kyle

"Discovery"

Supplies *Computer fonts:* Soli and Lemon Chicken, downloaded from the Internet.

"Circle of Life"

Supplies *Vellum:* Close To My Heart; *Computer fonts:* 2Peas Nevermind and 2Peas Circle Blocks, downloaded from *www.twopeasinabucket.com*; *Embossing powder:* UTEE, Suze Weinberg; *Stamping ink:* Tsukineko.

IDEAS TO NOTE: The pocket on the back of the layout holds personal thoughts on the "stuff" that matters to Leslie and her family. The title was inspired by the song "Stuff That Matters" by Tara Lyn Hart.

THE STUFF THAT MATTERS ...
THE THINGS THAT COUNT...
THEY DON'T COST MONEY -
THE THINGS WE REALLY CARE ABOUT.

"Stuff That Matters"

Supplies *Patterned paper:* Paper Fever; *Alphabet rubber stamps:* PSX Design (title), Hero Arts (journaling); *Stamping ink:* Memories; *Embroidery floss:* DMC.

"My favorite scrapbooking tool? I like just about everything. I love getting something new and seeing what unique things I can do with it."

LESLIE LIGHTFOOT • STIRLING, ONTARIO, CANADA

"Scrapbooking combines my love of photography with my love of crafting," says Leslie. She finds inspiration for her pages all around her—from advertising and graphic design to song lyrics and literature. "You can find inspiration everywhere you look," shares Leslie, "And I'm always looking!"

"Nature"

Supplies *Maruyama paper:* Magenta; *Vellum:* The Paper Company; *Computer font:* 2Peas Falling Leaves, downloaded from *www.twopeasinabucket.com*; *Fibers:* On the Surface; *Mini-brads:* Lost Art Treasures; *Other:* Black slide mount.

IDEA TO NOTE: Leslie used the slide mount, tied in place with fiber, to pull the eye to the photo subject.

"Life of Adventure"

Supplies *Computer font:* Kindergarten, package unknown; *Netting:* Magic Scraps; *Buttons:* Making Memories; *Embroidery floss:* Anchor.

"Water Yourself"

Supplies *Patterned papers:* Paper Fever (green), Doodlebug Design (blue); *Alphabet rubber stamps and stamping ink:* Hero Arts; *Page pebbles:* Making Memories; *Dimensional adhesive:* Diamond Glaze.

IDEA TO NOTE: Leslie's husband altered the quote to suit the photo.

"Eeyore"

Supplies *Handmade paper:* Jennifer Collection (blue swirl); *Patterned papers:* Karen Foster Design, Sue Dreamer; *Title:* Leslie's own design; *Other:* Safety pins and thread.

TIMESAVING TECHNIQUE

Like yours, my life is busy. On top of that, I'm not the most organized person in the world. So finding ways to save time is essential for me if I want to complete scrapbook pages. I use a variety of timesaving techniques, but my favorite? Go with the flow.

Here's what I mean. If I pull out some photos and inspiration doesn't come to me quickly, I don't force the page. I simply put the photos away until inspiration strikes. I select which page I'm going to work on by flipping through my photos and choosing the set that "speaks" to me. The page comes together quickly because I waited until I knew what I wanted to do with it. I always have a huge heap of photos, so the variety and opportunity is always there.

Next time you're stuck for a theme, pick up a different set of photos and just go with the flow. It will make scrapbooking fresh and, most importantly, fun.

—*by Leslie Lightfoot*

"Show Me the Way ... Daddy"

Supplies *Computer font:* Garamouche, Impress Rubber Stamps; *Netting:* Magic Scraps; *Chalk:* Craf-T Products.

"Magic"

Supplies *Patterned paper:* Karen Foster Design; *Vellum:* Autumn Leaves; *Computer font:* Aquiline, downloaded from the Internet; *Charm:* Forever Charms; *Modeling paste:* Liquitex; *Embossing powder:* UTEE, Suze Weinberg; *Wire hand:* Westrim Crafts; *Chinese coin:* Boxer Scrapbook Productions; *Antiquing medium:* Plaid; *Other:* Leaf, brads and transparency.

"My favorite product is glue dots. I use a lot of 'lumpy' embellishments, and more often than not, glue dots will do the trick when nothing else will."

AMIE LLOYD • BROKEN ARROW, OK

Amie began scrapbooking as a way to organize and display the hundreds of photos she'd taken of her son, Spencer, as a baby. "Spencer is still a favorite subject of mine," Amie says, "but as my interest has deepened, I've discovered so many aspects of life that are also worthy of being preserved." Now Amie scrapbooks as much for the creative outlet as to record her family's memories. The photos that end up on her layouts are the ones that "speak" to her. "The emotions and moods the photos evoke are the defining factor for every page I put together," shares Amie. "I believe that letting your pictures guide the layout is the single most important thing any scrapper can learn to do."

"Sacred Earth"

Supplies *Fiber:* Fibers by the Yard; *Computer fonts:* Unknown; *Ribbon:* All the Extras; *Wire leaves:* Westrim Crafts; *Brads:* Boxer Scrapbook Productions; *Stamping ink:* ColorBox, Clearsnap, Inc.; *Other:* Transparency.

"Summer in the City"

Supplies *Patterned paper:* Sonnets, Creative Imaginations; *Maruyama paper:* Magenta; *Textured paper:* Club Scrap; *Alphabet rubber stamps:* PSX Design; *Stamping ink:* Ranger Industries (blue), Excelsior (black); *Computer fonts:* Boomerang ("Summer"), Lainie Day ("in the City"), downloaded from the Internet.

"Smile Lines"

Supplies *Patterned paper:* Club Scrap; *Computer fonts:* 2Peas Cookie Dough (title), downloaded from *www.twopeasinabucket.com*, Dan's Hand (journaling), downloaded from the Internet; *Letter stickers:* Sonnets, Creative Imaginations; *Other:* Foam core.

CREATING MULTI-DIMENSIONAL LAYOUTS

Create interest on your layouts by adding dimension.

MATERIALS:

☐ 3 sheets of Square Mirror Print paper (from Club Scrap's Mocha Java kit)

☐ 2 sheets of 12" x 12" coffee-brown cardstock

☐ 3 sheets of brown or tan Flexi-Foam (by Fibre Craft) *Note:* I doubled up on each layer of craft foam for additional height; to do this, two more sheets will be necessary.

☐ Flea Market alphabet stickers (Sonnets, Creative Imaginations)

☐ Black transfer paper (Mona Lisa Products, Houston Art, Inc.)

☐ Black Zig Writer (EK Success)

☐ Computer fonts: Cookie Dough (Two Peas in a Bucket), Dan's Hand (downloaded from the Internet)

FOLLOW THESE STEPS:

❶ Cut two sheets of the Square Mirror Print paper down to 11" x 11". Lay your photos out on the two trimmed sheets and decide where you want each photo to go, and where you want to place the title and journaling. This is also the time to decide which photos will be shadowboxed, which ones will be popped up, and which will lie flat on the paper. Once you have it figured out, draw a rough sketch of your plan so you can refer back to it.

❷ Using a pencil, trace lightly around the photos that will be shadowboxed. Cut the areas out using a craft knife and a ruler.

❸ Cut two sheets of the craft foam to fit underneath the paper. For the shadowboxed items, use the holes in the printed paper as a guide, trace the shadowboxed areas onto craft foam, and cut out. Cut these holes wider and longer than the ones in the printed paper so that none of the craft foam will show when looking at the layout from different angles. Since the craft foam isn't supposed to show, your cuts don't need to be straight.

❹ Mount the popped-up photos on the extra craft foam. The bigger the foam sheets underneath, the better the stability, but make sure it doesn't show. The photos should have the appearance of floating.

❺ Cut various squares and rectangles out of the extra sheet of printed paper to use as accents, making sure they match the areas they'll be placed on. Mount these on the craft foam. Attach all foam-mounted pieces to the layout.

❻ Print journaling (Dan's Hand) and subtitles (2Peas Cookie Dough) on regular printer paper. Using transfer paper, trace all of the lettering onto the printed background sheets in the desired areas. Carefully go over the transferred lettering with a Zig Writer, using the fine point for journaling and the wider point for subtitles. Add letter stickers to complete title words.

❼ Mount both background sheets on the foam you cut for them, then attach all of it to the brown cardstock matting sheets. Attach shadowboxed photos to brown cardstock, showing through the holes that you cut out of the printed paper. Place them slightly off-center to enhance the shadowboxed effect.

—by Amie Lloyd

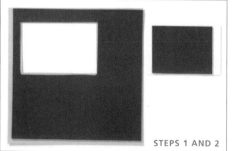

STEPS 1 AND 2

STEP 3

"Out in the Snow"

Supplies *Lettering template:* Unknown, Frances Meyer; *Computer font:* Texas Hero, downloaded from the Internet; *Stickers:* Class A 'Peels, Stampendous!; *Pen:* Zig Opaque Writer, EK Success; *Shaved ice:* Magic Scraps.

IDEAS TO NOTE: To save herself from having to precisely line up each cardstock strip, Amie cut the background paper apart, leaving space for the border. Then she tucked the ends of the cardstock strips underneath the edge of the background paper and adhered the ends.

"The Little Boy with the Flag"

Supplies *Patterned paper:* K & Company; *Computer fonts:* Ghostwriter, Chilly Moe, Butterbrotpapier and Piracy, downloaded from the Internet; *Rubber stamp:* Inkadinkadoo; *Stamping ink:* Tsukineko; *Embossing powder:* UTEE, Suze Weinberg; *Wooden stars:* Craft It with Woods, Crafts Etc.; *Antiquing medium:* Plaid; *Brads:* Boxer Scrapbook Productions; *Metallic wax finish:* Rub 'n Buff, Amaco; *Chalk:* Craf-T Products; *Other:* Elastic cord, cotton fabric and transparency.

How many times have my WISHES and my dREAMS and my pRAYERS for you hidden beneath my breath?

How many times have I looked at you, heart in my throat, hands in my pockets, a smile on my face, just wanting to say...

i hOpE yOu nEVER LOsE yOuR SEnSE Of

W O N D E R

from the book
i hOpE yOu dAncE
by Mark D. Sanders & Tia Sillers

"Wonder"

Supplies
Computer fonts: 2Peas Chestnuts and 2Peas White Sale by Melissa Baxter, downloaded from *www.twopeasina-bucket.com*; *Typewriter key cutouts:* Stampington.com; *Ribbon:* Memory Lane Paper Co.; *Ribbon and beaded trim:* Style-a-bility, Hirshberg Schutz & Co.; *Fibers:* Adornaments, EK Success; *Book label holder:* Twopeasina-bucket.com; *Background:* Nichol's own design; *Embroidery floss:* Coats & Clark; *Photo corners:* Making Memories.

"Paper is my favorite product. I love mixing and matching patterned papers to create my own custom backgrounds."

NICHOL MAGOUIRK • DODGE CITY, KS

Nichol's hands have always been busy creating one thing or another, and six years ago, she discovered that scrapbooking fills that creative need perfectly. "I feel an enormous sense of pride when my children look through their albums and exclaim, 'That's me!', " shares Nichol. Often, her best ideas come to her late at night, just as she's drifting off to sleep. Says Nichol, "I wake up the next morning eager to create!"

"Joy"

Supplies *Patterned paper:* Karen Foster Design; *Mesh:* Magenta; *Specialty paper:* Hobby Lobby; *Vellum:* Close To My Heart; *Metal letter tags and metal tags:* Making Memories; *Beads:* Blue Moon Beads; *Jewelry tag:* American Tag Co.; *Alphabet rubber stamps:* PSX Design; *Stamping ink:* Source unknown; *Letter stickers:* Stampendous!; *Computer font:* CK Newsprint, "Fresh Fonts" CD, *Creating Keepsakes;* *Paper clips:* Clipiola; *Flat-top eyelets:* Stamp Dr.; *Sun punch:* Marvy Uchida; *Embroidery floss:* DMC; *Metal tags:* Twopeasinabucket.com; *Sewing thread:* Coats & Clark; *Mini-brads:* Lost Art Treasures; *Photo corners:* Canson; *Other:* Date stamp.

"Time"

Supplies *Patterned paper:* Magenta; *Ribbon:* Close To My Heart; *Metal letters:* Making Memories; *Letter stickers:* Flavia; *Alphabet rubber stamps:* PSX Design; *Stamping ink:* Source unknown; *Glassine envelopes:* Anima Designs; *Flat-top eyelets:* Stamp Dr.; *Laminate tags:* Twopeasinabucket.com; *Embossing powder:* Comotion; *Embroidery floss:* DMC; *Thread:* Coats & Clark; *Photo corners:* Making Memories; *Purple beads:* Little Charmers, On the Surface; *Other:* Silver beads.

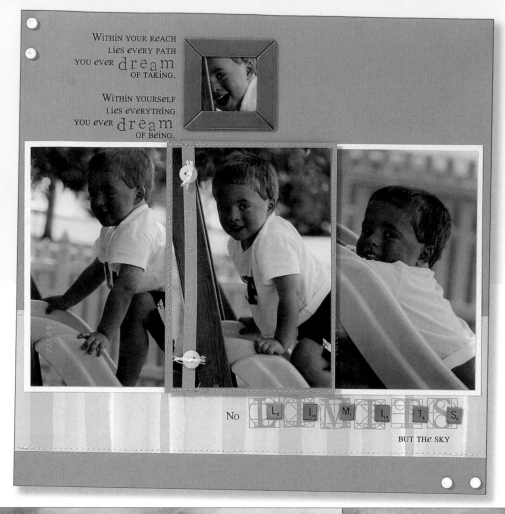

WITHIN YOUR REACH
LIES EVERY PATH
YOU *ever* dream
OF TAKING.

WITHIN YOURSELF
LIES EVERYTHING
YOU *ever* dream
OF BEING.

No **LIMITS**

BUT THE SKY

"No Limits"

Supplies *Patterned paper:* Paper Fever; *Metal frame:* Making Memories; *Computer font:* CK Chemistry, "Fresh Fonts" CD, *Creating Keepsakes;* *Scrabble tiles:* Limited Edition; *Alphabet rubber stamps:* Hampton Arts; *"Dream" stamp:* Dawn Hauser, Inkadinkadoo; *Flat-top eyelets:* Stamp Dr.; *Buttons:* Making Memories; *Thread:* Coats & Clark.

walk baRefoOt aCross

Sunshine
days
james kavanaugh

"Walk Barefoot across Sunshine Days"

Supplies *Patterned papers:* Magenta (flower), Karen Foster Design (green); *Vellum tags:* Making Memories; *Letter stickers:* Sonnets, Creative Imaginations; *Alphabet rubber stamps:* PSX Design; *Stamping ink:* Memories; *Date tag:* Nichol's own design; *Eyelets:* Impress Rubber Stamps; *Fibers:* Adornments, EK Success; *Beads:* Westrim Crafts; *Thread:* Coats & Clark; *Other:* Date stamp.

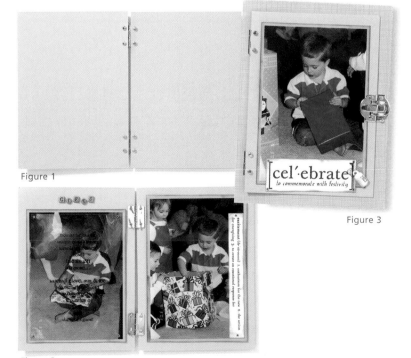

"Perfect Pumpkin"

Supplies *Patterned paper:* Magenta; *Vellum:* Close To My Heart; *Alphabet rubber stamps:* PSX Design; *Stamping ink:* Memories (black); ColorBox (brown), Clearsnap, Inc.; *Hinges and buckle clasp:* Hobby Lobby; *Walnut ink:* Anima Designs; *Rubber stamps:* Inkadinkadoo (clock and film strip), Hampton Arts (Chinese symbol and art), Stamp of Excellence (script background), Hero Arts (postage stamp); *Mini-brads:* Lost Art Treasures; *Other:* Date stamp, eyelets, canvas, craft pins, sandpaper, book label holder, tags, metal stamps and metal.

CREATING A HINGED MINI BOOK

I love to find ways to add more photos and journaling to a page without distracting from the look of the layout. One of my favorite ways to do this is by creating a hinged mini book. This eye-catching mini book can be adapted to fit any number of page themes, and it's easy to create. Follow these steps:

❶ To create the front and back of the book, trim two pieces of cardstock to 5" x 7". Attach two hinges to one side using mini brads (Figure 1).

❷ Mat photos or journaling on a coordinating piece of cardstock. Add eyelets, brads, etc., to the mat. Adhere each to the fronts of both pages and the back of the cover (Figure 2).

❸ Adhere the buckle clasp to the front cover of the mini book, and the closure to the layout using mini brads (Figure 3). Add adhesive to the back of the mini book and adhere to your layout, lining it up with the closure.

Optional: Hang a small jewelry tag or charm from the clasp.

—by Nichol Magouirk

Figure 1

Figure 2

Figure 3

terrie mcdaniel 2003

IDEA TO NOTE: Terrie used ink jet–sensitive Shrinky Dink film for the title and comments. She punched holes in the film prior to baking so she could thread the fibers through afterward.

Taylor made

For as long as I can remember, my Great Aunt JuJu has teased Mymee about all of the grandkids getting the good things from the Taylor side (Aunt JuJu and Daddy Bill's side of the family) and the sassy things from the Thompson side (Mymee's side of the family). Poor Mymee was always outnumbered but she always took it in great stride. They have always had the most fun with that and they still do it to this day.

Daddy Bill always used the term "sassy" to refer to when the kids and the wives were acting up! These days, my sisters and I use the word "spicy". No matter what you call it … in Maddie's case, the apple doesn't fall far from the tree!

Although it isn't unusual for Maddie to be less than willing to pose *properly* for a picture, on this particular day, she REALLY didn't want to pose … obviously. I realized that she was wearing my "Taylor Made" cap so I kept snapping away, giggling all the while. Mac bought it for me awhile back because he knew I'd love to wear something bearing my maiden name. How appropriate that Maddie gets caught on film being sassy while she's wearing this hat.

Madeline Taylor McDaniel

Straight A's in school?
"It's the Taylor side!"

Lead in the school play?
"She's a Taylor!"

The girls are being sassy?
"Must be the Thompson side !"

"I've used my Fiskars Micro-Tip Scissors and tape runner adhesive since I started scrapbooking. They provide the level of precision I need to handle the tiniest of accents."

"Taylor Made"

Supplies *Patterned paper:* American Crafts; *Plastic film:* Shrinky Dink; *Computer fonts:* P22 Garamouche, Typewriter and CB Wednesday, downloaded from the Internet; 2Peas Dreams, downloaded from *www.two-peasinabucket.com*; *Other:* Fibers, brads, tin heart and bookplate.

TERRIE MCDANIEL • LEAGUE CITY, TX

"I've always enjoyed taking pictures," explains Terrie, "but somehow, the photo albums I religiously kept organized didn't seem to cut it. The photos alone didn't do justice to the stories behind them." Terrie loves scrapbooking because it allows her to capture all the big and little stories in life—and everything that falls in between. Shares Terrie, "I'm fueled by the idea of passing down my family's stories to future generations."

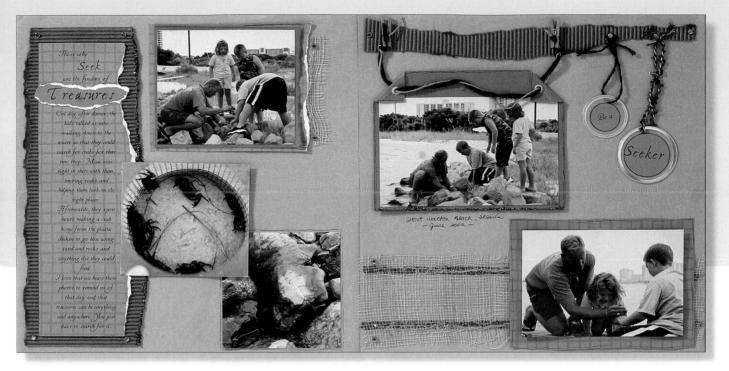

"Seekers"

Supplies *Patterned paper:* EK Success; *Corrugated paper:* DMD, Inc.; *Netting:* Magic Scraps; *Vellum tags:* Making Memories; *Computer font:* Corabael, downloaded from the Internet; *Fibers:* Adornaments, EK Success; *Other:* Brads, jute and clothespins.

"The Perfect Wave"

Supplies *Vellum:* Karen Foster Design; *Computer font:* 2Peas Beautiful, downloaded from *www.twopeasinabucket.com*; *Square punch:* McGill; *Pop dots:* All Night Media; *Other:* Brads.

IDEA TO NOTE: Terrie used her sewing machine without thread to create the stitched holes around the border of the journaling and focal-point photo.

"Love Letters to Mymee"

Supplies *Patterned paper:* Mustard Moon; *Vellum:* Paper Adventures; *Vellum tags:* Making Memories; *Computer font:* 2Peas Jack Frost, downloaded from *www.two-peasinabucket.com*; *Alphabet rubber stamps:* Limited Edition; *Stamping ink:* Tsukineko; *Photo corners:* Kolo; *Pen:* Source unknown; *Other:* Staples.

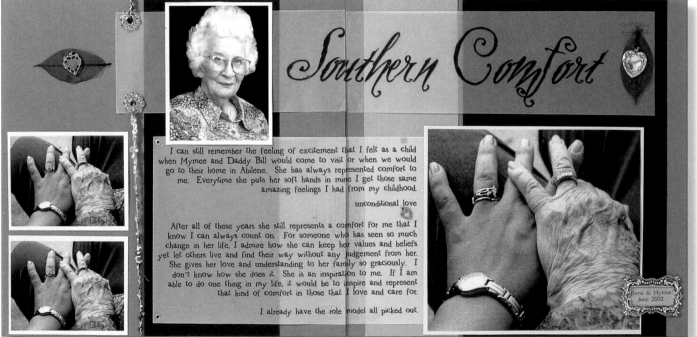

"Southern Comfort"

Supplies *Vellum:* The Paper Company; *Leaves:* Black Ink; *Frame:* Creative Imaginations; *Computer fonts:* Zothique Demo (title), downloaded from the Internet; 2Peas Flea Market by Sharon Soneff, downloaded from *www.twopeasinabucket.com*; *Charms:* Embellish It!; *Other:* Eyelets and fibers.

CREATIVE INSPIRATION

Movies. Books. TV shows. Slang terms. And oh yes, songs! My affinity for pop culture has been working its way into my scrapbooks for as long as I can remember. A phrase in a song or maybe even a line or two from a movie often evoke a mood or a feeling that inspires a theme for a layout. And why not? Artists put emotions and feelings into words we so often relate to. Incorporating them into layouts is a natural next step.

By integrating these tidbits of our time into my pages, I'm providing a glimpse into the world I live in. I often imagine my daughter relating the "classic" songs and movies of today back to the layouts in our family scrapbooks. Maybe someday she'll hear a song on the radio and smile when she thinks of the layout with the same name in her family scrapbook!

—by Terrie McDaniel

"Hunting Buddies"

Supplies *Patterned paper:* Source unknown; *Rusty metal hearts:* Darice; *Alphabet rubber stamps:* Hero Arts; *Stamping ink:* Tsukineko; *Embossing powder:* Source unknown; *Pop dots:* All Night Media; *Other:* Fibers and eyelets.

"A Black and White Christmas"

Supplies *Textured paper:* Club Scrap; *Computer fonts:* 2Peas Chestnuts ("A Black &"), 2Peas Gift ("White") and 2Peas Evergreen ("Christmas"), downloaded from *www.twopeasinabucket.com.*

"My favorite tools are things that cut: the Fiskar's Shape Cutter, Coluzzle knife and template, and Fiskar's micro-tip scissors. I use the Shape Cutter for cutting out letters from computer fonts. I use the Coluzzle to cut circles of various sizes and mats. And I use the micro-tips for letters and for detail work."

TRACY MILLER • FALLSTON, MD

Tracy's motivation to scrapbook comes from two things: her love of capturing her children on film and her desire to remember details about them. "I'm amazed by how quickly I forget details about my children at particular ages," says Tracy. "At the moment things are happening, I think, 'I will remember this,' but so often I don't. Scrapbooking allows me to capture those moments."

"Meredith Takes Flight"

Supplies *Computer fonts:* Cezanne and Garamouche, P22 Type Foundry; *Accent photos:* Shotz! by Danelle Johnson, Creative Imaginations; *Other:* Embossing powder.

IDEA TO NOTE: Tracy printed the journaling directly onto the photo and embossed it with clear embossing powder to set the ink.

"Buttons"

Supplies *Textured papers:* Strathmore (white), Paper Adventures (pink); *Computer fonts:* 2Peas Pancakes (title) and 2Peas Bad Hair Day (journaling), downloaded from *www.twopeasinabucket.com*; *Photo paper:* Epson; *Buttons:* Making Memories; *Pop dots:* All Night Media.

"Sibling Rivalry"

Supplies *Textured paper:* SEI; *Silver paper:* Artistic Enhancements; *Computer font:* Noodlescript, downloaded from the Internet; *Heart charm:* Making Memories; *Eyelets:* Making Memories (⅛"), Boxer Scrapbook Productions (1/16"); *Embossing powder:* Stampendous!; UTEE, Suze Weinberg; *Pop dots:* All Night Media.

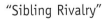

"Chubby Cheeks and a Big Head"

Supplies *Specialty paper:* Canson; *Computer font:* Tahoma, Microsoft Word; *Other:* Iron-on transfers.

IDEA TO NOTE: Tracy cut a slit in each matted circle to tuck the photo corners into.

"Love You"

Supplies *Patterned paper:* SEI; *Heart charms:* Card Connection; *Computer font:* Times New Roman, Microsoft Word; *Letter and border stickers:* SEI; *Jump rings:* Hirschberg Schutz & Co.; *Embossing powder:* Stampendous!; *Transparency film:* 3M; *Pop dots:* All Night Media.

IDEA TO NOTE: Tracy printed her journaling on a transparency and heat-embossed with clear embossing powder to set the ink.

CREATING CIRCLE ACCENTS

As you can tell from some of the layouts featured here, I love using geometric shapes on my pages. I find that circles add interest and complexity to the page without overwhelming my photos.

Here's how you can re-create the layout above:

MATERIALS:

☐ Black cardstock
☐ White cardstock
☐ Various shades of pink cardstock (SEI)
☐ Pink patterned paper (SEI)
☐ Coluzzle Cutting System with circle template and circle companion template
☐ SEI Elements and Letter stickers (for photo mat)
☐ Transparency film

FOLLOW THESE STEPS:

◆ In order to determine the circle placement, it's helpful to draw a sketch.

◆ Use the template to cut the circles from the black cardstock.

◆ Layer the black cardstock over the patterned paper.

◆ Make borders for the circles in the black cardstock by cutting a circle in the same size from pink cardstock. Then place the companion template over the circle and cut in the channel ¼" larger. Adhere that circle over the holes in the background cardstock.

◆ Journal on transparency film and adhere to the patterned paper so that it shows through the holes in the top paper.

◆ Attach charms with jump rings.

◆ Affix photo to mat, decorated with letter and border stickers.

◆ Attach black cardstock to patterned paper using pop dots.

Note: The placement of these circles was loosely based on product packaging from Bath & Body Works.

—by Tracy Miller

5 tips for better journaling

PHOTOGRAPHS ARE AN AMAZING record of moments in your life, but without your written memories alongside them, the stories just aren't complete. Journaling on your scrapbook pages doesn't have to be intimidating—just start with these five tips to get those words flowing.

❶ Carry a small notebook with you. No matter where you go, when memories drift back or someone says a particularly funny thing, jot them down and refer to your notebook later when you're creating scrapbook pages. You can also use your notebook to keep a record of the photos you're taking and any interesting details you think of that may not appear in the photos.

❷ Don't just tell the obvious. If you're writing journaling to go with a photograph, let the photograph speak for itself and fill in the missing details. Instead of writing, "In this photograph, Anna is wearing a white dress with embroidered flowers," you could say, "The dress Anna is wearing is an heirloom— my mother bought it for me when I was little and kept it all these years so my own daughter could wear it someday." Your journaling doesn't have to focus only on the event in the photo. If you notice something in the photograph that has a story, write about it while you have the opportunity!

❸ Include the who, what, where, when and why on your pages. Who's in the pictures, what are the events, details or stories surrounding the photograph, where and when was it taken, and why did you want to include it in your scrapbook? Don't just focus on the events captured in the photo—talk about the photo as if you were describing it to a good friend who wasn't there for the occasion.

❹ Read your journaling twice before including it on your page. Sometimes getting words on paper is such a relief we don't notice our errors until the journaling is already printed and on our page. Practice your journaling on scratch paper, read over it to make sure it expresses what you'd like to include, then create a final copy. But wait, you're not done yet! Read over the final copy twice more before attaching it to your page, making sure to correct any errors before it's too late.

❺ Journal in your own handwriting, at least once in a while. Even if you don't like your writing, your loved ones will enjoy seeing your memories written in the handwriting they remember. Take your time, draw guidelines and write carefully. Remember that you're leaving a legacy, and your handwriting is an important part of it.

As you're incorporating these tips into your journaling, remember that the extra effort will be worth the keepsakes you'll create! ♥

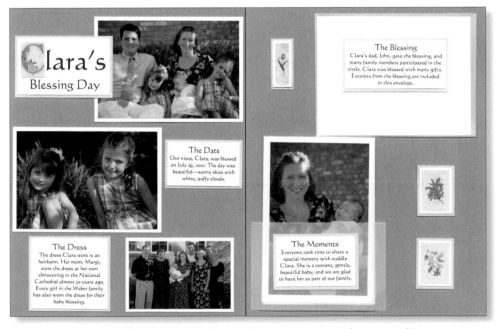

Include written memories with your photographs to complete the story on your layouts. **Supplies** *Vellum:* Paper Cuts; *Stickers:* K & Company; *Computer font:* Calligraph421 BT, WordPerfect, Corel."

IDEA TO NOTE: The chain in the upper left-hand corner holds a list of Maya's family's favorite adventure spots.

"Because journaling is often a focal point of my work, my computer has become my favorite tool. My computer makes it easy to manipulate text on a page, and it makes the text easier to read. I especially love the way fonts help set the tone of a layout."

"These Are Days to Remember"

Supplies *Rubber stamps:* Stampin' Up! (trees and large sprigs), Close To My Heart (small sprigs); *Stamping ink:* Tsukineko; *Computer font:* McBooHmk, downloaded from the Internet; *Eyelets:* Making Memories; *Other:* Chain.

MAYA OPAVSKA • REDMOND, WA

When Maya began scrapbooking five years ago, she resisted expressing her feelings on her pages, hesitant to be too personal. Now heartfelt journaling is a hallmark of her layouts. "The more I spoke from my heart," Maya explains, "the more I realized I had things I needed to share." And the more she shared, the more she realized she was speaking to those she loves. "I hope my pages will help my children remember all the happy times we've shared together as a family," says Maya. "I hope they'll hear my voice even after I'm gone, and feel how much they were loved."

"Is This Love?"

Supplies *Computer fonts:* AliceLight and Papyrus, downloaded from the Internet; *Stamping ink:* Tsukineko, Stampin' Up!; *Pen:* Zig Writer, EK Success; *Charms:* Making Memories; *Snaps:* Coffee Break Design; *Square eyelets:* Emagination Crafts; *Gold cord:* Stampin' Up!; *Embossing powder:* UTEE, Suze Weinberg; *Pop dots:* Glue Dots International; *Double-stick tape:* Wonder Tape, Suze Weinberg; *Other:* Copper plant tags and metal punches.

IDEA TO NOTE: Maya sponged the background paper with several colors of ink to match the photo.

IDEAS TO NOTE: The envelope at the top contains a photo of Maya and her grandfather taken in 1980. She designed the envelope enclosure at the bottom of the layout, which contains vital statistics about her grandfather.

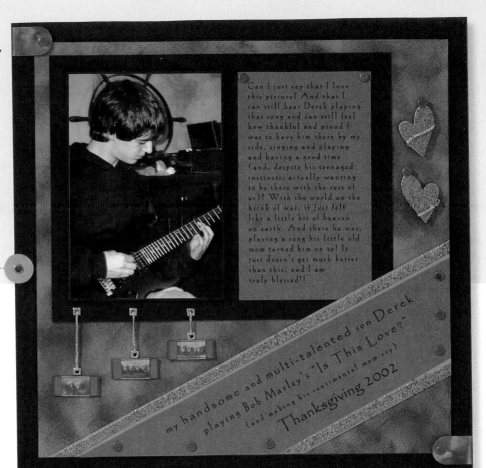

Can I just say that I love this picture? And that I can still hear Derek playing that song and can still feel how thankful and proud I was to have him there by my side, singing and playing and having a good time (and, despite his teenaged instincts, actually wanting to be there with the rest of us)? With the world on the brink of war, it just felt like a little bit of heaven on earth. And there he was, playing a song his little old mom turned him on to! It just doesn't get much better than this, and I am truly blessed!!

my handsome and multi-talented son Derek playing Bob Marley's "Is This Love?" (and making his sentimental mom cry) Thanksgiving 2002

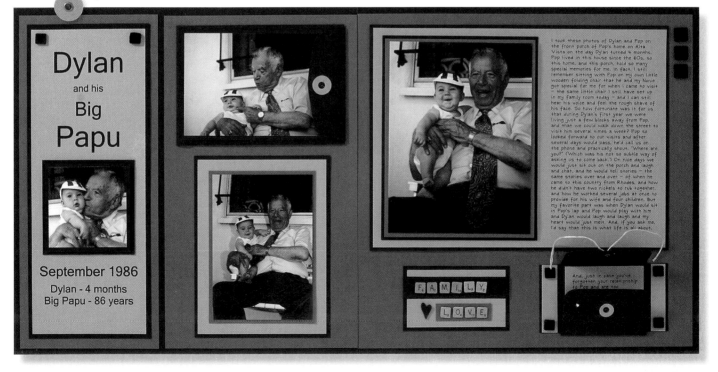

Dylan
and his
Big Papu

September 1986
Dylan - 4 months
Big Papu - 86 years

I took these photos of Dylan and Pop on the front porch of Pop's home on Alta Vista on the day Dylan turned 4 months. Pop lived in this house since the 60s, so this home, and this porch, hold so many special memories for me. In fact, I still remember sitting with Pop on my own little wooden folding chair that he and my Nonie got special for me for when I came to visit — the same little chair I still have set up in my family room today — and I can still hear his voice and feel the rough shave of his face. So how fortunate was it for us that during Dylan's first year we were living just a few blocks away from Pop, and that we could walk down the street to visit him several times a week? Pop so looked forward to our visits and after several days would pass, he'd call us on the phone and practically shout, "Where are you?" (Which was his not so subtle way of asking us to come back.) On nice days we would just sit out on the porch and laugh and chat, and he would tell stories — the same stories over and over — of when he came to this country from Rhodes, and how he didn't have two nickels to rub together, and how he worked several jobs at once to provide for his wife and four children. But my favorite part was when Dylan would sit in Pop's lap and Pop would play with him, and Dylan would laugh and laugh and my heart would just melt. And, if you ask me, I'd say that this is what life is all about.

FAMILY
♥ LOVE

And, just in case you've forgotten your relationship to Pop and are too...

Dylan and His Big Papu"

Supplies *Computer fonts:* Sans Serif (title), Microsoft Word; CK Journaling (journaling), "The Best of Creative Lettering" CD Vol. 2, *Creating Keepsakes; Buttons and eyelets:* Making Memories; *Scrabble tiles:* Limited Edition; *Fibers:* Two Busy Moms, Leeco Industries; *Punches:* EK Success (heart), Emagination Crafts (circles); *Stamping ink:* Marvy Uchida; *Foam squares:* Therm O Web.

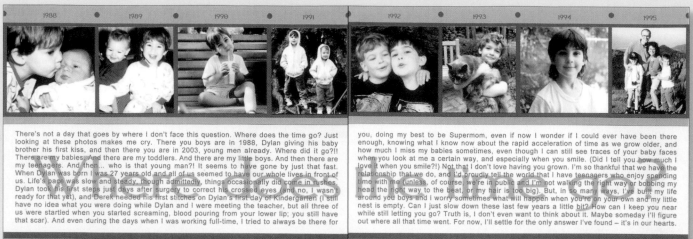

"Where Does the Time Go?"

Supplies *Patterned paper:* SEI; *Computer fonts:* Aquaduct (title), downloaded from the Internet; Arial (journaling), Microsoft Word; *Punches:* Emagination Crafts.

"Mikaela"

Supplies *Patterned paper:* Club Scrap; *Vellum:* The Paper Company; *Computer fonts:* Boulder (title) and Architect (journaling), downloaded from the Internet; *Metal studs and rings:* ScrapWorks.

"It's a Small World After All"

Supplies *Vellum:* The Paper Company; *Rubber stamps:* Uptown Rubber Stamps (double globe), Club Scrap (single globe); *Stamping ink:* Tsukineko; *Computer fonts:* Aquaduct and Boulder (title), downloaded from the Internet; Arial Narrow (title and journaling), Microsoft Word; *Snaps:* Doodlebug Design; *Eyelets:* Making Memories; *Pen:* Zig Writer, EK Success.

IDEA TO NOTE: The block under the journaling is a pocket that holds maps of Maya's travels.

UNIFYING TWO-PAGE LAYOUTS

When creating two-page layouts, I love to play with different ways of tying the two pages together. You're probably familiar with the simplest and most common technique—framing the pages with a single border—but there are several other methods you can use to create unity between two pages. Try these ideas:

◆ **Look at the two pages you're designing as one.** If you're working with 12" x 12" pages, look at them as one 24" x 12" page. Don't be afraid to ignore the line between the pages as you're laying things out. You can jiggle elements around to get them in exactly the right place with respect to the center line as you get closer to gluing things down, but this approach almost always yields a design that flows well across both pages.

◆ **Use borders, text and/or alignment to create strong horizontal or diagonal lines that span both pages.** Try spanning the title, a subtitle, a quote or even the journaling across both pages (in the case of journaling, you just need to use larger text so it's easy to follow as you read across the pages).

◆ **Try color-blocking in three vertical blocks (or two blocks of different widths) so that one of the blocks crosses the center line.**

◆ **Consider splitting photographs or other elements across the center line.** This works particularly well on landscape-oriented photographs with logical dividing lines. In some cases, you can even split embellishments or borders.

◆ **Try clustering photographs or other elements around the center line so they form a cohesive block.** The shape itself isn't so important—it's the clustering that matters here.

Creating unity on two-page layouts doesn't have to be a challenge. Just experiment to discover what works best with your design.

—*by Maya Opavska*

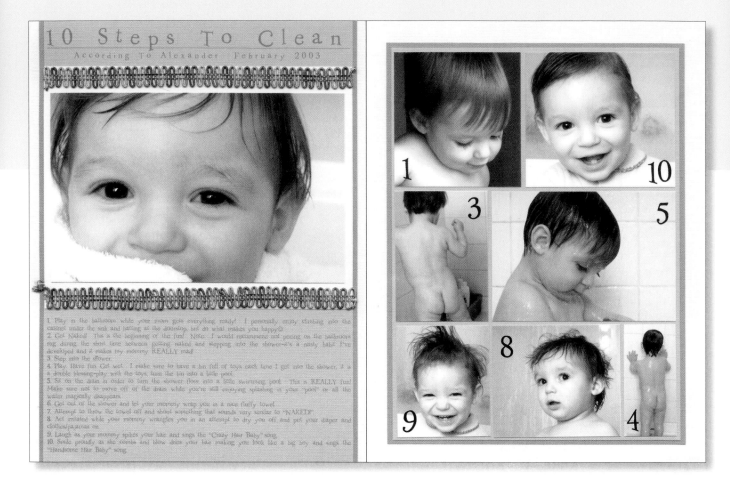

"My favorite scrapbooking tools are simple:

my camera, my printer, cardstock, Hermafix

tabs and a good paper cutter."

"10 Steps to Clean"

Supplies *Textured paper:* Bazzill Basics; *Computer font:* 2Peas Flea Market by Sharon Soneff, downloaded from *www.twopeasinabucket.com; Other:* Trim.

MARISSA PEREZ • ISSAQUAH, WA

Marissa loves everything about scrapbooking—from photography to storytelling to design. "I love having the opportunity to create beauty on a blank page," says Marissa, "and I love documenting our family's stories." Marissa's inspiration comes from her son, Alex. "As a child, I loved turning the pages of my mother's and grandmother's photo albums," she says. "I hope my son's children and grandchildren will enjoy this legacy, too."

An American Classic

I LOVE this photo of Alex! It looks like it should be on some Ralph Lauren ad. I am continually amazed by Alex's good looks. He has the same "All American Boy" thing going that his dad does. The amazing smile, the shiny flowing hair, the sparkly eyes all perfectly accentuated by a warm, gregarious spirit. I look forward to watching him grow and change. I know that he will always keep those classic good looks and his fun, flirty personality!

"An American Classic"

Supplies *Computer font:* Times New Roman, Microsoft Word; *Other:* Postage stamp.

"A Letter to Alexander"

Supplies *Computer font:* Source unknown.

IDEA TO NOTE: Marissa scanned the two photos of her son sleeping and applied a slight under-painting technique to them using Adobe Photoshop 7. Then she printed the photos onto cardstock and gently ripped the edges.

A Letter To Alexander

Monday

June 24, 2002

7:46 am

Dearest Alexander-
As I laid you down on my bed a moment ago, frustrated by the fact that you had awoken at 6:00am ready to party and now close to 2 hours later when I am ready to start my day you nod off into a sleepy smiled dream land next to your dad, I was over-come by your perfection! your face is art to me! Those long, dark, curly eyelashes. your faultless soft, fair, pink skin. your perfectly rounded nose (the only thing that keeps you from being an exact replica of your father) your soft, round cheeks. your impeccably formed mouth. your little chin. I adore you. My gaze moves down as I examine your soft little body. your legs and feet are bare and like velvet. I love your square, broad feet- just like Daddy's! you bring your hand to your face and smile, obviously dreaming of a calm, sweet place. you will be 9 months old on Thursday! How can that be? It seems like just yesterday you were a teeny 6lb. 14oz. crying creature being handed to me. So very different from the crawling, babbling boy you are today! But your spirit is the same! you are pure sunshine! It has been a fascinating journey, which I know will continue as you grow. to watch your personality begin to take form these last 9 months! As I look at your little bod I realize you are more parts toddler than infant these days. your body has stretched and lengthened preparing to take off and examine the world. I am grateful for you. I am grateful for the amazing change you have brought to my life. what was I before I was your mother? Thank you for choosing me to be your mother! I love you always! Mama

"First Bike"

Supplies *Computer font:* 2Peas Flea Market by Sharon Soneff, downloaded from *www.twopeasinabucket.com;* *Other:* Mesh.

IDEAS TO NOTE: Marissa used her camera's macro lens to zoom in and capture all of her son's tiny parts. She formatted the photos into a square using Adobe Photoshop 7 and had them printed on a Fuji Frontier printing machine.

As I looked at these photos the first time my gut reaction was "Who is that boy riding my baby's bike!!!" Alexander has grown up so much in every facet of his life in the last month. His molars are forcefully pushing their way through his gums. He is finally putting on some chub and has that distinctive toddler shape-belly hanging over his pants and chubby little fingers and legs. His vocabulary is taking off like a rocket. His understanding of the English language is absolutely phenomenal. He has swiftly gone from scooting and crawling to running everywhere he goes. His obsession with books has been rekindled and he will sit and read with me for a half hour at a time.

This bike was a Christmas gift from Aunt Bec and Uncle Peter. I think it certainly wins the prize as his most loved present from Christmas 2002! He rides it in the house and on the sidewalk outside our patio. He and Anna take turns riding it when she comes over to play.

As his 18 month birthday looms ever closer I am forced to accept the fact that he is officially a toddler, one literal and figurative step further from babyhood and closer to being a full fledged boy. Part of me is sad, as is always the case as he reaches a milestone. But another part of me is excited by the realization that even through all the insanity of our daily existence I really like him! I truly enjoy the person he is becoming. I like that he will wave, smile or talk to anyone he comes in contact with, something the shy part of my personality still struggles with. I love that he is a sweetie, giving loves to all the other babies and toddlers at church. I love that he likes to read and explore and play and investigate the world. He is my sweetheart and I am grateful to get to spend so much time with him each day! February 2003

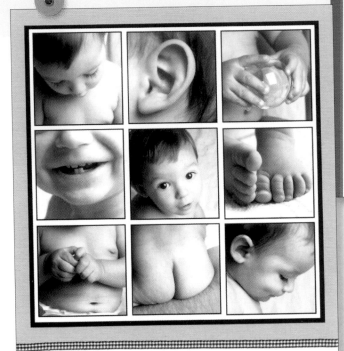

Parts & Pieces, Age One
Alexander November 2002

"Parts & Pieces"

Supplies *Textured paper:* Bazzill Basics; *Computer font:* 2 Peas Flea Market by Sharon Soneff, downloaded from *www.twopeasinabucket.com.*

"Visions of Sugarplums"

Supplies *Computer font:* Garamouche, downloaded from the Internet.

IDEAS TO NOTE: Marissa created the photo border along the top of the layout using Adobe Photoshop 7. She converted the large photo to black and white, and lightened and reduced it. Then she burned the file to a CD and had it printed on a Fuji Frontier printing machine at a local store.

This photo is linked to one of my earliest memories. One night as my mom was finishing up her performance as the Sugarplum Fairy in Riverside's production of The Nutcracker my Grampy carefully snuck me backstage to prepare to take my mom flowers. I was a tiny three and a half year old sprite of a girl with strawberry blond hair and a shy, sweet spirit. I vividly remember carefully walking down the metal steps to get backstage. I can still see their grate-like design and the tiles below. I don't remember how we got back stage or being handed the flowers and I'm sure that my memory of being on the stage is heavily supplemented by the video footage I have seen and my mom's account of the tale. I scurried out onto the stage carrying an enormous bouquet of flowers which swept the ground as I walked. The audience of course let out a unified "Awwww" as I walked past the other dancers and proceeded to center stage where my mom stood. I stuck my arms out and she took both me and the flowers into her arms for a gigantic hug. Her partner Edward bent down to try to get a hug from me as well at which point I realized just how many people were sitting looking at me and just how bright the stage lights were and immediately bolted back across the stage to the safety of my Grampy's arms, which of course caused the audience to chuckle. I have always been so proud of my mom and the amazing things she is able to accomplish. Kyle was 10 months old when this photo was taken and thereshe was onstage, the most beautiful Sugarplum Fairy ever! I am grateful for the snippets of memory that I have of this wonderful time in both our lives.

Photo taken December 1980. Journaling written January 2003

Visions of Sugarplums

Ready, Set, Squeal!

Taking pictures of bored kids who'd rather be somewhere else? Do what Wendy Sue Anderson of Heber, Utah, does: scream or squeal. "It gets the kids' attention," says Wendy, "and in seconds I'm getting big, genuine smiles or even laughter from my children. You can see the big difference in the photos here."

WENDY SUE ANDERSON

Gather Family Stories

Family get-togethers are ideal times to gather family stories. Next time you're chatting with family members, ask the following "starter" questions. Get more details later from the people who can supply them.

- ◆ Who in the family knows the most about our ancestors?
- ◆ What interesting tidbits do you know? Was someone an immigrant? A Pony Express rider? A teacher?
- ◆ Have you heard any inspiring or humorous stories?
- ◆ What are your memories of our great-grandparents or grandparents?

Break a Pattern

While you can reinforce a shape by repeating it on a page, do it too many times and the results can be boring. Break the pattern! Here, Angie Cramer of Redcliff, Alberta, Canada, enlarged the photo of the plate of food, then trimmed it to fit in the upper left-hand corner of her page. Note how the curve of the plate offsets the three square photos below and adds visual interest.

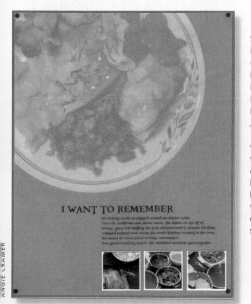

I WANT TO REMEMBER

ANGIE CRAMER

Supplies *Vellum:* Paper Adventures; *Computer font:* Freebooter, downloaded from the Internet; *Other:* Mini brads. *Journaling excerpt:* ". . . the smell of turkey roasting in the oven, the sound of voices joined in lively conversation, how good everything tasted, the cherished moments spent together."

Smarter Journaling

The next time you get photos back from the developer, grab a sheet of paper or sit down at your computer. Take a few minutes to jot down or type the "who, what, when, why and where" details behind the pictures. Scrapbooking the specifics later will be much easier—and more accurate!

This is also a good time to record your thoughts and feelings as you look at the photos, along with any miscellaneous ideas. Store the notes with the related photos.

LISA HANSON

Life brings Simple Pleasures to us everyday it is ...up to us to Make them WONDerful Memories

"Life Memories"

Supplies
Patterned paper: Making Memories;
Mesh: Magenta;
Flower buttons and eyelet letters: Making Memories;
Ball chain: Westrim Crafts; *Computer font:* 2Peas Jack Frost, downloaded from *www.twopeasina-bucket.com.*

"I love Making Memories' product line. From their watercolor

papers to their Details collection, they're all must-haves!"

VANESSA REYES • LAKE PORT, CA

Vanessa's passion for scrapbooking stems from her desire to preserve her family's memories. "I've always deeply valued family bonds," shares Vanessa. "Scrapbooking allows me to tie all my memories, values, wishes and hopes into a keepsake I can pass on to future generations."

"Water Everywhere"

Supplies *Patterned paper:* Karen Foster Design; *Page accents:* Fresh Cuts, EK Success; *Fibers:* Rubba Dub Dub; Adornaments, EK Success; *Shaved ice and microbeads:* Magic Scraps; *Other:* Page pebbles, beads and clips.

IDEA TO NOTE: A sparkling mix of shaved ice, beads and microbeads mimic the look of water.

IDEA TO NOTE: Vanessa lashed twigs with wire to create the frame and accent piece.

"Autumn"

Supplies *Patterned paper:* Making Memories; *Mesh:* Magenta; *Vellum:* Paper Adventures; *Computer fonts:* CK Cursive, "The Best of Creative Lettering" CD Vol. 2, *Creating Keepsakes:* 2Peas Dragonfly, 2Peas Flea Market by Sharon Soneff and 2Peas Cookie Dough, downloaded from *www.twopeasinabucket.com*; *Die cuts:* Li'l Davis Designs; *Chalk:* Craf-T Products; *Craft wire:* Artistic Wire Ltd.

Our beautiful Polynesian princess. A delightful mix of Tongan and Guamanian **HERITAGE** your name has a meaning that is heavenly and was chosen especially for **YOU** Though you are miles away from our islands, you show an untaught love & **APPRECIATION**

IDEA TO NOTE: Vanessa tied individual bunches of fibers along the top of the layout.

"Polynesian Princess"

Supplies *Patterned paper:* Making Memories; *Vellum:* The Paper Company; *Computer fonts:* 2Peas Dreams, downloaded from *www.twopeasinabucket.com*; Fontdinerdotcom Loungy, downloaded from the Internet; *Eyelet letters:* Making Memories; *Fibers:* Adornaments, EK Success; *Paper-pieced flowers:* Vanessa's own design.

KEEPING THE FOCUS ON YOUR PHOTOS

When I first started scrapbooking, I fell in love with all the beautiful papers and unique embellishments. I used them on all of my layouts—even if they didn't correspond to my photos. Soon I noticed that many of my most precious pictures were getting lost in all the fancy decorations.

Since then, I've learned to keep the focus on my photos by taking that beautiful smile or special moment and putting it center stage. I still love to use all the latest products when they apply, but now I know it's the memories I want to preserve, not the latest trends.

—*by Vanessa Reyes*

Tall oaks from little acorns grow — David Everett

"Tall Oaks"

Supplies *Patterned paper:* Frances Meyer; *Computer fonts:* Papyrus (title), Microsoft Word; misc. fonts, packages unknown; *Other:* Eyelets and hemp.

"After taking the time to learn the basics of photo-editing software, I can improve the appearance of most of my older photos. It's one of the best things I've done to improve the quality of my work."

KAREN RUSSELL • GRANTS PASS, OR

Karen has always been drawn to photography—the clean lines, the sharp contrasts and, especially, the stories the images tell. "I'm primarily a self-taught photographer," Karen explains. "I've spent a lot of time reading photography books and magazines, and just hanging out in the camera shop asking questions." Karen lets her photos set the direction of her scrapbook pages. "From color choices to journaling, I let the photos dictate the page design," says Karen. "And if I love a photo, I want to be sure it's the focal point of my layout, so I enlarge it ... the bigger the better."

IDEA TO NOTE: Karen used an air art gun with a pen to create the brown-speckled look on the brown cardstock.

"Free Spirit"

Supplies *Patterned paper:* Colorbök; *Metal letters:* Making Memories; *Letter stickers:* Sonnets, Creative Imaginations; *Dog tag:* Chronicle Books; *Computer fonts:* Unknown; *Pen:* Zig Writer, EK Success; *Other:* Fiber, watch crystal, buttons and eyelets.

"Be Something"

Supplies *Patterned paper:* Source unknown; *Computer fonts:* Papyrus, French Script and Edwardian Script, downloaded from the Internet; *Pewter stickers:* Magenta; *Metal words and glass pebble:* Making Memories; *Eyelets:* Impress Rubber Stamps; *Photo corners:* Kolo; *Other:* Bookplate, buttons, brads and beads.

"Oceanside"

Supplies *Computer font:* CK Bella, "The Best of Creative Lettering" CD Vol. 2, *Creating Keepsakes; Embossing powder:* Stampin' Up!; *Stamping ink:* VersaMark, Tsukineko; *Other:* Charms, seashells, fibers and foam core.

SHAKER BOXES AND RECESSED PHOTOS

Recessed photos, shaker boxes and windows are all great ways to create interest and dimension on a page. I love the look of these boxes and they're so much fun to create. I've included my technique here, but feel free to experiment with different shapes and sizes.

MATERIALS YOU'LL NEED:

☐ Foam core
☐ Cardstock
☐ Transparency film
☐ Photos
☐ Items to go inside shaker box
☐ X-acto knife (or square punch)
☐ Cutting mat
☐ Metal ruler

FOLLOW THESE STEPS:

◆ Use an X-acto knife or square punch to cut out "windows" in your cardstock for photos and shaker boxes in the desired locations.

◆ Place the cardstock on top of the foam core and trace the outline of the squares onto the foam core.

◆ Use an X-acto knife and metal ruler to begin cutting out the squares on the foam core (be sure to cut out the squares slightly larger than the traced outline so you won't be able to see the foam core underneath the cardstock).

◆ Cut out a piece of transparency film that is slightly bigger than the size of the square on the cardstock, then adhere the transparency film to the backside of the cardstock square that you'll be using for the shaker box (this will create the window for your shaker box).

◆ Adhere the cardstock to the foam core.

◆ Adhere your photos to the underside of the foam core, being sure to line them up so they show through the cardstock squares on the front side.

◆ Place items inside the shaker box portion of the foam core.

◆ Cut a piece of cardstock and securely adhere it to the backside of the foam core

so the items inside the shaker box won't slip out (this will also secure your photos).

—by Karen Russell

"Lasting Friendship"

Supplies *Patterned paper:* Cut from a greeting card; *Computer fonts:* Scriptina (title), downloaded from the Internet; misc. fonts, packages unknown; *Pewter alphabet charms:* Magenta; *Other:* Heart charm, fabric, eyelets, buttons and fiber.

IDEA TO NOTE: Karen used Adobe Photoshop to take most of the color out of the photo.

"Wonder"

Supplies *Patterned paper:* Scrap-Ease; *Pewter alphabet charms:* Magenta; *Metal words and frame:* Making Memories; *Stickers:* Magenta; *Computer font:* 2Peas Gingersnap, downloaded from *www.twopeasinabucket.com*; *Other:* Brads and raffia.

IDEAS TO NOTE: After printing the text on the canvas paper, Lisa embossed it to create a raised finish. She used masking tape to mark off the edges she didn't want painted, painted the field and removed the tape, leaving a smooth edge.

"Time with You"

Supplies *Canvas paper:* Canson; *Computer fonts:* Terracotta, P22 Type Foundry; LainieDaySH, downloaded from the Internet; *Rubber stamps:* Hero Arts (script), Inkadinkadoo (large clock face), Limited Edition (small clock face), Stampabilities (key), Raindrops on Roses (escutcheon); *Stamping ink:* Memories (silver), Stampin' Up! (blues); *Watch face:* Mato Fev; *Heart charm:* Crafts Etc.; *Embossing powder:* All Night Media; *Acrylic paint:* Delta; *Large eyelet:* Creative Imaginations; *Silver clasp:* Paper Parachute; *Embroidery floss:* DMC; *Other:* Handmade ribbon and watch crystal.

PLAYING

KISSING

LAUGHING

LOVING

HUGS

LEARNING

PRECIOUS

MY FAVORITE THING

SPENDING *Time* WITH YOU.

"My favorite scrapbooking tool is my Making Memories Tool Kit. I'm painfully organized, and I just adore having all the little tools I need in a compact case!"

LISA RUSSO • OSWEGO, IL

"I've never had any 'crafty' hobbies, so I was surprised by how obsessed I became with scrapbooking," says Lisa. "Now I can't even go two days without playing with my 'stuff'!" Lisa finds inspiration everywhere—from magazines to scrapbooking friends—but relies on her photos to guide her work: "These mini works of art are perfect jumping-off points for creating layouts."

"Smile"

Supplies *Tag:* Lisa's own design; *Computer font:* 2Peas Flea Market by Sharon Soneff, downloaded from *www.twopeasinabucket.com*; *Snaps:* Making Memories; *Eyelet:* Creative Imaginations; *Watercolors:* Angora; *Walnut ink:* Tom Norton Designs; *Stamping ink:* ColorBox, Clearsnap, Inc.; *Gesso:* Liquitex; *Other:* Fibers.

IDEA TO NOTE:
Lisa created the middle strip by applying gesso to watercolor paper with a sponge and using the edge of the sponge to create wavy texture. After it dried, she painted it with watercolors.

Smile...
And the whole world smiles with you.
- Aidan at 3 1/2

CREATING YOUR OWN WATERCOLOR BACKGROUND

One of my favorite ways to add texture and color to regular background paper is to create my own. Painting your own background paper is easier than it looks and is very forgiving. Here is one of my favorite methods:

MATERIALS YOU'LL NEED:

☐ Heavy watercolor paper

☐ Acrylic gesso

☐ Triangle-shaped cosmetic sponge

☐ Watercolors and watercolor paintbrush

FOLLOW THESE STEPS:

◆ Squeeze a liberal amount of gesso onto your watercolor paper. Using a cosmetic sponge, "paint" the gesso across the paper in a wavy pattern. Use the thin (pointed) edge of the sponge to carve wavy lines into the gesso. Allow to dry.

◆ Using diluted watercolors, paint a variety of colors across the gessoed paper, following the line of the waves you created. Allow to dry.

◆ Using an X-acto knife, cut a wavy strip (following the gesso pattern), and adhere to your page with brads or snaps.

—by Lisa Russo

"I love to get my hands on paper! The possibilities are endless: tearing, crumpling, mixing, chalking, stamping, inking, folding, stitching. Your choice of paper and how you use it can affect the entire mood of your layout."

"Winter's Playground"

Supplies *Patterned papers and letter stickers:* Sonnets, Creative Imaginations; *Vellum:* The Paper Company; *Computer font:* CK Bella, "The Best of Creative Lettering" CD Combo, *Creating Keepsakes; Fibers:* Adornments, EK Success; *Beads:* Little Charmers; *Punches:* EK Success (small snowflake), QuicKutz (large snowflake); *Metal photo corners, snowflake charms, vellum tags, eyelets and brads:* Making Memories.

JULIE SCATTAREGIA • CARMEL, IN

"My layouts are often emotion-driven," shares Julie. "If I feel strongly about something, you can bet it will wind up on a layout." Julie finds inspiration in the talented work of her scrapbooking friends, home décor magazines and song lyrics. She uses that inspiration to capture her family's memories. Says Julie, "I never want my kids to guess how I felt about the important things in life."

"If Only"

Supplies *Patterned paper:* Sonnets, Creative Imaginations; *Vellum:* The Paper Company; *Computer font:* CK Bella, "The Best of Creative Lettering" CD Combo, *Creating Keepsakes; Rubber stamps:* Limited Edition (small tag), Stampabilities (pocket watch), Inkadinkadoo (heart); *Stamping ink:* Ranger Industries (sepia), Tsukineko (cocoa), Close To My Heart (black); *Fibers:* Adornaments, EK Success; *Eyelets, brads and page pebble:* Making Memories; *Embossing powder:* Stampendous! (tiger eye), Ranger Industries (copper); *Ribbon:* C. M. Offray & Son; *Photo corners:* Canson; *Craft feathers:* Fibre Craft; *Other:* Microbeads, mesh, charm, printed letter tiles, antique rulers and photos.

CREATING A COLLAGE TAG

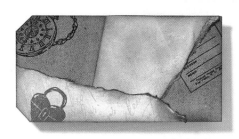

Want to create a simple yet elegant page accent? Try a collage tag. It's great for a heritage page but can add a bit of sophistication to any style of layout. Although the instructions appear lengthy, a collage tag is fast and easy to create—no measuring necessary! Here's how:

◆ Using a sponge applicator, ink the sides of the tag.

◆ Stamp one image near the top of the tag and a second image near the end of the tag.

◆ Tear two strips of paper, ink the sides and randomly apply to the tag. It's okay to cover a portion of the stamped images, but avoid covering them entirely.

◆ Turn the tag over, trim the excess and apply ink to the tag's edge.

◆ Stamp a third image directly on the paper covering the tag.

◆ Cut two small pieces of mesh. Pull out random fibers from the mesh for that not-so-perfect look.

◆ Ink the mesh and apply one piece near the end of the tag and one near the top of the tag. Turn the tag over and trim the excess.

◆ Ink the edges of two heritage photo cards. Adhere the photo cards to the tag, overlapping at a slight angle.

◆ Position the antique ruler against the top of the heritage photo cards and adhere to the tag.

◆ Turn the tag over and trim the excess photo cards and ruler. Ink the sides of the tag where the photo cards have been trimmed.

◆ Ink the edges of the tile letters ("Time") and adhere to the left, bottom corner of the heritage photo card near the top of the tag.

◆ Apply glue to the ends of the craft feathers and slide under the heritage photo card.

◆ Apply glue to random areas of the tag and sprinkle with microbeads.

◆ Allow to dry. To finish, set eyelet and attach tassel to tag.

—by Julie Scattaregia

"Journey of Love"

Supplies *Patterned paper:* Sonnets, Creative Imaginations; *Vellum:* The Paper Company; *Computer font:* CK Sketch, "The Best of Creative Lettering" CD Combo, *Creating Keepsakes; Wire expressions and stickers:* Sonnets, Creative Imaginations; *Eyelet ampersand:* Making Memories; *Rubber stamp:* Hero Arts; *Stamping ink:* Ranger Industries; *Embossing powder:* Stampendous!; *Mesh:* Magic Mesh; *Fibers:* Adornaments, EK Success; *Photo corners:* Canson; *Other:* Buttons.

Journey Of love

Aidan, you and Daddy definitely have a "guy thing" going on! Without a doubt, there is a magical bond between a

DAd&SON

Yesterday, you told me that when you grow up, you're going to be a Daddy and have one son. "I'm going to play construction and cars with him. I'm going to talk on the phone at work and wrestle other Daddies all day long, because that's what Daddies do."

You continued with, "But I don't want to be an adult yet. I'm still just a big boy." So true, Aidan. Your journey has only begun. Along your way, remember this, "A great man is one who has not lost the child's heart." (Mencius) We love you, big boy!

It's hot and humid, and we're headed to the

SPRINKLER PARK

What better way to beat the summertime heat!

alexa · aidan

refresh · revive · relieve · soothe · savor · shrivel

"Sprinkler Park"

Supplies *Patterned papers:* All About Me (blue), Colors By Design (multi-colored), Making Memories (yellow); *Vellum:* The Paper Company; *Computer font:* CK Stenography, "Fresh Fonts" CD, *Creating Keepsakes; Lettering template:* Khaki, QuicKutz; *Letter stickers:* Sonnets, Creative Imaginations; *Brads, eyelet charm, tag and eyelets:* Making Memories; *Fibers:* Adornaments, EK Success; *Swirl clips:* Clipiola.

"The Day That Wasn't"

Supplies *Vellum:* Postmodern Design; *Computer font:* CK Typewriter, "Fresh Fonts" CD, *Creating Keepsakes; Metallic rub-ons:* Craf-T Products; *Eyelets and eyelet letters:* Making Memories; *Ribbon:* Moon Rose; *Colored pencils:* Prismacolor, Sanford; *Pen:* Zig Millennium, EK Success; *Square punch:* Fiskars; *Walnut ink:* Postmodern Design; *Other:* Chipboard.

"My favorite tool is my sewing machine. It reminds me of both of my grandmothers, who spent hours and hours in front of their sewing machines when I was a little girl."

TRACIE SMITH • SMITHTOWN, NY

A multi-tasker at heart, Tracie loves scrapbooking because it allows her to try a variety of new things and incorporate them into one project. Tracie doesn't scrapbook chronologically, preferring to think of her albums as journals. "As I think of things I want my children and other family members to know," she explains, "I write the story and gather the appropriate photos to illustrate it. This is a hobby that leaves a priceless heirloom for future generations, and that makes me feel good about what I do."

"I'm Everything I Am"

Supplies *Ribbon:* The Ink Pad; *Beads:* Licorice Beads, Embellees; *Heart charm:* Ink It!; *Chalk pencils:* Creatacolor; *Square tiles:* Magenta; *Pen:* Zig Writer, EK Success.

IDEA TO NOTE: To create shine on the cardstock blocks and strips, Tracie used a sponge brush to coat them with Crystal Lacquer.

"Moments"

Supplies *Pen:* Zig Writer, EK Success; *Rubber stamp:* Renaissance Art Stamps; *Stamping ink:* Stampin' Up!; *3-D lacquer:* Crystal Lacquer; *Tag:* Making Memories; *Colored pencils:* Prismacolor, Sanford; *Other:* Fibers.

"You and Me, by the Sea"

Supplies *Pen:* Zig Millennium, EK Success; *Modeling paste:* Liquitex; *Hemp:* Stampin' Up!; *3-D lacquer:* Crystal Lacquer; *Seashells:* Magic Scraps; *Beads:* JewelCraft, Hirschberg Shutz & Co.; *Chalk pencils:* Creatacolor; *Watercolors:* Royal Talens; *Stamping ink:* Adirondack, Ranger Industries; *Other:* Foam stamp.

IDEAS TO NOTE: Tracie adapted the idea for her frame from the Magic with Modeling Paste tip on page 92. She painted Crystal Lacquer over the top to create a shiny texture.

FRAMING TECHNIQUES

We use beautiful frames to display our most treasured photos around our homes. Why not use frames to draw attention to the photos on our scrapbook pages? Finding inspiration is easy. Take a look around your home, stroll down the frame aisle at your local department store, or browse through a mail-order catalog. You're sure to find an array of ideas. To create the frame shown here, follow these four easy steps:

❶ Determine the frame size you need. For my 4" x 6" photo, I created a 1½" frame. Make sure to cut the inside opening smaller than the photo if you want a snug look.

❷ Use a sponge brush to paint burlap with Radiant Pearls. Make sure you have a full container—it took approximately one jar to create the frame here.

❸ Pour clear embossing powder over the Radiant Pearls and use a heat tool to melt it into the burlap.

❹ Add embellishments as finishing touches.

—by Tracie Smith

"Camel Ride"

Supplies *Fiber:* Adornaments, EK Success; *Pen:* Galaxy Marker, American Crafts.

"My all-time favorite tool is the Staedtler hot foil pen. I love to use it to heat-emboss a metallic title directly onto dark background paper or cardstock. It also makes it easy to add accent marks to pre-made letters and laser cuts."

HEIDI STEPANOVA • EAST LANSING, MI

"I usually design my best pages while I'm driving," says Heidi. "I think not having everything in front of me lets my imagination exaggerate the aspects of the photos that mean the most to me." Before she even picks up her supplies, Heidi has often planned the entire layout, including color, placement and embellishments—all she has to do is work out the final details.

IDEAS TO NOTE: Heidi printed her title onto white paper, then traced the image with a hot foil pen to transfer the font. To create the frame, she removed the protective coating from the back of a mirror with paint remover, then used a mixture of vinegar and table salt to remove the silver on the mirror.

"A Reflection of You"

Supplies *Computer font:* Scriptina, downloaded from the Internet; *Hot foil and silver pens:* Staedtler; *Beads:* Halcraft; *Mirrors:* Darice; *Brads:* Scrap Arts; *Border stickers:* Mrs. Grossman's; *Pen:* Zig Writer, EK Success.

"Splish Splash"

Supplies *Lettering template:* Giggly, Crafter's Workshop; *Die cut:* Sizzix, Provo Craft; *Pen:* Pigma Micron, Sakura; *Dimensional adhesive:* Diamond Glaze.

IDEAS TO NOTE: Heidi covered the die cuts with Diamond Glaze to create a wet look.

"Feeding the Birds"

Supplies *Vellum:* Paper Adventures; *Mirrors:* Darice; *Beads:* Zuma Beads; *Mesh:* Avant Card; *Computer font:* Bradley Hand ITC, downloaded from the Internet.

IDEA TO NOTE: Heidi used a glass-etching solution to etch the lighthouse and birds into the mirrors.

Feeding the Birds
Walt Disney World, December 2002

While we were at Magic Kingdom with Nana, Pa, Grandma, MeMa and Sam, we made a special trip down to the docks in Frontierland to split a turkey leg with the birds. Two turkey legs were $8 and fed the 9 of us, along with a dozen or so birds. This bird was our favorite because he was very gentle with his beak and not at all afraid of the kids.

CREATING A MIRROR FRAME

Adding mirrors to scrapbook pages can create a variety of moods, from quiet reflection to sparkling excitement. Using a mirror as a frame focuses this mood around a special photo, decorative accent or piece of memorabilia. Follow these steps to re-create this look:

◆ Use a permanent marker to sketch or trace the shape you want on the back of the mirror. Remember that if the shape is asymmetrical, you'll need to sketch the reversed image (Figure 1).

◆ A mirror typically has two layers: a protective outer layer made of gray or black plastic or paint, and an inner silver layer that provides the reflection through the glass. Use a piece of fine-grit sandpaper to rough up the outer coating over the shape you want to create. Be careful not to use much pressure or sand into the glass.

◆ Use a razor blade to scrape away the remaining backing within your shape. As you remove the gray outer layer, the inner layer of the mirror that provides the reflection will have a copper or golden look (Figure 2).

◆ Combine a half-cup of table salt with just enough apple-cider vinegar to make a thick paste (about one teaspoon). Lay your mirror on a flat, solid surface and vigorously rub with the salt and vinegar mixture until all of the inner backing is removed, leaving a clear glass opening. Rinse well.

◆ To attach the photo you wish to frame, place a strong adhesive tape within the remaining gray border on the back of the mirror, then position the mirror above your photo and attach. You may need to trim the edges of the photo down to the size of the mirror (Figure 3).

◆ To finish the edges of the mirror and provide some protection, run adhesive tape along the edges, then cover with a fiber or strand of beads (Figure 4).

—*by Heidi Stepanova*

sisters.

SiSTeRs aRe SPeCial

JoDi, YOU aRe BeaUtiFuL INSiDe aNd OUt! I aM SO BLeSSed tO HaVe YOU aS mY SiSTeR aNd fRieNd. I LoVe yOU!

KiNdS OF FRieNdS

JoDi 4NiTe   LoNi LeaH

"My favorite scrapbooking tool is my sewing machine. I use it to sew around photo mats, around the edge of a page, or directly onto a photo. I love the homemade feel the sewing machine adds to my scrapbook pages."

"Sisters"

Supplies *Vellum:* Paper Adventures; *Letter stickers:* Mrs. Grossman's; *Alphabet rubber stamps:* PSX Design; *Stamping ink:* ColorBox, Clearsnap, Inc.; *Brads:* Making Memories; *Mini-eyelets:* Scrapbook Attic; *Other:* Twine and silk flowers.

LONI STEVENS • PLEASANT GROVE, UT

The daughter of an Air Force audio/visual officer, Loni grew up digging through boxes of photographs he'd taken over the years. She was always struck by how a single photo can evoke so many memories. That's why Loni fell in love with scrapbooking. "It encompasses everything I'm passionate about—photography, creativity, writing and family history," explains Loni. "I love documenting the photos I'm so proud of in an original, creative way. Without the photos, it would be hard to share the stories I want to tell."

"Tough"

Supplies *Specialty paper:* Source unknown; *Vellum:* Paper Adventures; *Alphabet rubber stamps:* PSX Design (antique), Hero Arts (print); *Stamping ink:* ColorBox, Clearsnap, Inc.; *Metal letters and brads:* Making Memories; *Computer font:* 2Peas Chestnuts, downloaded from *www.twopeasinabucket.com*; *Other:* Newspaper clipping.

"I'll Take Care of You"

Supplies *Patterned paper:* Magenta; *Alphabet rubber stamps:* Hero Arts (print), PSX Design (antique); *Stamping ink:* ColorBox, Clearsnap, Inc.; *Computer fonts:* 2Peas Evergreen and 2Peas Think Small, downloaded from *www.twopeasinabucket.com*; *Label holder:* Making Memories; *Eyelets:* Doodlebug Design; *Other:* Date stamp, raffia, twine and large buttons.

"Nauvoo Temple Dedication"

Supplies *Patterned paper:* Liz King; *Vellum:* Paper Adventures; *Alphabet rubber stamps:* PSX Design; *Stamping ink:* ColorBox, Clearsnap, Inc.; *Computer fonts:* Gilligan's Island, Michaels and Scriptina, downloaded from the Internet; Arial, Microsoft Word; *Envelope:* Memory Lane Paper Co.; *Skeletonized leaves:* Black Ink; *Eyelets:* Prym-Dritz; *Other:* Date stamp, twine, mini-buttons, fabric and brads.

"Leah, My Namesake"

Supplies *Patterned paper:* Keeping Memories Alive; *Paper flowers:* Natural Paper Company; *Computer fonts:* Scriptina, Typewriter New Roman and Pan Roman, downloaded from the Internet; *Raffia:* Memory Lane Paper Co.; *Other:* Button.

"Day after Thanksgiving"

Supplies *Patterned paper:* Scrap-Ease; *Vellum:* Paper Adventures; *Computer font:* 2Peas Jack Frost, downloaded from *www.twopeasinabucket.com*; *Eyelets and craft wire:* Making Memories; *Spiral clips:* Clipiola; *Other:* Date stamp, buttons and beads.

ACHIEVING BALANCE ON A LAYOUT

Balance is one of the most important keys to a visually pleasing layout. When the balance is off, something just doesn't feel right. Here, I've listed some techniques that will help you ensure your pages are balanced every time:

◆ Every item you add to a layout has visual weight. Consider this as you add accents to the page. Larger items weigh more than smaller items. Be sure to use the size that will create balance on your page.

◆ When choosing colors for a layout, keep in mind that each color has a visual weight. For example, a dark color weighs more than a light color. To keep things in balance, choose colors that are in your photos or that complement them.

◆ When creating a two-page layout, make sure each side is in harmony with the other. Both sides of the layout should "weigh" the same visually.

◆ If there's an empty spot on your layout that's throwing off the balance, fill it with a brad or two or a torn piece of paper to equally distribute the weight across the layout.

—by Loni Stevens

sara tumpane

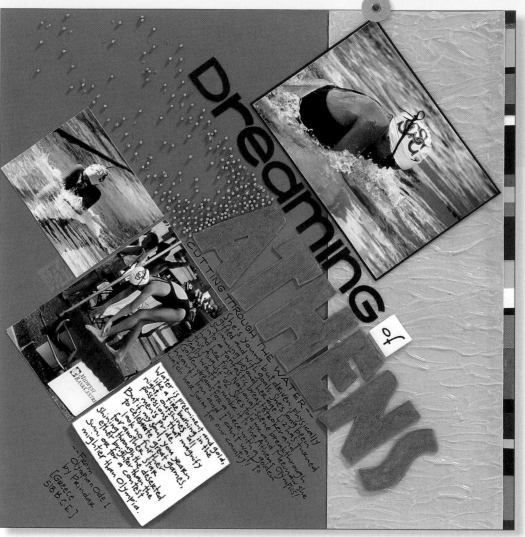

IDEAS TO NOTE: The word "Dreaming" in the title is Sara's own design. She painted "Athens" using a mixture of Pearl Ex and Crystal Lacquer.

"I love my paint brushes.

I use them for practically everything!"

"Dreaming of Athens"

Supplies *Modeling paste:* Liquitex; *Computer font:* Tribeca, downloaded from the Internet; *Beads:* Willow Bend (blue), Accent2 (clear); *Pigment powder:* Pearl Ex, Jacquard; *Clear gloss:* Diamond Glaze, JudiKins; *Pen:* Sharpie, Sanford; *Clay:* Paperclay; *Craft paint:* Plaid.

SARA TUMPANE • GRAYSLAKE, IL

Although Sara started scrapbooking to preserve her family photos, she's gravitated to exploring her creative side. "I've always loved art, from painting to sketching to sculpting to photography," shares Sara. "I love scrapbooking because it combines all the creative things I'm drawn to. I start with a blank canvas and end up with a work of art that tells a story."

"Linebacker Personality"

Supplies *Clay:* Paperclay; *Snaps:* Making Memories; *Computer fonts:* CK Broad Pen (title lines), "Fresh Fonts" CD, *Creating Keepsakes*; Arial Black and Andy, Microsoft Publisher; Times, downloaded from the Internet; *Clear gloss:* Diamond Glaze, JudiKins; *Other:* Transparency and football tag.

"The Joys of Summer"

Supplies *Modeling paste:* Liquitex; *Clay:* Paperclay; *Craft paint:* Plaid; *Metal letters and snaps:* Making Memories; *Plastic school letter tiles:* The Paper Magic Group, Inc.; *Rubber stamps:* Hero Arts; *Stamping ink:* Rubber Stampede; *Clear gloss:* Diamond Glaze, JudiKins; *Pens:* Zig Writer, EK Success; Slick Writer, American Crafts.

When the midwest summer sun has us all sweltering into August, we happily look forward to seeing the Jameses and to tasting

iowa Sweetness

corn Corn CORN corn corn CORN corn CORN Corn CORN

There is nothing better grown on this planet than fresh, juicy Iowa sweet corn... hot and dripping with butter that dribbles down your chin—mmm! Our annual "cornfest" with our friends the Jameses is easily one of our favorite traditions! Shopping for our corn this year at the farmers Market, we opted for the bargain of a BUSHEL BAG of honey "cream" and a few dozen "Bodacious." Each summer we get together—either at their house in Cedar Rapids or they come to our house (with a trunk full of corn!) + we include friends + neighbors. This year Lisa + her sister Cam, Julie + her daughter Jessie, and the Bushs also joined us. I never thought I'd see the word "BODACIOUS" associated with corn, but this new variety we tried...delicious doesn't even come close...more like "sweetly perfect"! If you don't eat at least 3 ears, you're considered a wuss! Our time together is always anticipated, enjoyed + remembered fondly.... Pass the wet naps!!

when you're **tubin'** goose Creek Lake

....this happens?

how long can you hold on til...

july '02

What's more fun than tubin'? Driving the boat + seeing how long it takes for someone to flip on that big boat wake... or perhaps where the waves converge at the "point"? On this rare visit to the lake, Lizzie, Tim and I each got our share of wipe-outs! And it's not so bad — that is, til the pain sets in the next day!!

"Iowa Sweetness"

Supplies *Patterned paper:* Flavia, Colorbök; *Clear gloss:* Diamond Glaze, JudiKins; *Embossing powder:* Ranger Industries; *Colored snaps and alphabet snaps:* Making Memories; *Computer fonts:* Times, downloaded from the Internet; Juliet, Microsoft Publisher; *Nailheads:* Prym-Dritz; *Beads:* Crafts, Etc!; *Craft paint:* Plaid; *Pens:* Sharpie, Sanford; Zig Writer, EK Success; *Pop dots:* Glue Dots International; *Other:* Fabric and green hemp.

"Tubin'"

Supplies *Modeling paste:* Liquitex; *Clay:* Paperclay; *Craft paint:* Plaid; *Clear gloss:* Diamond Glaze, JudiKins; *Pen:* Zig Writer, EK Success; *Glue dots:* Glue Dots International; *Title:* Sara's own design.

"Deer Valley Hike"

Supplies Craft paints: Plaid, Delta; Clear gloss: Diamond Glaze, JudiKins; Computer fonts: Scrap Rhapsody ("Flowers"), "Lettering Delights" CD Vol. 2, Inspire Graphics; Desdemona ("Quiet"), Dragonwick ("Winding Trail"), Jamiro ("Forests") and Laser Let ("Mountains"), Microsoft Publisher; Chicken Shack, downloaded from www.two-peasinabucket.com; Duality ("Beauty"), Dyer ("Cool"), Juliet ("Alone"), Depot ("Aspens"), Evadare ("Sara + Tim"), Mufferraw ("Slope Signs"), Mendoredondo ("Breathe"), Deaf Crab ("Spectacular Day") and Day of the Tentacle ("Sunshine"), downloaded from the Internet; Pen: Uniball Gel Tropics, Sanford; Other: Transparency.

CRAFT PAINT

I've always loved to paint, so I figured, why not try it in my scrapbooks? I'd already worked with watercolors, so I decided to experiment with craft paints. I love the effects! With craft paints, the creative options are endless. Plus, they're extremely easy to use, and since they're pH neutral and dry quickly, they're a great fit for scrapbooking. The guidelines below will help you get started:

1 Pick up your supplies. Craft paints are available in a rainbow of colors at your local craft store, usually for less than $1.00 per bottle. You'll even find "glossy" and metallic formulas. Don't worry about buying expensive brushes. Inexpensive, "flat" bristle brushes from your craft store (in various widths) work great.

For mixing paints, you may also want to pick up a small, plastic mixing palette with several wells; a square of cardboard works well, too. You'll also need a small cup of water nearby for rinsing your brushes. Clean-up is basically soap and water.

2 When starting out, use small amounts of paint (a quarter-sized dollop will generally do). You can always pour more paint if needed. However, if you're mixing a custom color, be sure to mix enough of the color to cover the area. It's next to impossible to mix the exact same color again!

3 Brush the paint on in thin layers. If you put it on too thickly, the moisture content in the paint can cause your paper to ripple. Try various patterns and color combinations to create the effect you want for your page.

4 Allow your paint to dry for at least 5–10 minutes (it should be dry to the touch) before putting your page in a page protector.

Once you've got the basics down, try experimenting. Paint a custom background, or apply color to smaller areas for a color-blocked look. You can even cut or punch accents out of your painted paper. Just have fun!

—by Sara Tumpane

Figure 1. Create a rustic look with a modeling-paste background, hemp string and a pressed leaf. *Page by Julie Turner.* **Supplies** *Modeling paste:* Liquitex; *Tags:* American Tag Co.; *Powdered pigment:* Pearl-Ex, Jacquard Products; *Pressed leaf:* Nature's Pressed; *Adhesive:* Perfect Paper Adhesive, USArtQuest; *Other:* Hemp string. *Ideas to note:* Julie made her photo mat by wetting, crumpling, then ironing dry a piece of cardstock. To give her tags and photo mat an aged look, Julie mixed a small amount of antique gold Pearl-Ex powder with Perfect Paper Adhesive, then brushed the mixture on the tag and mat edges.

Magic with Modeling Paste

I frequently add texture to my layouts with handmade paper, yet I like to try different techniques, too. While experimenting one day, I used modeling paste to create textured background paper for my son's picture in Figure 1.

To create a texture that looked like an old plaster wall, I took a palette knife and spread a thin coat of modeling paste over a piece of heavy cardstock (Figure 1a). Next, I dragged a painter's comb through the wet paste (Figure 1b) to give

the appearance of plaster. I accented the shabby look with a hemp string tie and journaling tags.

— *Julie Turner, Gilbert, AZ*

Figure 1a. Use a palette knife to spread a thin coat of paste over heavy cardstock.

Figure 1b. Drag a painter's comb through the wet paste for dramatic effect.

"My favorite tool is definitely a black Zig Writer by EK Success. I've got about three in my purse, five in my desk at work, and bunches more in my scrapbook room. I use them for everything: scrapbook layouts, cards, writing checks, grading papers ... you get the idea!"

"Love Each Other Together"

Supplies *Textured paper:* Source unknown *Vellum:* Paper Accents; *Alphabet rubber stamps:* Hero Arts; *Compass rubber stamp:* Stampabilities; *Stamping ink:* VersaMark, Tsukineko; *Stickers:* Jolee's Boutique, Sticko; *Metal hearts:* Making Memories; *Metal frame:* Impress Rubber Stamps; *Fibers:* Fibers by the Yard, Rubba Dub Dub; *Pen:* Zig Writer, EK Success; *Paper yarn:* Twistel, Making Memories.

JOY UZARRAGA • CLARENDON HILLS, IL

Joy's passion for photography was ignited when her parents gave her a camera for winning a piano competition at nine years old. She's been taking photos ever since. Joy's advice to other scrapbookers? "Make sure *you* are in your scrapbooks. When I pass my albums on to my children, I want them to know who I was, where I've been and what my dreams were for myself and for them. If I've accomplished this, then I've succeeded as a scrapbooker."

"Sweetly"

Supplies *Patterned paper:* Paper Adventures; *Vellum:* Paper Accents; *Embossed paper:* Jennifer Collection; *Computer font:* 2Peas Crumbly Gingersnap by Melissa Baxter, downloaded from *www.twopeasinabucket.com*; *Sticker:* Jolee's Boutique, Sticko; *Flower rubber stamp:* All Night Media; *Fibers:* Fibers by the Yard (green), Making Memories (blue); *Ribbons:* Bucilla Corp. (silk), source unknown (gingham); *Metal-rimmed tags:* Avery; *Mini-brads:* Creative Impressions; *Pen:* Slick Writer, American Crafts; *Embossing powder:* UTEE, Suze Weinberg.

MONOCHROMATIC COLOR SCHEMES

I have to admit that more than half of the layouts in my albums have a monochromatic color scheme. After all, who can go wrong using different values (lightness or darkness) of one color? Monochromatic schemes are easy to manage because the colors go well together, resulting in pages with a clean, sophisticated look. More importantly, taking a monochromatic approach will help ensure your photos are the main focus of your pages. Here are some guidelines to follow when using a monochromatic color scheme:

◆ **Select a color that is prominent in your photo(s).** If you use black-and-white film, or like to convert photos to black and white, select a color that will help set the mood of your layout.

◆ **After you've decided on a background color for your layout, use different values of that color when adding other elements, such as photo mats and embellishments.**

◆ **For a more serene effect, select values that are closer together on the color wheel.** For a bold contrast, combine a pale tint (a color that has been lightened with white) with a dark shade (a color that has been darkened with black).

◆ **Use a monochromatic scheme to help establish a mood on a layout.** Select greens, blues or browns for a soothing effect, and reds and oranges for a more exciting or playful mood.

—by Joy Uzarraga

IDEAS TO NOTE: Joy embossed the edges of the photo mat to create texture. She also crumpled and chalked the cardstock behind the slide frames before stamping them.

"Let Laughter Live"

Supplies *Patterned paper:* Scrappin' Dreams; *Alphabet rubber stamps:* Hero Arts; *Stamping ink:* ColorBox, Clearsnap, Inc.; *Embossing powder:* PSX Design; *Fibers:* Fibers by the Yard; *Chalk:* Craf-T Products; *Other:* Slide frames.

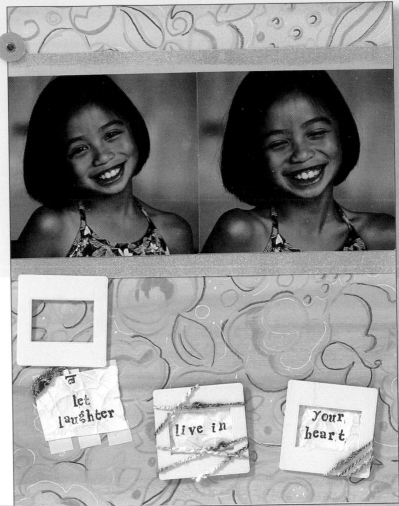

"Dream"

Supplies *Computer fonts:* Cezanne and Garamouche, P22 Type Foundry; *Letter stickers:* Sonnets, Creative Imaginations; *Mesh:* Avant Card.

Become a mother

Travel to Australia

Learn how to play the harp

Become a home-owner

Adopt a child from another country

Help Ronald through MBA school

Open a photography studio

Take an Alaskan cruise

These are the dreams that I hope to fulfill in the next ten years of my life. I've been a *dreamer* ever since I was a little girl. Throughout my *childhood,* I wanted to be so many different things when I grew up. An acrobat in the circus, a missionary doctor in a *faraway* land, an architect, an haute couture fashion designer, a make-up artist, a professional singer, a marine biologist, an *orthodontist...* the *possibilities* were endless! When I was old enough to read chapter books, I eagerly read through *Little Women* by Louisa May Alcott. Somewhere in it's *pages,* Jo March, the heroine, tells her sisters, "I could have been a *great* many things." Ever since I first read this statement, I knew that it would have great meaning in my life. It has been my motto, one that I frequently refer to. It is an *idea* that continually inspires me to keep *searching* for my dreams. Now that I am a grown up, I have come to the *realization* that I *have* become a great many things. A school teacher, a loving wife, a faithful friend. I also realize that my dreams from childhood are quite different than the *dreams* that I have today. However, one thing is certain. I will always be a *dreamer.*

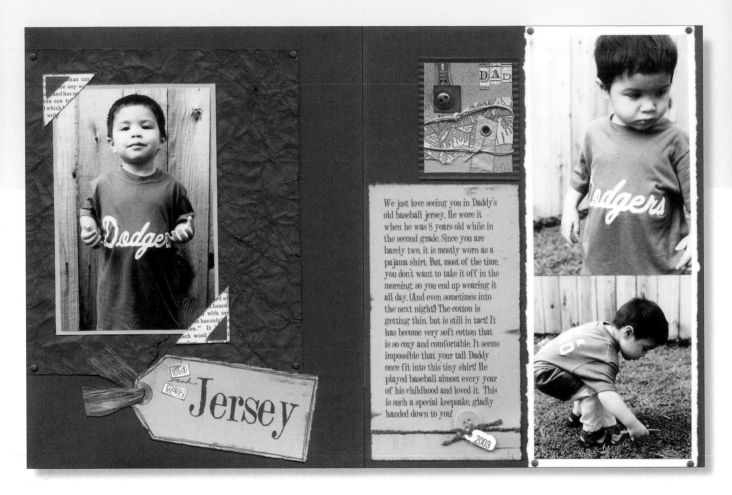

We just love seeing you in Daddy's old baseball jersey. He wore it when he was 8 years old while in the second grade. Since you are barely two, it is mostly worn as a pajama shirt. But, most of the time, you don't want to take it off in the morning, so you end up wearing it all day. (And even sometimes into the next night!) The cotton is getting thin, but is still in tact! It has become very soft cotton that is so cozy and comfortable. It seems impossible that your tall Daddy once fit into this tiny shirt! He played baseball almost every year of his childhood and loved it. This is such a special keepsake, gladly handed down to you!

"If I could own every shade of brown, green and blue cardstock, I would be a happy girl. I love using different shades of these colors—they just seem so natural to me."

"Old and Worn Jersey"

Supplies *Computer fonts:* 2Peas Evergreen and 2Peas Vintage Fun Blocks, downloaded from *www.two-peasinabucket.com; Accents:* Fresh Cuts, EK Success; *Tag:* Avery; *Fibers:* On the Surface; *Paper yarn:* Twistel, Making Memories; *Pen:* Pigma Micron, Sakura; *Stamping ink:* Stampin' Up!; *Other:* Brads.

JAMIE WATERS • S. PASEDENA, CA

Jamie used to think scrapbooking was only for "event" photos. "I would feel overwhelmed and often give up," shares Jamie. "When I was introduced to the simple, 'moment' layouts, I knew instantly that was what I wanted to do for my children." Simple, however, doesn't mean ho-hum. Jamie loves to add texture to her pages. "Whether it's handmade paper, metal or ribbon," says Jamie, "I love the depth and feel texture adds."

"Your Little World"

Supplies *Handmade paper:* Artistic Scrapper; *Computer fonts:* 2Peas Think Small and 2Peas Flea Market by Sharon Soneff, downloaded from *www.twopeasinabucket.com; Dog tag:* Chronicle Books; *Tag:* Avery; *Hemp:* Stampin' Up!.

Your little world
at two years old

Daddy and Mommy,
Sissy and Budgie,
Fruit snacks,
Buzz Lightyear,
Spiderman,
Nick Jr.,
Books,
Snuggles,
Bubbles,
Coloring,
Babies & Bluelu juice,
Trips to the park.
How innocent, how fun,
how big your world is.

PHOTO BY TARA WHITNEY

"THE REAL VOYAGE OF DISCOVERY CONSISTS NOT IN SEEKING NEW LANDSCAPES BUT IN HAVING NEW EYES."
-MARCEL PROUST

discover

explore

"Discovery"

Supplies *Specialty paper:* Magenta; *Batik paper:* Jennifer Collection; *Computer font:* CK Chemistry, "Fresh Fonts" CD, *Creating Keepsakes; Letter stickers:* Sonnets, Creative Imaginations; *Metal Accents:* Conchos, ScrapWorks; *Fibers:* Artistic Enhancements; *Wire mesh:* Art Form; *Eyelets:* Making Memories; *Other:* Brads.

"Joy"

Supplies *Patterned paper:* Making Memories; *Stickers:* Sticko (big flower); Debbie Mumm (small flower), Creative Imaginations; *Rubber stamps:* Stampin' Up!; *Stamping ink:* Tsukineko; *Fibers:* Artistic Enhancements; *Square punch:* Marvy Uchida; *Buttons, eyelets and page pebble:* Making Memories; *Other:* Mesh.

USING ACCENTS EFFECTIVELY

Like most scrappers, I love embellishments. When used effectively, they add the perfect finishing touch to a page without overwhelming the photos. When I shop for embellishments, I'm usually drawn to non-theme, neutral accents that can be used for a variety of layouts. I also tend to choose accents in muted colors that won't compete with my photos.

On my layouts, I try to place accents in visual triangles to draw the eye throughout the design. For additional interest, I often mix embellishments. Certain textures complement each other well, and I like to challenge myself to see how I can use my supplies. For example, I'll pair a dog tag with textured paper, add corrugated cardstock to a Fresh Cut accent, or adhere Maruyama mesh to the middle of a cut-out circle.

Pick up a handful of your favorite embellishments and experiment. You're sure to discover dozens of fresh ways to accent your pages!

—by Jamie Waters

Today you came up to me singing this song by the Backstreet Boys. I thought, "Eek, my 4 year old knows the Backstreet Boys!" I looked at you a little funny, and you giggled. Your typical coy little giggle, which of course makes me laugh out loud! I think this boyish charm of yours is so very cute, Cammy. When you are happy, the whole world knows it. You radiate. There is just something about you. We walk around the mall and strangers come up to me and say the sweetest things about you. They don't even know the half of it! You are lovely and amazing, my beautiful boy. Please don't ever stop singing songs. You are larger than life, Cameron!

Larger than **Life**

"Larger Than Life"

Supplies *Computer fonts:* 2Peas Nevermind and 2Peas Block Font Circles, downloaded from *www.two-peasinabucket.com*; *Mesh:* Magenta; *Fiber:* On the Surface; *Other:* Brads and washers.

"Lovely and Amazing"

Supplies *Specialty paper:* Artistic Scrapper; *Patterned paper:* Karen Foster Design; *Stickers:* Debbie Mumm, Creative Imaginations; *Rubber stamps:* PSX Design; *Ribbon:* Crackerjack; *Tag:* Impress Rubber Stamps; *Brads:* Making Memories.

Lovely and Amazing

CK
expert tips for scrapbookers

a farewell to friends

Three scrapbookers record a tender relationship

FOR CHILDREN OF MILITARY PERSONNEL, station changes can be difficult. Verity Koons knew her children would struggle when their close play-mates, Megan and Lucas Markos, left Mannheim Army Base in Germany to return to a base in the United States. Verity and her friend Mary Markos wanted the children to remember their special relationship, so Verity took photos of the children shortly before the Markos family left.

Verity sent these tender photos to *Creating Keepsakes* and asked for scrapbooking ideas. We gave the photos to three talented scrapbook-ers—Kristi Banks, Cathryn Zielske and Eva Flake—and asked them to capture the friend-ship on 8½" x 11" layouts. Following are their interpretations. ♥

After sharing four years together in Mannheim, Germany, Delainey and Dacey had developed a very close bond with friends Megan and Lucas. Now it was time to bid farewell. These photos were taken to preserve forever the love and friendship they shared.
January, 2001

"Remember"

by Kristi Barnes
Kaysville, UT

SUPPLIES

Square punch: EK Success
Letter eyelets, heart clip, seed beads and
foam mounting squares: Making Memories
Computer font: CK Constitution,
"Fresh Fonts" CD, *Creating Keepsakes*
Ribbon: C.M. Offray & Son
Other: Vellum envelope

KRISTI'S APPROACH

Blue represents friendship, and that's just how Kristi wanted to depict these gentle photos. "I chose the title 'Remember' and used script letters, rather than block, for the center M and E to give the effect of 'Remember ME,' " she says.

Kristi included a wire loop threaded with beads to denote unity and togetherness. The vellum envelope tied with ribbon and sealed with an X and O represent the memories the children will always have and their promise to stay in touch.

Kristi used extra photos of the children's faces to create a border that shows each child's unique character and personality.

After sharing four years together in Mannheim, Germany, Delainey and Dacey had developed a very close bond with friends Megan and Lucas. Now it was time to bid farewell. These photos were taken to preserve forever the love and friendship they shared.

true
friends

JANUARY 2001

"Remember"
by Cathryn Zielske
St. Paul, MN

SUPPLIES

Computer fonts: CK Newsprint (journaling), "Fresh Fonts" CD; CK Cursive ("Friends"), "The Best of Creative Lettering" CD Combo, *Creating Keepsakes*

Fiber: Rubba Dub Dub, Art Sanctum

Photo paper: Matte Heavyweight, Epson

Other: Metal grommet

Idea to note: Cathy scanned her photos at high resolution (1200 dots per inch), then resized them in a photo software program. She printed them at 300 dpi onto archival quality photo paper.

CATHRYN'S APPROACH

When Cathryn saw the photos, her heart skipped a beat. "I knew I wanted to let the photos shine," she says. "They tell so much about the children's relationships with one another." To make the photos work well on 8½" x 11" pages, Cathryn resized the pictures in Adobe Photoshop. "If you have a great photo," she says, "why not make it large and dramatic?"

Cathryn chose a soft color palette and simple embellishments because she felt the photos didn't need much in the way of external enhancements. Notes Cathryn, "Black-and-white film is so timeless, I really wanted to support that with a clean, minimalistic approach to design."

"Delainey, Dacey, Lucas, Megan"

by Eva Flake
Mesa, AZ

SUPPLIES

Patterned vellum: Autumn Leaves

Silver metallic paper: Accu-Cut Systems

Vellum: Paper Adventures

Chalk: Craf-T Products

Fiber: On the Surface

Leaf punch: The Punch Bunch

Photo corners: Pioneer Photo Albums

Computer fonts: CK Elegant and CK Constitution, "Fresh Fonts" CD, *Creating Keepsakes*

Vellum tag: Eva's own design

Other: Buttons and ribbon

Idea to note: Eva created the tag with her circle cutter. She made the silver frame, then adhered the vellum under it.

EVA'S APPROACH

Eva wanted to create a warm, inviting layout to match the warmth of the children's friendship. "The kids look so peaceful and happy in these photos," she says. "It made me sad that they don't live near each other anymore." She chose to include a touching quote that describes relationships.

Eva chose subtle colors that evoke a calm and peaceful mood. The button flowers emphasize the beauty of the quote, while the ribbon and bows help symbolize the children's lasting ties.

"Creatures of the Sea"

Supplies *Vellum:* Paper Adventures; *Craft wire:* Westrim Crafts; *Beads:* Blue Moon, Crafts Etc., Halcraft; *Computer font:* Vivaldi, Microsoft Word; *Pen:* Zig Millennium, EK Success; *Other:* Fibers.

"The greatest compliment I can receive about a completed page is for someone to comment first on the pictures and then on the design. That's when I feel I've done things right."

BRENDA ARNALL • PACE, FL

Inspired by an artistic mother who learned to draw and paint after her children were grown, Brenda believes creativity is "cultivated." She developed her own creative reservoir as a scrapbook store owner, attending various workshops and trade shows. Brenda also relies on her husband, traveling companion and fellow photographer, Wayne, who "is the best when it comes to shopping for scrapbook supplies," she says. Whenever they head off on a road trip, he always makes sure she has her list of local scrapbook stores handy.

"Arches"

Supplies *Patterned paper:* Two Busy Moms; *Circle punch:* McGill; *Computer font:* Scrap Oval (journaling), "Lettering Delights Deluxe" CD Vol. 2, Inspire Graphics; *Lettering template:* Chunky ("Arche"), Provo Craft; Doodle-E-Do ("S"), Cut-It-Up; *Pen:* Zig Millennium, EK Success; *Fibers:* On the Surface.

TRY THIS BORDER TECHNIQUE

Patterned paper adds variety and a splash of color to scrapbook pages. Here's a technique for creating an eye-catching border and title with patterned paper that's perfect for any layout:

1 Tear your background cardstock down the full length of the paper where you want to insert the patterned paper strip. Tear another strip of the background cardstock to adhere to the other side of the patterned paper strip.

2 Punch staggered holes down the cardstock strips, about ⅛" in from the torn edges. (Mark the location with a pencil first to keep the holes aligned.)

3 Thread a large-eyed needle with your favorite fiber and stitch loosely to lace the cardstock pieces together, crisscrossing from one side to the other. Start the first stitch at the back of the paper, but stitch from front to back on subsequent stitches so you'll end your last stitch in the back. Leave plenty of room between the cardstock pieces.

4 Cut a strip of patterned paper about 4" wide. Adhere the laced cardstock to the patterned paper, leaving 2" of the patterned paper showing. Tighten the fiber and adhere the ends under the corners of the torn cardstock. Trim any excess cardstock so your page is the appropriate size for your album.

5 To make the title, cut out the letters, then use a pencil to draw two parallel, slightly wavy lines through the middle of them. Trim along the lines to cut your letters in half. Mount the top portions of the letters on the patterned paper, then adhere the bottom portions, leaving a small strip of patterned paper in between. Cut out the letters.

—Brenda Arnall

"Rustic Cabin"

Supplies *Computer fonts:* Yikes! (title), downloaded from the Internet; Scrap Hap'nen (journaling), "Lettering Delights" CD Vol. 3, Inspire Graphics; *Stickers:* Debbie Mumm, Creative Imaginations; *Brads:* Creative Trends; *Pens:* Zig Millennium and Zig Scroll & Brush, EK Success; *Chalk:* Craf-T Products; *Other:* Jute. *Idea to note:* Brenda created the leaf embellishment in Adobe Photoshop, using a Deluxe Cuts die cut as a pattern.

"Soulmates"

Supplies *Patterned paper:* Rocky Mountain Scrapbook Company; *Vellum:* Paper Adventures; *Fibers:* On the Surface; *Eyelets:* Stamp Studio; *Computer font:* Pristina, Microsoft Word; *Pen:* Zig Writer, EK Success. *Idea to note:* Brenda converted the photos to sepia using Adobe Photoshop.

What one loves in childhood stays in the heart forever.

comrade * friend * buddy * mate * amigo * pal * chum
—GRAYSON

"Yee-haw cowboy" * "You're my favorite deputy" * "There's a snake in my boot" * "Howdy partner"
"My name's —WOODY
"You're my favorite deputy"

begs * pleads * whines * bargains for
—ROOT BEER

acoustic * electric * ABC song * loud
—GUITAR

snow * rain * worker man * brown and COWBOY!
—BOOTS

Two years old

"My inspiration for layout composition comes from magazine ads and CD covers. I've also always noticed movies that are made in letterbox format. It gives me two borders to either leave alone, put stitches across or embellish."

"What One Loves in Childhood"

Supplies *Computer font:* Spumoni LP, downloaded from the Internet; *Silver beads:* Source unknown; *Embroidery floss:* DMC.

CATHY BLACKSTONE • COLUMBUS, OH

"A good picture inspires me to scrapbook," shares Cathy. While she started out scrapbooking all of her photos, Cathy became overwhelmed after her second child was born. "The solution that by far makes me the happiest is to scrapbook just my favorite photos."

A teacher turned stay-at-home mom, Cathy has combined her love of teaching and scrapbooking as a scrapbook instructor. "I'm so flattered by the people who fill up my classes every week and keep coming back—that is the ultimate compliment."

"Muddy Buddies"

Supplies *Computer fonts:* Fingerprints Inside and Minya Nouvelle, downloaded from the Internet; *Embroidery floss:* DMC; *Chalk:* Craf-T Products; *Other:* Beads.

"A layout isn't complete until something is stitched down to it by hand or by machine!"

"Today You Are You"

Supplies *Computer font:* Mr. Larry Tate, downloaded from the Internet; *Photo corners:* Kolo. *Idea to note:* Cathy created the borders by stitching across the strips with her sewing machine.

IDEA TO NOTE: Showcase your child's growth by including snapshots taken throughout the year on one layout.

"Seasons"

Supplies *Computer font:* CK Sketch, "The Art of Creative Lettering" CD, *Creating Keepsakes; Flower punch:* 2 Grrrls; *Chalk:* Craf-T Products; *Embroidery floss:* DMC.

We had a perfect day at the patch. You discovered that you could turn around and sit on the pumpkins and bounce up and down like a wild child. It sounds silly, but it was adorable and you were incredibly proud of yourself!

October 2001

"Pumpkin Patch"

Supplies *Computer font:* Thanksgiving, downloaded from the Internet; *Buttons:* Hillcreek Designs; *Craft wire:* Darice; *Chalk:* Craf-T Products; *Other:* Fabric.

"We Wish We Were Fish"

Supplies *Shadow-block rubber stamp:* Impress Rubber Stamps; *Stamping ink:* Making Memories; *Computer fonts:* Baby Kruffy (title) and Cher (journaling), downloaded from the Internet; *Fish:* Cathy's own design. *Idea to note:* Cathy stamped the shadow block stamp in two shades to resemble tiles.

"Ellie"

Supplies *Vellum:* Paper Adventures; *Computer font:* Little Days, downloaded from the Internet; *Circle punches:* Family Treasures (large), McGill (medium).

border variations

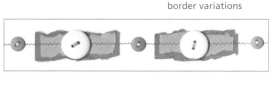

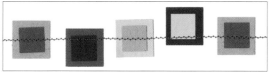

s e w n   b o r d e r   i d e a

Create this eye-catching border with just a few basic punches and your sewing machine. You can accent the simple shapes with charms or buttons, or tear and chalk the punches for more dimension. Here's how to create the border at left:

❶ Punch three rectangles and five squares from cardstock.

❷ Adhere the rectangles to the background strip, making sure they're evenly spaced.

❸ Cut out a heart and adhere it to the center square. Adhere the squares to the rectangle and heart (see border at left).

❹ Draw a straight line down the middle of the border using a ruler and pencil.

❺ Sew over the line and erase any visible pencil marks.

❻ Add charms tied with embroidery floss for a finishing touch.

—*Cathy Blackstone*

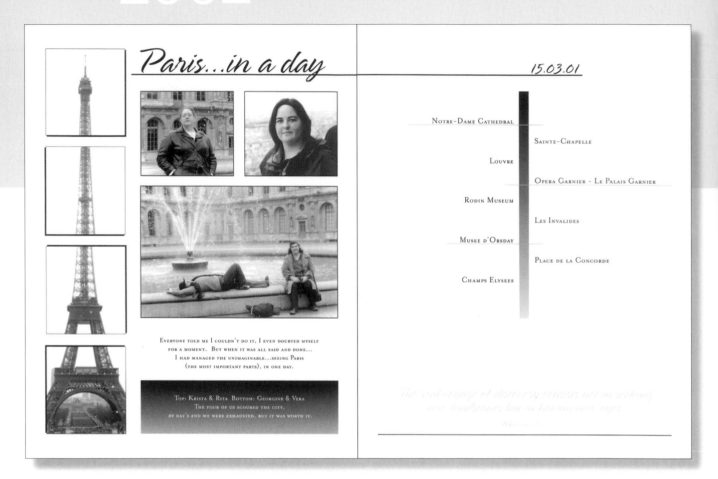

Paris...in a day

15.03.01

Notre-Dame Cathedral

Sainte-Chapelle

Louvre

Opera Garnier - Le Palais Garnier

Rodin Museum

Les Invalides

Musee d'Orsday

Place de la Concorde

Champs Elysees

EVERYONE TOLD ME I COULDN'T DO IT. I EVEN DOUBTED MYSELF
FOR A MOMENT. BUT WHEN IT WAS ALL SAID AND DONE...
I HAD MANAGED THE UNIMAGINABLE...SEEING PARIS
(THE MOST IMPORTANT PARTS), IN ONE DAY.

TOP: KRISTA & RITA BOTTOM: GEORGINE & VERA
THE FOUR OF US SCOURED THE CITY,
BY DAY'S END WE WERE EXHAUSTED, BUT IT WAS WORTH IT.

"Scrapbooking helps me highlight and showcase my pictures.

As an avid photographer, I love working with my photos

and coming up with new ideas and designs."

"Paris ... in a Day"

Supplies *Computer fonts:*
Mrs. Eaves Petite Caps and
Bustamalaka-Light & Aqualine,
Adobe.

KRISTA BOIVIE • NORTH LAS VEGAS, NV

"I've always been drawn to clean, classic designs," says Krista. "Years ago, I began a file

of photographs, articles and ads that have struck me in some way; I frequently go

through my files to get design ideas and photographic inspiration."

As a graphic designer, Krista uses a computer daily in her work, but only recently start-

ed creating her scrapbook pages on the computer. "Now that I'm using the computer as

my primary equipment to scrapbook, I feel more freedom with my designs."

"Every dreamer knows that it is entirely possible to be homesick for a place you've never been to, perhaps more homesick than for familiar ground." - Judith Thurman

07.08.01 - 18.08.01

"Europe 2001"

Supplies *Computer fonts:* Carpenter ICG and Throhand Ink-Roman, Adobe.

IDEA TO NOTE:
Krista created her entire layout with QuarkXPress.

selecting fonts

Fonts come in so many varieties that selecting which one to use on a scrapbook page can be a difficult task. For me, selecting fonts is a personal process. I do, however, have a few rules I follow when choosing fonts for my layouts:

❶ Use fonts to unify layouts. When I have multiple scrapbook pages for an event, I choose one or two common fonts to use throughout the spread.

❷ Limit the number of fonts on one page. In general, don't use more than three different fonts on a layout. Too many fonts can detract from the layout's design.

❸ Have fun with fonts! Don't be afraid to use fonts that are different, wacky or weird. Fonts add dimension to a scrapbook page and help complete its design.

—*Krista Boivie*

"Three colors I can't live without?

Black because it's classic; red because it's

my favorite color—it gives photos an added

punch, and it looks great with black;

and tan because it works with almost

any color scheme."

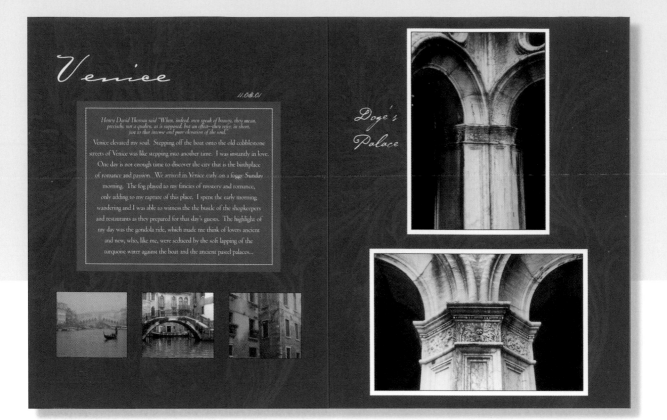

"Venice"

Supplies *Computer fonts:* Carpenter ICG and Throhand Ink-Roman, Adobe; *Background pattern:* Krista's own design

"Paris"

Supplies *Computer fonts:* Carpenter ICG, Throhand Ink-Regular and Throhand Ink-Italic, Adobe

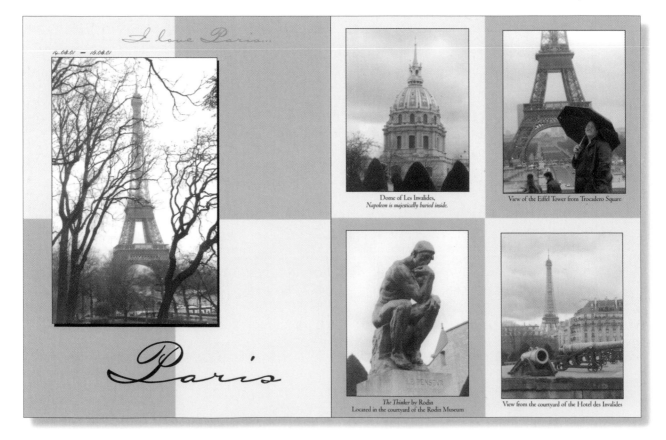

Portraits

self-portraits

Photography 101

"Photography 101"

Supplies *Computer font:* Andale Mono, Adobe.

August 15 - 18, 2001

Chicago

...my kind of town

"Chicago"

Supplies *Computer fonts:* Bodoni Book and Kaufman, Adobe.

helpful hint

Using my computer to design my scrapbook pages gives me ultimate control and freedom to manipulate the images and the page itself. I'm a perfectionist, and computer programs help me line up my titles and journaling perfectly.

When scrapbooking, I prefer using programs such as Adobe PageMaker, Adobe InDesign, QuarkXPress and Corel Draw; they allow me the control and manipulation I need. Although the programs can seem difficult to use, once you've learned the basics, you have limitless possibilities.

—*Krista Boivie*

"Time"

Supplies *Patterned paper:* Scrap-Ease; *Computer font:* Times New Roman, Microsoft Word; *Eyelets:* Impress Rubber Stamps; *Fibers:* On the Surface; *Rubber stamps:* Museum of Modern Rubber (melting clock), Hero Arts (old script), Magdalaina (fancy script), Above the Mark (crackle, clocks and gears); *Stamping ink:* Adirondack, Ranger Industries; VersaMark, Tsukineko; *Chalk:* Stampin' Up!; *Clock numbers and hands:* Walnut Hollow.

Time is stealing my baby girl! I remember bringing her home from the hospital – it seems like yesterday. We put her in the bassinet and stared at her for hours. I remember when she crawled, walked, ran. Now she's three and not really a baby anymore. I look at this picture and see a little girl. Full of spunk and energy. Witty and charming and daring and loving. Unfortunately, time won't slow down. And neither, I suppose, will Emma.
December, 2001

"For me the 'dessert' of a layout is always the title. I love to create interesting

and eye-catching titles. My techniques vary depending on the layout,

but the title is often the element I spend the most time on."

KAREN BURNISTON • LITTLETON, CO

Karen's geometrical pages show her background in engineering, but it's her attention to the world around her that shines through the most on her pages. She once drew an idea for a color scheme from a bird she saw while walking. And her motivation to scrapbook comes from her almost-four-year-old twins Karl and Emma. "I see how a good picture can tell a story, and I'm passionate about recording that story, especially for my kids."

"Karl Is My Candid Kid"

Supplies *Vellum:* Paper Adventures, Making Memories; *Computer fonts:* Snap ITC (title) and Pooh (journaling), downloaded from the Internet; *Eyelets:* Doodlebug Design; *Pen:* Zig Writer, EK Success; *Colored pencils:* Prismacolor, Sanford; *Square punch:* Marvy Uchida.

IDEAS TO NOTE: Karen created the title by tracing a computer font onto vellum and coloring the back of the letters with colored pencils. To create the circle and square accents, she randomly punched circles inside of squares and rearranged the dots, offset from the holes, for a shadow effect.

"Twins"

Supplies *Computer font:* Viner Hand ITC, package unknown; *Eyelets:* Doodlebug Design; *Circle and square punches:* Marvy Uchida; *Colored pencils:* Prismacolor, Sanford; *Other:* Ribbon.

"Roaming the Red Rocks"

Supplies *Patterned paper:* Scrap-Ease; *Vellum:* Hot Off The Press; *Computer font:* VAG Rounded Thin, package unknown; *Lettering:* Traced from letter stickers by Mary Engelbreit, Creative Imaginations ; *Names and subtitle:* Karen's own designs; *Pen:* Zig Writer, EK Success; *Colored pencils:* Prismacolor, Sanford; *Eyelets:* Album Memories; *Other:* Ribbon.

IDEA TO NOTE: Karen created the title by tracing the outline of the letter stickers onto vellum, coloring the back of the letters with colored pencils and adding a black shadow.

IDEA TO NOTE: To create the "Threedom" and "Play" title blocks, Karen traced the outline of the letter stickers on vellum, added a shadow, and colored the back of the letters with colored pencils.

"Threedom"

Supplies *Handmade paper:* Two Hands Paperie; *Vellum:* Paper Adventures; *Eyelets:* Rubber Baby Buggy Bumpers; *Alphabet rubber stamps:* Rubber Stampede; *Craft wire:* Artistic Wire Ltd.; *Pen:* Zig Writer, EK Success; *Colored pencils:* Prismacolor, Sanford; *Other:* Beads and studs.

FUN PHOTO IDEA:
Karen lay on the ground to snap the photo of her daughter on the swing with the blue sky behind her.

"Windows"

Supplies *Vellum:* Paper Adventures; *Rubber stamps:* Magdalaina ("W," "N," "O" and "S"), Above the Mark (compass, crackle in "D"), Rubber Stampede (bricks on journaling block); *Stamping ink:* Adirondack, Ranger Industries; *Lettering:* Karen's own design; *Chalk:* Stampin' Up!; *Pens:* Zig Writer, EK Success; American Crafts; *Quote:* Author unknown.

SHADOW-BOX LETTERING TECHNIQUE

I love to create eye-catching titles with everything from stamps and vellum to computers and my own handwriting. This shadow-box letter technique on the layout above can be adapted to fit a number of page themes. Here's how:

❶ Start by sketching thick block letters on cardstock and cutting them out (Figure 1). Use a ruler and craft knife to cut out the centers of the letters.

❷ Turn the letters over and attach thin strips of mounting tape or adhesive pop-up dots (Figure 2). (Adhere pieces of transparency film under the letters to create a window box look.)

❸ To create the backing pieces for the letters, stamp an image on white cardstock using clear watermark ink. Lightly brush chalk across the image with a cotton ball and watch the image appear (Figure 3).

❹ If desired, stamp a quote or saying over the image, and add detail with colored pencils. Repeat, varying the stamped images for each letter.

❺ Adhere the letters over the stamped images and trim (Figure 4).

—*Karen Burniston*

Figure 1

Figure 2

Figure 3

Figure 4

"Imagine"

Supplies *Vellum:* Paper Adventures; *Computer font:* Papyrus, downloaded from the Internet; *Square punch:* Marvy Uchida; *Silver word pebble:* Source unknown.

To know is nothing at all; To imagine is everything.

"When I get scrapper's block, I like to look through scrap-booking magazines and idea books. This usually gets me going again."

MELISSA CALIGIURI • WINTER PARK, FL

A passionate photographer, Melissa started scrapbooking as a way to turn her photos into lifelong memories. Single-photo layouts are her trademark, and Melissa's three active boys provide her with plenty of photo opportunities. "If I only had three colors of cardstock to use, they would have to be blue, tan and white," explains Melissa. "Since I mostly create boy layouts, I seem to use these colors often. These basic colors seem to go with a lot of my photos."

BROTHERS

A PAL, A CONFIDENT, A FRIEND, THERE TO SHIELD OR TO DEFEND. BRAVING LIFE'S EVER CHANGING WEATHER BY STANDING STEADFASTLY TOGETHER.

WITH A BROTHER YOU SHARE A COMMON HISTORY OF ALL THAT IS, AND WHAT CAN BE, AS CHILDHOOD TEARS AND INNOCENT FEARS MELT INTO MEMORY OVER THE YEARS.

MUCH TO THE HUMAN HEART'S DELIGHT, LOVE DOES INDEED MAKE ALL THINGS RIGHT. THROUGH EVERY JOY, AND ANY STRIFE, A BROTHER IS A FRIEND FOR LIFE!

"Brothers"

Supplies *Computer font:* Harman, Microsoft Word.

Summer Days

I love seeing my boys all tan and and towheaded during the summer. Griff loves to be outside barefoot in just his shorts, a real Florida boy!

"Summer Days"

Supplies *Computer font:* Yippy Skippy, downloaded from the Internet; *Stickers:* David Walker, Colorbök; *Flower paper clips:* Pier 1 Imports; *Eyelets:* Impress Rubber Stamps.

"Conner"

Supplies *Patterned paper:* Scrap-Ease; *Computer fonts:* Sarah Caps (title) and McGannahan, downloaded from the Internet; *Large square punch:* Marvy Uchida; *Leaf charm:* Embellish It!, Boutique Trims Inc.

"Pumpkin Patch"

Supplies *Specialty paper:* Black Ink; *Wood beads:* Source unknown; *Computer font:* Fabulous 50s, downloaded from the Internet; *Fibers:* On the Surface.

"The Boys of Summer"

Supplies *Computer font:* Desyrel, downloaded from the Internet; *Straw speckles:* Judi-Kins; *Chalk:* Craf-T Products; *Other:* Seashells.

"Take several pictures during a shoot so you have lots of photos to choose from. Use a zoom lens to capture your subjects' expressions, and snap the photos when they're not paying attention to the camera. Be aware of what's in the background, too."

timesaving tip To save time, I place my photos directly onto the background cardstock without matting them. This technique creates a clean, fresh look, and leaves me more time to create other pages.

Photos without mats look best mounted on solid cardstock that's either lighter or darker than the photos. The contrast will keep photos from floating on the page. For an effect that's even more striking, I use only one or two photos on the page.

—Melissa Caligiuri

renee camacho *2002*

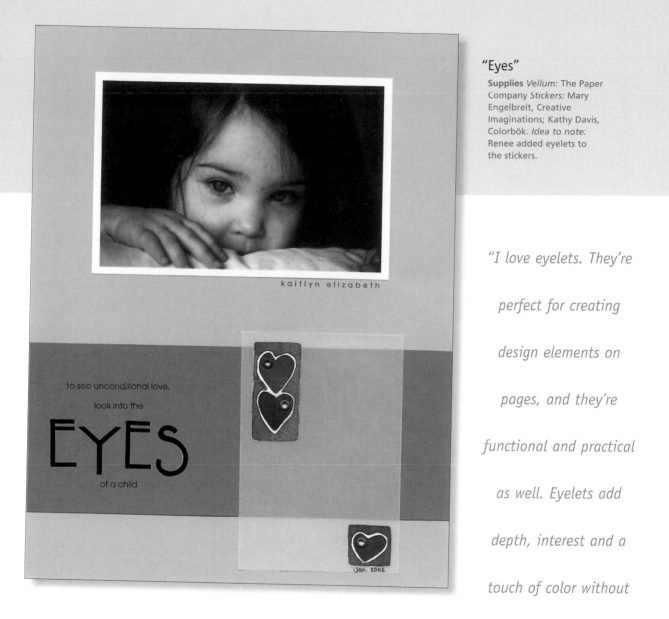

kaitlyn elizabeth

to see unconditional love,

look into the

EYES

of a child

Jan. 2002

"Eyes"

Supplies *Vellum:* The Paper Company *Stickers:* Mary Engelbreit, Creative Imaginations; Kathy Davis, Colorbök. *Idea to note:* Renee added eyelets to the stickers.

"I love eyelets. They're

perfect for creating

design elements on

pages, and they're

functional and practical

as well. Eyelets add

depth, interest and a

touch of color without

all the bulk."

RENEE CAMACHO • NASHVILLE, TN

Lovingly referred to as the "eyelet queen" by her friends, Renee is never without her little black book of sketches. When she finds herself stumped for page ideas, she pulls out her sketchbook to get the scrapbook ball rolling again.

Renee's favorite color of cardstock is blue, which she uses to mat close-ups of her blue-eyed husband and kids. "It takes the focus straight to the features I love the most ... their eyes!"

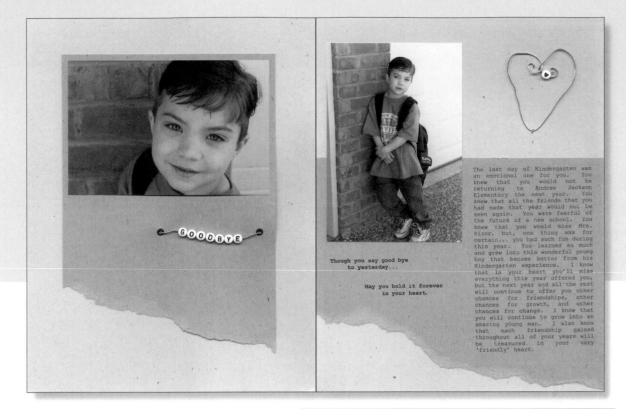

"Goodbye"

Supplies *Computer font:* Courier New, downloaded from the Internet; *Letter and heart charms:* Impress Rubber Stamps; *Eyelets:* Impress Rubber Stamps; *Craft wire:* Source unknown.

free-form shapes Whimsical shapes and photo mats can create a fun, funky feel on your layouts. Keep these hints in mind when working with shapes:

❶ Use free-form designs in patterned paper. In this example, I layered vellum over the top of the patterned paper, then cut out funky squares in the vellum to let the pattern show through in places.

❷ I also cut an imperfect window for the photo out of vellum. I then cut out vellum squares in the same funky square shape and overlapped them in the empty parts of the layout.

Try this technique with different patterns like stripes, circles and splashes of color. This will help your patterned paper become part of the layout, and not just an individual element.

—*Renee Camacho*

"Fresh, Clean, Pure"

Supplies *Patterned paper:* Paper Fever; *Vellum:* The Paper Company; *Eyelets:* Impress Rubber Stamps; *Computer fonts:* Pristina, downloaded from the Internet; *Creative lettering idea:* Title was inspired by a layout by Jennifer Wohlenberg in the February 2002 issue of *Creating Keepsakes*

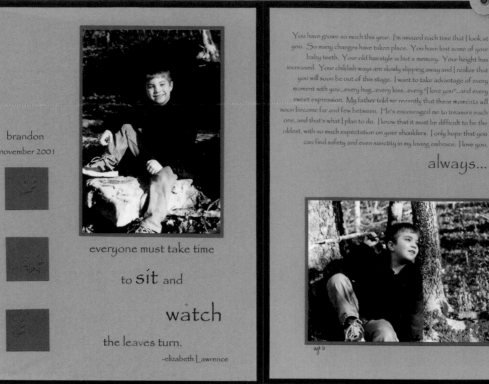

"Sit and Watch"

Supplies *Computer font:* Papyrus, downloaded from the Internet; *Pen:* Zig Millennium, EK Success; *Punches:* EK Success.

IDEA TO NOTE: Renee cut out the letters from the photo mat, making sure to leave the negative space untouched.

"Joy"

Supplies *Patterned paper:* Paper Fever; *Vellum:* The Paper Company; *Lettering template:* Block Lowercase, ABC Tracers, Pebbles for EK Success; *Pens:* Zig Memory System and Zig Millennium, EK Success.

w o r d   h i n t s

Although I have an extensive collection of fonts, I have favorites that I use all the time. I also have several rules of thumb for selecting the right font, the right formatting and the right placement of text:

◆ For journaling, always choose a font that's readable and easy on the eye. The font should also complement the look you're trying to create. I tend to like the cleaner lines of Bell Gothic and Century Gothic fonts.

◆ Try using bolder, larger fonts for emphasis. I also like to format some lines off-center to draw the reader's attention.

◆ I find inspiration for the placement of my journaling from magazines. Most graphic designers try to stay away from straight block formats and lean toward a more free-form style.

—Renee Camacho

"Hug O' War"

Supplies *Computer font:* Unknown; *Star charms:* Source unknown; *Square punch:* EK Success.

"Harmony"

Supplies *Rubber stamps:* Impress Rubber Stamps (square and flower); *Stamping ink:* ColorBox, Clearsnap, Inc.; Crafter's Workshop; *Pens:* Zig Memory System and Zig Writer, EK Success; *Eyelets:* Impress Rubber Stamps.

"I hate to have my creative flow interrupted, but with three kids that's almost impossible. So to take advantage of the time granted to me, I make sure my layouts are simple and to the point."

d e s i g n   h i n t s   I seldom crop my photos. I simply lay them out on the cardstock as is to determine the perfect placement, then I decide where I want the title and the journaling to go, and if I need any other accents. Here are some tips for creating balance on layouts:

◆ Follow the rule of threes. Placing accents in odd numbers or in a triangular pattern will draw the eye throughout the layout.

◆ In "Sit and Watch" (page 124), I drew the layout together by placing three squares on one side, and the journaling and two other squares on the opposite side.

◆ Position your text in line with your photos to keep the text from running off the page.

◆ If you use one particular color on one side of the layout, use it again on the other side.

—Renee Camacho

It doesn't really matter how you spell it . . . sunkissed or sunkist because neither word can be found in the dictionary. However, a fairly accurate definition for these "words" would be . . . one whom the sun has shone upon and kissed . . . or would that be kist? Both of these photos were taken in . . . Disney land!

"I love to add embellishments to my layouts.

Deciding what type to use and where to place them is

an ongoing process as the layout evolves, but that's

part of the fun—being creative!"

"Sun-kissed Sunkist"

Supplies *Patterned papers:* Carolee's Creations (light-yellow speckled), Provo Craft (all other patterned papers); *Punches:* Family Treasures (small sun), Darice (mini-sun and flower); *Computer fonts:* Yippy Skippy (title), downloaded from the Internet; CK Sketch (journaling), "The Art of Creative Lettering" CD, *Creating Keepsakes; Eyelets:* Impress Rubber Stamps.

ANGIE CRAMER • REDCLIFF, AB, CANADA

"I scrapbook for the here and now—for my family," explains Angie. "I communicate to them that the details of their lives, whether big or small, are very important to me." When Angie finds it difficult to journal about older photos, she watches home movies filmed around the time she's writing about. "The videos contain a wealth of information that enables me to relive the moment or event, making it fresh in my mind."

"Crystal Cathedral"

Supplies *Computer fonts:* Arial Black ("Crystal"), Avenida ("Cathedral") and Tempus (journaling), Microsoft Word; *Stickers:* Class A'Peels, Mark Enterprises; *Clear rhinestones:* The Beadery. *Ideas to note:* Angie chose title fonts that matched the lettering in the church bulletin. She also made an interactive flap, which reveals additional photos (see image at left).

"The Gardens"

Supplies *Patterned papers:* Anna Griffin (green floral), Provo Craft (beige and green marble); *Computer font:* Papyrus, Microsoft Word; *Stickers:* Provo Craft; *Scissors:* Regal edge, Fiskars.

sticker tip

For me, stickers are often the perfect page accents, especially when I don't have time to create something from scratch. From colorful and cute to serious and classy, there's a sticker out there to suit almost any layout. Try these tips for using stickers:

◆ Take your photos along with you when you shop for stickers. This way you'll be able to choose stickers that complement your photos.

◆ Cut the sheet of stickers apart, leaving the backing intact. Then you can experiment with different positions on your layout until you find the one you like best.

◆ Stickers made of clear material can sometimes get lost on dark backgrounds. Try backing them with lighter-colored cardstock and cutting them out before adhering them to your page.

—*Angie Cramer*

"Nickelodeon Splash"

Supplies *Computer font:* Abadi MT (title), Microsoft Word; CK Sketch (journaling), "The Art of Creative Lettering" CD, *Creating Keepsakes; Letter stickers:* Alphabitties, Provo Craft; *Punches:* Darice (circle), EK Success (rectangle); *Beads:* Westrim Crafts.

STEP-BY-STEP BEADING

Want an attention-grabbing title? Adding a beaded border will help your titles pop. Follow these easy steps to re-create the "Sweet Dreams" title below:

❶ Cut cloud shapes from patterned paper and white cardstock. Adhere the pieces together, then attach them to a piece of patterned vellum (Figure 1).

❷ Poke small holes about 1" apart around the edge of the cloud.

❸ Cut a piece of craft wire long enough to go around the outer edge of the bottom cloud. Thread the beads on the wire.

❹ Insert one end of the wire through the front of the paper in the first hole, leaving a 1" tail. Tape the tail down in back.

❺ Bend the beaded wire around the edge of the cloud design.

❻ Tack the beaded wire to the vellum using a needle and thread. Bring the needle through the first hole from back to front. Bring the thread over the beaded wire, and insert the needle back down into the first hole. Continue tacking down the wire using the pre-poked holes (Figure 2).

❼ Remove any excess beads from the wire, and insert the wire into the last hole. Trim to leave a 1" tail, and tape it down in back.

❽ Repeat Steps 3–7 with the second cloud.

❾ Mat the design on patterned paper, securing it with pins and sequins.

❿ Adhere the cut-out title or letter stickers, and mat the completed design on white cardstock (Figure 3).

—*Angie Cramer*

Figure 1

Figure 2

Figure 3

"Snowflakes"

Supplies *Vellum:* Paper Adventures; *Handmade paper:* Source unknown; *Punches:* Darice (small snowflake), EK Success (folk heart); *Computer font:* Angelina, downloaded from the Internet; *Eyelets:* Impress Rubber Stamps; *Other:* Ribbon.

IDEA TO NOTE: Each panoramic photo opens to reveal more photos and journaling.

"The Magic of Snow"

Supplies *Vellum:* Paper Adventures; *Computer fonts:* Papyrus (title) and Lucida Handwriting (journaling), Microsoft Word; *Border stickers:* Michel Studios; *Eyelets:* Impress Rubber Stamps.

taunya dismond 2002

"Lasting Legacy"

Supplies *Patterned paper:* Source unknown; *Computer fonts:* Bradley Hand, Microsoft Word; CK Calligraphy, "The Best of Creative Lettering" CD Combo, *Creating Keepsakes; Rubber stamp:* Magenta Rubber Stamps; *Stamping ink:* VersaColor, Tsukineko; *Fibers:* On the Surface, Rubba Dub Dub; *Eyelets:* Doodlebug Design; *Beads:* Source unknown; *Other:* Paper crimper.

Lasting Legacy

Three generations of Dismond men
(L-R: Samuel, Charles Jr., Charles Sr. and Larry)

"My purpose for scrapbooking is to preserve my precious photographs,

memorabilia and recollections. I tend to see it primarily as a way to record

those events and people that are important in my life."

TAUNYA DISMOND • LEE'S SUMMIT, MO

The daughter of a semi-professional photographer, Taunya says she inherited her father's role as family photographer and historian. "I firmly believe that scrapbooking is not just about creating spectacular, creative pages, it's also about preserving memories, celebrating life and passing on traditions." While Taunya began scrapbooking with the sole intention of safely preserving photos, she now enjoys the creative side of scrapbooking, and loves "scouring" for embellishments that enhance her photos and convey the message she wants to send.

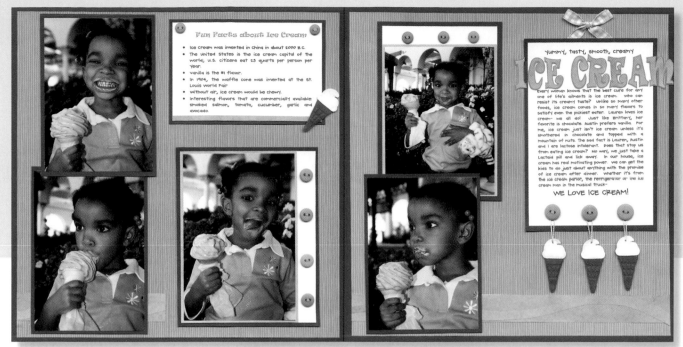

"Ice Cream"

Supplies *Patterned papers:* Doodlebug Design (green), Making Memories (pink); *Computer fonts:* Ravie, downloaded from the Internet; CK Handprint, "The Best of Creative Lettering" CD Combo, *Creating Keepsakes; Buttons:* Hillcreek Designs; *Embossing template:* Dreamweaver; *Chalk:* Stampendous!; *Embroidery floss:* DMC; *Other:* Bow.

d e s i g n   t i p

My favorite technique when designing a page is to create a visual triangle. By placing similar shapes, textures, embellishments or colors throughout my page in a triangular fashion, I create an effective, well-balanced design that draws my audience in and leads them through the layout. While many techniques come and go, the visual triangle is tried and true."

—*Taunya Dismond*

"To My Daughter"

Supplies *Patterned paper:* Colors By Design; *Computer font:* Coraband, Microsoft Word; *Lettering template:* EK Success; *Paper yarn:* Twistel, Making Memories; *Beads:* Source unknown.

IDEA TO NOTE: The mat opens up to reveal more photos and journaling.

"Mr. Sandman"

Supplies *Computer fonts:* Pristina, downloaded from the Internet; Bradley Hand, Microsoft Word; *Charms:* Embellish It!; *Eyelets:* Doodlebug Design; *Fibers:* On the Surface; *Brads:* American Pin & Fastener

"Making Waves"

Supplies *Computer font:* CK Toggle, "The Best of Creative Lettering" CD Combo, *Creating Keepsakes; Lettering template:* Block, ABC Tracers, Pebbles for EK Success; *Eyelets:* Doodlebug Design; *Embroidery floss:* DMC.

stitching tip I used my wavy decorative ruler to create this simple stitched design on my journaling block. Follow these steps for re-creating the look:

❶ Trace a wave design on the back of cardstock.

❷ Poke holes along the shape of the design with a needle. (Use a smaller needle so your holes will be less noticeable.)

❸ Back-stitch the design with the desired fiber or embroidery floss. Bring the needle through the back of the paper at hole 2, leaving a small tail and taping it down in back. Bring the needle down at hole 1. Bring the needle up at hole 3 and down at hole 2. (See example above.) Repeat for the entire wave.

Use this technique to stitch flowers or stars on your backgrounds, or trace a zigzag ruler and stitch to make mountains on a journaling block for an outdoor layout.

—Taunya Dismond

"Personal Rainbow"

Supplies *Patterned papers:* Karen Foster Design, Bo-Bunny Press; *Computer fonts:* Think Small, downloaded from *twopeasinabucket.com*; Mostlios, downloaded from the Internet; *Fibers:* Rubba Dub Dub. *Idea to note:* Jennifer created the background by piecing strips of colored paper together and covering the seams with matching fibers.

"When selecting colors for a layout, I choose colors that complement the photo and represent the 'feel' of the memory. If the colors in the photo don't match the mood, I simply change the photo to black and white."

JENNIFER DITZ McGUIRE • CINCINNATI, OH

"I draw my inspiration for scrapbooking from thinking about the people in the future who will be paging through my album," shares Jennifer. Jennifer lets her husband do all her journaling. "It's a great way to include him in my hobby, and it adds a personal touch that both of us will be able to look back on and enjoy." Jennifer began scrapbooking after living in Italy for almost a year. "I wanted to make sure I captured the feel of those fantastic places," she says.

"Greet Each Day"

Supplies *Computer font:* Mandingo, downloaded from the Internet; *Sun accent:* Jennifer's own design.

IDEA TO NOTE: To create the border and sunrays, Jennifer moistened the cardstock, then tore and curled it.

"Greeting from Italy"

Supplies *Patterned papers:* Paper Adventures, Karen Foster Design; *Mulberry paper:* PrintWorks; *Alphabet rubber stamps:* PSX Design; *Stamping ink:* Source unknown; *Computer font:* 39 Smooth, downloaded from the Internet; *Embossing powder:* PSX Design; *Postcard charm:* Darice; *Italian postage stamps:* Purchased on eBay; *Creative lettering idea:* Jennifer stamped the letters on mulberry paper, then embossed them.

memorabilia tips

I've collected a lot of memorabilia, especially while living in Italy and traveling throughout Europe, and I love putting it in my scrapbook along with my photos. Here are some tips for preserving your precious items:

◆ Photocopy or scan and print all the paper items that aren't acid free, then adhere them to your pages.

◆ Save an original piece of memorabilia by making a vellum envelope to insert it in, then simply adhere the envelope to your layout.

◆ Save yourself a little time by purchasing a pre-made memory pocket at your local scrapbook store.

—Jennifer Ditz McGuire

"Mom"

Supplies *Patterned papers:* K & Company, Karen Foster Design; *Vellum:* Pixie Press; *Computer font:* Liberty BT, downloaded from the Internet; *Flower stickers:* Darice; *Fibers:* Rubba Dub Dub; *Paper yarn:* Twistel, Making Memories; *Charms:* Embellish It!; *Leaf accent:* Black Ink; *Buttons:* Dress-It-Up, Cut-It-Up; *Chalk:* Craf-T Products. *Creative lettering idea:* Jennifer created the title entirely from embellishments.

"Gathering Memories"

Supplies *Computer font:* Problem Secretary, downloaded from the Internet; *Page accents:* Clip art from Microsoft; *Beads:* Better Beads; *Embossing powder:* Suze Weinberg.

IDEAS TO NOTE: Jennifer positioned the font on top of the clip-art images and applied several layers of embossing powder. She cracked the pieces for an antique look and adorned them with beads.

"Created for Love"

Supplies *Mulberry paper:* Black Ink; *Fuzzy paper:* Source unknown; *Vellum:* Paper Adventures; *Computer font:* Santa's Sleigh, downloaded from the Internet; *Mini-envelope template:* Stampawayusa.com; *Paper yarn:* Twistel, Making Memories; *Flower punch:* EK Success.

IDEAS TO NOTE: Using an envelope template, Jennifer created her own mini vellum envelopes to use as page accents. To create the flowers, she punched the shapes from fuzzy paper and made the stems by cutting a tiny hole in the center of each flower, feeding the Twistel through and tying a knot.

"God Loves Me"

Supplies *Computer font:* International Playboy, downloaded from the Internet; *Glass beads:* Halcraft; *Glue dots:* Glue Dots International.

Beaded letters add dimension and color to a layout (this technique works best on solid, bold colors of cardstock). Here's how to create this unique look:

1 Print the title on regular printer paper.

2 Lay the title over the cardstock and cut out the letters with a craft knife.

3 Place the cut cardstock over another piece of cardstock that is the same size and color.

4 Lightly trace the letters onto the background cardstock. Remove the top piece of cardstock and cover the sketched letters with Wonder Tape (by Suze Weinberg).

5 Remove the release paper from the tape and sprinkle on the glass beads. Press them down to secure them to the tape.

6 Adhere the top piece of cardstock and photos with adhesive pop dots (see layout).

—*Jennifer Ditz McGuire*

IDEAS TO NOTE: Jennifer created the title by sketching a tower based on a clip-art image. She cut out the word "Pisa" and mounted it on cardstock with Glue Dots by Glue Dots International before adhering it to the rest of the title piece.

"Pisa"

Supplies *Computer font:* Grumble, downloaded from the Internet; *Lettering template:* Better Letter, Déjà Views, The C-Thru Ruler Co.; *Colored pencils:* Prismacolor, Sanford; *Chalk:* Craf-T Products

When Alix is not out running, playing soccer or being a natural tomboy, she enjoys the sweeter things in life! Flowers, pretty dresses, and jewelry share equal space with her collection of rocks and frogs. All combined, this is our Alix! 03/99

Add texture to your scrapbook pages with crumpled tissue paper. *Page by Heather Lancaster.* **Supplies** *Tissue paper:* Sunrise Printed Tissue; *Patterned paper:* Keeping Memories Alive; *Lettering template:* ABC Tracer, Pebbles for EK Success; *Heart punch:* Family Treasures; *Pen:* Zig Writer, EK Success; *Other:* Raffia. *Idea to note:* Heather created her own photo corners with raffia.

Crumpled Tissue Paper

Have you ever noticed the variety of patterned tissue papers in scrapbook and craft stores? The papers are perfect for creating interesting page backgrounds! You can add depth and texture by crumpling them slightly for a fun or classic look. Here's how:

❶ **Choose the tissue paper you want.** Keep in mind that a lighter-colored pattern will show off the crumpled look better than a darker colored pattern. Also, choose a smaller design that won't overwhelm your photos.

Always test tissue paper with a pH testing pen before using the paper in your scrapbook. You can deacidify tissue paper with Archival Mist spray or purchase acid-free tissue paper through an archival supply store.

❷ **Cut your tissue paper.** It should be approximately 1" larger than your page on each side since the paper will shrink when you crumple it. Remember which way the pattern will face and cut accordingly.

❸ **Crumple the cut tissue paper into a ball.** Next, uncrumple it, being careful not to rip the paper. If you see a spot that's still smooth, crumple the paper some more! Once you're satisfied with the texture of the tissue, gently smooth it out. Take care not to flatten it too much.

❹ **Adhere your tissue paper to a piece of cardstock.** The Xyron machine offers the easiest method, but you can also use acid-free spray adhesive. Carefully place the tissue paper onto the cardstock, pressing it firmly into place.

❺ **Use scissors to trim the excess tissue paper from the sides of your page.** Your paper is now ready and you can actually get started on your masterpiece!

Try using this technique for title lettering or for photo mats. The crumpled look can be elegant or fun, and it offers a distinctive new paper option for those of us who just can't get enough!

—*Heather Lancaster,*
Calgary, Alberta, Canada

mechelle felsted 2002

IDEA TO NOTE: Mechelle cropped in on the photos of her children, matted the pictures and placed them on top or to the side of the scenic photo to create a 3-D look.

"It's hard to say which I love more: the written word or the image captured on paper. Scrapbooking allows me to use two mediums I love to preserve the memories of the people I cherish."

"Waves Snatch at My Toes"

Supplies *Vellum:* Graphix; *Lettering idea:* Mechelle adapted the lettering from the CK Cursive and CK Penmen fonts on "The Best of Creative Lettering" CD Vols. 2 and 3 by *Creating Keepsakes*; *Pen:* Pigma Micron, Sakura; *Gemstone:* Halcraft; *Glass spheres:* Tinybeads; *Embossing tape:* Gary M. Burlin Co.; *Other:* Bathroom scrubber.

MECHELLE FELSTED • FLAGSTAFF, AZ

Mechelle's husband Jim says if Mechelle scrapbooks any more, they'll have to add another room onto their house just for the albums—Mechelle says it would be her favorite room. Her creative inspiration comes mostly from her children, and Mechelle says she's learned some of her favorite techniques from them. One afternoon, her young son Corbin decided he had waited long enough for his turn with the paper trimmer and started to tear his photos. "I discovered a new technique that I now love!" laughs Mechelle.

IDEA TO NOTE: Mechelle laid vellum strips over the title to draw attention to it.

"Falling Leaves"

Supplies *Vellum:* Hot Off The Press; *Lettering:* Mechelle adapted the lettering from the CK Bella and CK Penman fonts on "The Best of Creative Lettering" CD Vol. 3 by *Creating Keepsakes; Leaves:* Mechelle pressed real leaves from her yard and included them on her layout; *Circle punch:* Punch Line; *Jute:* DC & C Supplies; *Pen:* Pigma Micron, Sakura.

CREATE A VELLUM WINDOW

Want to pique the interest of those who pore through your scrapbooks? A vellum window is a wonderful way to give the viewers a sneak preview of what's to come. These easy steps will help you:

1. Adhere two sheets of cardstock, back-to-back, with double-sided adhesive tabs.
2. Determine the size and position of the window you want to create, and mark it lightly with a pencil.
3. Cut along the lines with a craft knife and cutting mat. Erase any visible pencil marks.
4. Gently pull apart the two pieces of cardstock and adhere the vellum in the window opening. Re-adhere the cardstock with permanent adhesive.
5. Complete the rest of the layout, making sure the photo behind the vellum window is placed appropriately.

—*Mechelle Felsted*

"Blessed with Children"

Supplies *Patterned paper:* Geographics; *Specialty papers:* Provo Craft; *Vellum:* Graphix; *Leaf accents:* Source unknown; *Lettering:* Mechelle's own design; *Pen:* Pigma Micron, Sakura.

"We've Never Told Him He Can't Fly"

Supplies *Vellum:* Hot Off The Press; *Specialty papers:* Provo Craft; *Lettering:* Mechelle's own design; *Eyelets:* Doodlebug Design; *Beads:* Halcraft; *Craft wire:* Anchor Wire; *Pen:* Pigma Micron, Sakura

"Forever May It Wave"

Supplies *Specialty papers:* Provo Craft; *Vellum:* Graphix; *Computer font:* CK Bella, "The Best of Creative Lettering" CD Vol. 3, *Creating Keepsakes; Flag ribbon:* Ribbon by the Yard; *Brads:* NSI Innovations.

"If I get scrapper's block, I work on a page for my child's scrapbook. This helps some of my best creativity flow."

"It's Elementary"

Supplies *Vellum:* Graphix; *Specialty papers:* Provo Craft; *Computer font:* CK Handprint, "The Art of Creative Lettering" CD, *Creating Keepsakes; Brads:* NSI Innovations; *Pen:* Pigma Micron, Sakura.

IDEA TO NOTE: Mechelle included color and sepia photos on her layout to add visual interest.

heidi gnadke 2002

The color of one of Reilly's favorite toys.

The color of the only M&M Reilly could not identify.

The color of the alarm Reilly recently set off at a local restaurant.

The color of Reilly's favorite blanket.

Reilly easily learned to identify all of his colors except for the color RED, despite the fact that many of his favorite things were RED. Grandpa tried to teach him his colors by giving Reilly any M&M he could correctly identify. Try as Reilly might, he could not identify any RED M&M. Grandpa later decided to buy Reilly a big RED ball to see if that would help him learn this ambiguous color. Grandpas tactic seems to have worked because now when we ask Reilly to identify something RED he says "RED, like my ball".

"The Color Red"

Supplies *Patterned paper:* Rocky Mountain Scrapbook Company *Computer fonts:* Freestyle Script ("The Color") and Orange Fizz ("Red"), downloaded from the Internet; *Eyelets:* Impress ; Rubber Stamps; *Jute:* Darice.

"I often bring my photos with me to the scrapbook store to help me select papers. Picking out the right paper for the style, color and mood of the layout makes such a difference in the end result of the page."

HEIDI GNADKE • CENTERVILLE, MN

When scrapper's block hits, Heidi heads straight for her three-ring binder full of ideas, sketches, notes and printouts. And if that doesn't work, Heidi says she enjoys getting feedback from her husband: "Once in a while he gives me a good idea or gets my wheels turning—or at least I get a great big laugh out of what he comes up with!" A self-proclaimed perfectionist, Heidi's detail-oriented personality shows through in her carefully planned embellishments and precisely cut titles.

"Carefree"

Supplies *Patterned papers:* Keeping Memories Alive (brown), Creative Imaginations (crackle); *Buttons and buckles:* JHB International; *Chalk:* Stampin' Up!

IDEA TO NOTE: *Idea to note:* Heidi scanned, reduced and printed out pictures to create the "photo border."

"Lessons in Love"

Supplies *Computer fonts:* Angelina ("Lessons in") and CAC Pinafore ("Love"), downloaded from the Internet; *Memorabilia pocket:* The C-Thru Ruler Co.; *Chalk:* Stampin' Up!

FRAMING TECHNIQUE

Create a rustic weathered frame to showcase your photos of a day at the farm, or use it on a heritage layout to complement the aged look of black-and-white photos. I created a large frame for my focal-point photo, and three smaller frames for my complementary photos (see "Carefree" layout). Follow these steps:

❶ Measure your photo and select the desired frame width. I chose to make a 1" wide frame for a 4" x 6" photo.

❷ Select a sheet of dark-colored cardstock with a white or light-colored back. Cut strips of cardstock the width of the frame and the length of the sides of the photo plus the frame width on each end. (In my case, I cut two 1" x 6" strips and two 1" x 8" strips.)

❸ Miter one frame corner by placing a shorter strip on top of a longer one, aligning the two ends to make a 90° angle. Cut a diagonal line from the outside corner to the inside corner. Repeat to miter the remaining corners.

❹ Sand the mitered strips to make the frame look weathered, then adhere the strips together, matching up the mitered corners.

❺ Punch ⅛" circles out of silver paper for nailheads and adhere to the corners of the frame.

—*Heidi Gnadke*

"Autumn"

Supplies *Patterned papers:* Rocky Mountain Scrapbook Company; *Vellum:* Paper Adventures; *Computer fonts:* Papyrus (title), Microsoft Word; Bud Null, downloaded from the Internet; *Gold sun:* American Art Clay Co.; *Rake, sun and wind:* Adapted from clip art by Microsoft Picture It! ; *Hearts:* Heidi's own designs; *Buttons:* Dress-It-Up, Cut-It-Up; *Jute:* Darice; *Other:* Leaf charms.

IDEA TO NOTE: Each letter on this layout lifts up to reveal a portion of Heidi's son's memorable autumn experience.

IDEA TO NOTE: Heidi used key words and pictures to describe her son's autumn experience.

TITLE TECHNIQUE

Capture the colors, sights and feel of autumn by using key words and photos instead of traditional journaling. I used Microsoft Picture It! to create this look, but you can re-create it using various photo-editing programs. Here's how:

❶ Scan a piece of leaf patterned paper.

❷ Type the first letter, select a font, and change the font style to outline. I made my letters approximately 4" x 10½" to fit a 12" x 12" page.

❸ Electronically combine the letter and the scanned paper together, laying the letter over the leaf pattern.

❹ Crop around and inside the letter to cut away the excess leaf pattern.

❺ Print out the letter on transparency paper appropriate for your printer and cut to the desired size.

❻ Frame the edges of the transparency with strips of cardstock. Create cardstock hinges and attach the letters to the background with mini brads.

❼ Repeat for the remaining letters.

—*Heidi Gnadke*

"#3 of Four"

Supplies *Computer fonts:* Victorian LET (title) and Poor Richard (journaling), downloaded from the Internet; *Pressed flowers:* Heidi's own designs; *Chalk:* Stampin' Up!; *Other:* Ribbon and charms.

"My biggest inspiration for scrapbooking is the feeling I get while I'm creating a layout, and when I'm finished with a layout I'm really proud of."

"Look-Alike"

Supplies *Patterned paper:* Making Memories (blue); Debbie Mumm, Creative Imaginations (cream striped); *Computer fonts:* Euphororgenic SP (title) and Marker Fine Point Plain (journaling), downloaded from the Internet; *Shirt:* Heidi's own design; *Buttons:* Dress-It-Up, Cut-It-Up.

IDEA TO NOTE: Denise used sand (adhered with embossing tape) to create a textured border around the journaling and focal-point photo.

"I like my pictures to be the focus of attention on my layouts. One way I do this is by enlarging one of my photographs, and using smaller photos to complement the enlarged shot."

"Jayden and Madi"

Supplies *Patterned paper:* Texas Art Supply; *Computer font:* CK Journaling, "The Best of Creative Lettering" CD Vol. 2, *Creating Keepsakes; Foam core:* Source unknown; *Embossing tape:* Inkits; *Other:* Sand, seashells and transparency paper.

DENISE HOOGLAND • BELLAIRE, TX

Planning is key for Denise, who emphasizes arranging all the elements on a page before adhering anything down. She also recommends "sleeping" on a layout when a creative block sets in. "I tend to develop a lot of creative ideas at night before I fall asleep," she says. Denise's mother introduced her artistic daughter to scrapbooking in 1994, and she's been hooked ever since. "The most important features of my layouts are my photos. I tailor my layouts to emphasize the uniqueness of each photograph," shares Denise.

"Abbey at the Park"

Supplies *Patterned papers:* Close To My Heart, Texas Art Supply; *Vellum:* Paper Cuts; *Craft wire:* Artistic Wire Ltd.; *Computer fonts:* Britanic Bold, Microsoft Word; CK Journaling and CK Penman, "The Best of Creative Lettering" CD Combo, Creating Keepsakes.

"Curiosity"

Supplies *Patterned papers:* Texas Art Supply, Close To My Heart; *Vellum:* Paper Cuts; *Pens:* Zig Millennium and Zig Platinum, EK Success; *Computer font:* CK Journaling, "The Best of Creative Lettering" CD Vol. 2, *Creating Keepsakes; Colored pencils:* Prismacolor, Sanford; *Fibers:* Artsanctum.com; *Embroidery floss:* DMC; *Flower accents:* Denise's own designs.

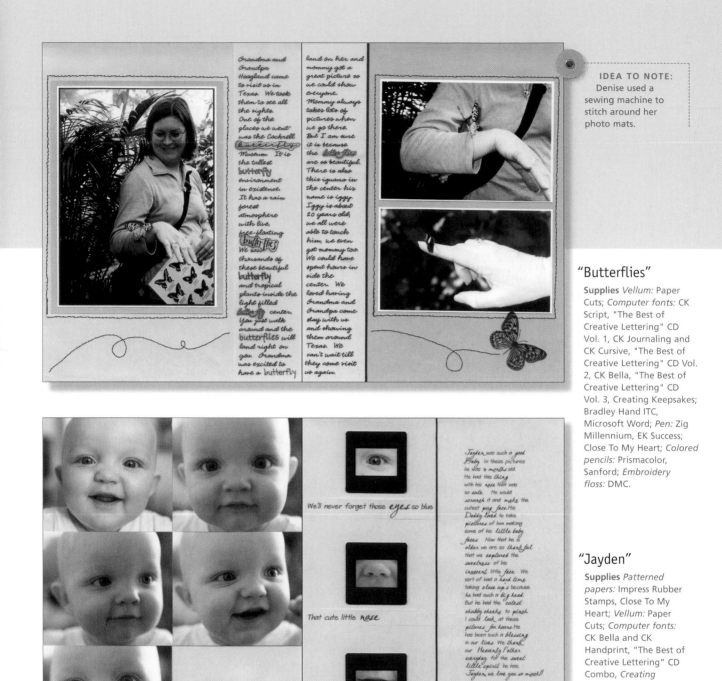

"Butterflies"

Supplies *Vellum:* Paper Cuts; *Computer fonts:* CK Script, "The Best of Creative Lettering" CD Vol. 1, CK Journaling and CK Cursive, "The Best of Creative Lettering" CD Vol. 2, CK Bella, "The Best of Creative Lettering" CD Vol. 3, Creating Keepsakes; Bradley Hand ITC, Microsoft Word; *Pen:* Zig Millennium, EK Success; Close To My Heart; *Colored pencils:* Prismacolor, Sanford; *Embroidery floss:* DMC.

"Jayden"

Supplies *Patterned papers:* Impress Rubber Stamps, Close To My Heart; *Vellum:* Paper Cuts; *Computer fonts:* CK Bella and CK Handprint, "The Best of Creative Lettering" CD Combo, *Creating Keepsakes; Square punch:* Family Treasures; *Slide film covers:* Impress Rubber Stamps.

creative framing Do you have a box of old slides and slide holders lying around in a box in your attic or basement? It's time to dust them off and transform them into useful embellishments for your scrapbook pages! Here's how I created small vignettes of my son's face in my "Jayden" layout shown above:

❶ I used a 2" square punch to cut out images of my son's eyes, nose and mouth from photos.

❷ I centered each photo inside a slide frame and adhered them to my layout. I included a thought about each cute little feature.

—Denise Hoogland

IDEA TO NOTE: Denise cut slits in the paper to the left of her photo and weaved fibers, string and sheer flowers through the slits.

"Hello Kitty"

Supplies *Patterned paper:* The Scrapbook Place *Computer fonts:* Bradley Hand ITC, Microsoft Word; CK Cursive, "The Best of Creative Lettering" CD Combo, *Creating Keepsakes; Sheer flower accents:* Impress Rubber Stamps; *Fibers:* Artsanctum.com; *Beads and paper adhesive:* Inkits; *Other:* String.

"Zion Canyon"

Supplies *Patterned papers:* Close To My Heart, Texas Art Supply; *Vellum:* Paper Cuts; *Computer fonts:* CK Bella, CK Cursive and CK Script, "The Best of Creative Lettering" CD Combo, *Creating Keepsakes.*

try this technique Unify a two-page layout by adhering a photo in the center, half on one side and half on the other. Here's how to create this look:

❶ Adhere several large photographs to both pages to define the corners of the layout.

❷ Cut the smaller photo in half and adhere it to the center of the two pages.

❸ Print the page title on vellum and adhere it over the photo for a soft look that won't detract from the other photos.

—*Denise Hoogland*

2002
danelle johnson

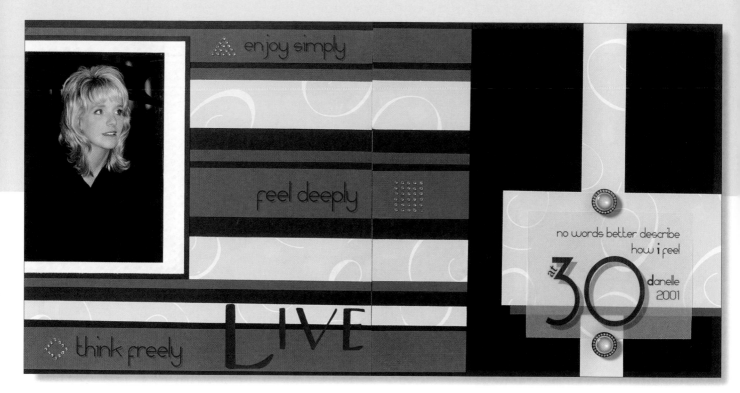

"I want my scrapbooks to reflect all the pieces of my world,

not just the people. I want to look back and remember

the sights, sounds and times as much as I possibly can,

so I scrapbook all these aspects of my life."

"Live"

Supplies *Patterned papers:* Treehouse Designs (green), source unknown (white); *Letter stickers:* Mrs. Grossman's; *Computer fonts:* Mamma Gamma and New Yorker, downloaded from the Internet; *Beads:* Greensleeves Buttons & Baubles & Beads; *Fibers:* Rubba Dub Dub; *Body tattoos:* Source unknown.

DANELLE JOHNSON • LINDSBORG, KS

A visual learner, Danelle says she "visually archives" bits and pieces of the world around her to use on her layouts. "I keep a running list of pages I want to do, with notes beside each that I can refer to when I feel like creating a special page," Danelle explains. "I find such satisfaction in adding page ideas to my list and checking off pages I've completed." Danelle also prefers to hide journaling or use it as a design element on her pages.

"Bethany Lutheran Church"

Supplies *Computer fonts:* Metro and Mariah, downloaded from the Internet; *Jewelry pieces and stones:* Halcraft, Regal Beading and Stones.

IDEA TO NOTE: Danelle designed the embellishments to coordinate with her photos.

"As They Build"

Supplies *Patterned papers:* Dana Simson, Colorbök; *Glossy paper:* Source unknown; *Letter stickers:* Mrs. Grossman's; *Computer fonts:* Metro, Invisible Killer and Speed Bowling, downloaded from the Internet; *Buttons:* JHB International; *Pop dots:* All Night Media.

IDEA TO NOTE: The photo on the left page opens to reveal journaling.

"I find today's media technology most fascinating, whether it's television or print. I believe my scrapbooking style strongly reflects my love for technological trends."

"Refresh"

Supplies *Computer fonts:* Rubberstamp, Quikscribble, Heliosphan, Metro, Stigmata, Print 151, Premi, Gargantum, Garamound and Dirty Ego, downloaded from the Internet; *Beads:* Blue Moon Beads.

IDEAS TO NOTE: Danelle used clear beads to re-create the water droplets in her photo.

GRAPHIC LETTERING TECHNIQUE

Figure 1

Figure 2

Figure 3

Introduce the power of words to your layouts. Repeating one word in several different fonts and colors creates a powerful, yet subtle way of telling a story. I used Microsoft Picture it! to design the words for "Refresh," but other photo-editing programs will produce the same results. Here's how to create an eye-catching page title like this one:

❶ Type the word in black in several fonts of your choice, creating a new text block for each word. Overlap the text blocks so the words will be closer together.

❷ Change the colors of the words, varying the shades from light blue to gray to black (Figure 1).

❸ Select the shadow option from the font styles menu to create shadows on the words (Figure 2).

❹ Rotate two of the text blocks to make the words vertical.

❺ Add any other words or phrases and place them among your other text blocks (Figure 3).

❻ Print the text on a piece of scratch paper to ensure proper placement, then print it onto the desired cardstock.

—Danelle Johnson

IN EVERY GRAIN OF SAND THERE IS A STORY OF THE EARTH.

his LAND his PEOPLE his STORY

pull

IDEAS TO NOTE: Danelle preserved soil from the area in a miniature bottle and included it on her layout. The photo on the bottom left opens up to reveal the story. Danelle printed the large photo on watercolor paper to soften the effect.

"His Land, His People, His Story"

Supplies *Patterned papers:* Anna Griffin (gold striped and green), Paper Patch (brown wash); *Letter stickers:* Mrs. Grossman's; *Computer fonts:* Anna and Heather, downloaded from the Internet; *Metal tags and miniature bottle:* Twopeasinabucket.com; *Fibers and stone:* Rubba Dub Dub.

So EXTRAORDINARY is NATURE with HER choicest   pull

TREASURES
treasures

IDEAS TO NOTE: The front of the layout pulls down to expose a second page. The second page includes additional photos hung together and arranged to flip upward.

"Nature's Treasures"

Supplies *Patterned papers:* Magenta Rubber Stamps (cells), Carolee's Creations (green splatter), Making Memories (striped and solid lime); *Computer fonts:* Enviro, Microsoft Word; SF Intoxicated Blues, Scratch and Diner-FATT, downloaded from the Internet; *Beads:* Rubba Dub Dub.

2002
helena jole

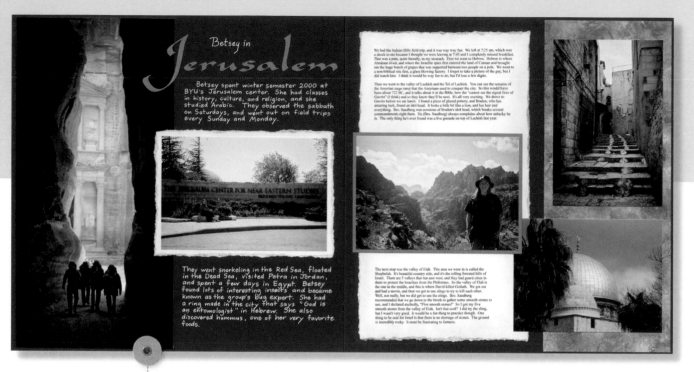

IDEAS TO NOTE: Helena enlarged a photo to 8" x 12" and trimmed it to create a panoramic shot. She also printed out some text on cardstock from an e-mail her sister sent from Jerusalem, then ripped and chalked the edges.

"Betsy in Jerusalem"

Supplies *Patterned paper:* Tuscany Papers, Scrap-Ease; *Title:* Helena scanned the alphabet "Legend Hand" from the book *Written Letters: 33 Alphabets for Calligraphers* by Jacqueline Svaren, then traced the letters onto cardstock and cut them out with a small utility knife. ; *Computer font:* Times New Roman, Microsoft Word; *Pen:* Milky Gel Roller, Pentel; *Chalk:* Craf-T Products.

"I've been consciously trying to apply certain design principles to my pages—like creating visual triangles, using odd numbers, and following the 'if you use it once, use it twice' principle of color."

HELENA JOLE • TACOMA, WA

"Gee, a lot of scrapbooking is just sitting and looking at things," says Helena's husband. And Helena admits she does a lot of "squinting" while choosing just the right colors for a page. When Helena was a child, her parents bought reams of tracing paper for her, and she traced everything she could get her hands on. Helena applies the same technique today, tracing designs from greeting cards, clip art, design books and even embroidered wall hangings.

"Berry Pickin' Time"

Supplies *Stencil pattern:* Adapted from a blackberry pattern (berries) and a strawberry pattern (leaves); *Computer font:* Brush Script BT, Corel Draw; *Pen:* Pigma Micron, Sakura; *Chalk:* Craf-T Products (Helena added fuchsia chalk to red cardstock to make the berry color.)

IDEA TO NOTE: Helena printed out two copies of the berry pattern—one back-facing and the other front-facing. She traced the back-facing pattern onto cardstock and cut out the pieces with a small utility knife (she numbered the small parts to help her keep track of them). Then she traced the front-facing pattern onto the background cardstock to create a guide for gluing the small pieces in place.

STENCILED PAPER PIECING

Figure 1

Figure 2

Figure 3

Creating paper-piecing patterns using stencils is one of my favorite techniques, and the end result is a simple, yet sophisticated accent for any page. All you need is a stencil of your choice, a craft knife, a cutting mat and cardstock. Here's how I created the elegant grapevine above:

❶ I printed out two copies of the stencil design, reversing the design for one of the copies.

❷ I transferred the *reversed* design onto the desired color of cardstock with tracing paper (Figure 1). *Note:* If you're using dark-colored paper, try using yellow or white transfer paper so the design will show up better.

❸ To make assembling the pieces easier, I numbered the grapes while tracing them. To add dimension to the grapes, I decided to cut a few from lighter-colored paper—rather than numbering those, I labeled them with a letter.

❹ I transferred the *reversed* leaves and vines design onto green cardstock, and cut out all the pieces using a craft knife and cutting mat.

❺ I transferred the forward-facing stencil pattern onto the background cardstock (Figure 2), tracing just inside the lines so when I adhered the cut-out pieces, the pencil lines wouldn't show.

❻ I adhered the cut-out pieces to the background cardstock, using the traced design and the numbered pattern as a guide (Figure 3).

—*Helena Jole*

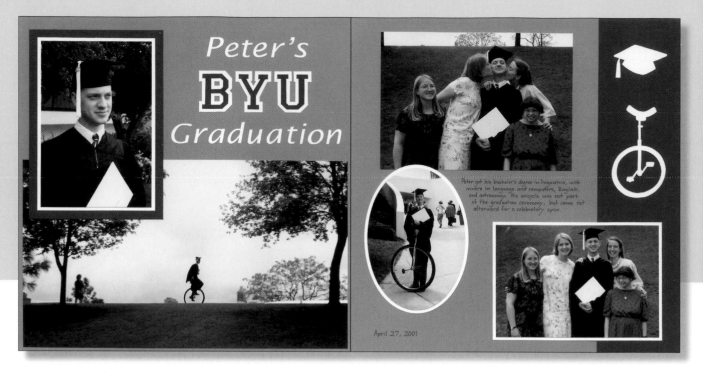

"Peter's BYU Graduation"

Supplies *Computer fonts:* Lucida Sans, Microsoft Word; Princetown, Corel Draw; *Graduation cap and unicycle:* Helena's own designs, based on clip-art images and photos she found online; *Pen:* Pigma Micron, Sakura. *Idea to note:* Helena enlarged one photo to 8" x 10".

"Mists of the Avalon"

Supplies *Vellum:* Paper Adventures; *Computer font:* President, Corel Draw; *Pen:* Pigma Micron, Sakura.

IDEAS TO NOTE: Helena printed out two copies of the title—one front-facing and the other back-facing. She traced the back-facing title onto cardstock and cut out the letters with a small utility knife. She placed the front-facing title over the large photo and made pinpricks following the pattern of the title as a guide for adhering the letters. Also, Helena folded the vellum around the edge of the paper and glued it on the back so adhesive wouldn't show on the front.

"Duck Duck Goose"

Supplies *Computer font:* Futura, Corel Draw; *Duck:* Adapted from Corel Draw clip art; *Pen:* Pigma Micron, Sakura.

"I've taken a lot of art classes (drawing, bookbinding and calligraphy) and find that I use a lot of skills from those classes as I scrapbook."

"Quidi Vidi"

Supplies *Pen:* Milky Gel Roller, Pentel; *Title:* Helena scanned the alphabet "Italic Hand" from the book *Written Letters: 33 Alphabets for Calligraphers* by Jacqueline Svaren, then traced the letters onto cardstock and cut them out with a small utility knife.

IDEAS TO NOTE: Helena tore blue cardstock and layered it over another shade of blue paper to create the background.

shannon jones 2002

IDEAS TO NOTE: Shannon made the mosaic background by wrapping squares wih different colors of cardstock, then lining them up. Shannon also tore a sheet of vellum and applied pink chalk to the torn edge.

If thou art merry, praise the Lord with singing, with music, with dancing, and with a prayer of praise and thanksgiving.
D & C 136

Andelyn Louise
September 2001

"If Thou Art Merry"

Supplies *Specialty paper:* Source unknown; *Computer font:* Page Italics, Microsoft ; *Chalk:* Craf-T Products; *Square punch:* Marvy Uchida; *Other:* Ribbon.

"I love chalk! I can change the whole color of my cardstock,

make clouds, waves, shadows, sunsets and beach scenes,

add texture—the list could go on and on."

SHANNON JONES • MESA, AZ

Neat, tidy and uncluttered—that's how Shannon describes her scrapbooking style.

While she often finds ideas from advertisements, bed and bath decor, book covers and clothes, she comes up with many of her own ideas in the wee hours of the morning. "I often dream about scrapbooking and wake up and remember a great page I was working on," shares Shannon. "Sometimes I write the idea down, and sometimes I even get up and work on it."

"Puerto Peñasco"

Supplies *Vellum:* The Paper Company; *Computer font:* Curlz, Microsoft; *Pen:* Zig Millennium, EK Success; *Fibers:* Rubba Dub Dub; *Embroidery floss:* DMC; *Sun and colored string design:* Shannon's own designs.

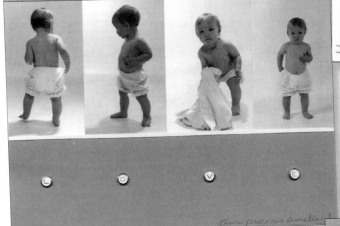

"Her Beauty Outshines"

Supplies *Patterned paper:* Bo-Bunny Press; *Computer font:* Page Italics, Microsoft Word; *Flower accents:* MERI; *Chalk:* Craf-T Products; *Other:* Ribbon.

"Baby Love"

Supplies *Lettering idea:* Shannon wrote the word "Baby" with watercolor pencils, then went over the letters with a wet cotton swab. To create the word "Love," Shannon cut small circles out and laid them inside the small metal frames. ; *Metal circle frame studs:* Memory Lane; *Pen:* Zig Millennium, EK Success; *Colored pencils:* Memory Pencils, EK Success; Staedtler, Inc.

IDEA TO NOTE: To create the look of a sunset on the background paper, Shannon rubbed cotton balls in several colors of chalk and blended them together on her page.

picture-perfect sunsets

Timing is everything when it comes to taking photos during the few minutes before the sun sets—you only have about 30 minutes of prime sunset time. Here are my tips for capturing fabulous shots during these golden minutes of the day:

- ◆ Have your subject wear soft, natural colors that complement the shades of the sunset in your area.
- ◆ Position your subject facing directly into the sun, or slightly turned to one side.
- ◆ If you're running out of precious sunset time, position a white or silver reflector facing the sun to collect a few more rays.
- ◆ Turn off your flash for this photo shoot—the sun will provide all the light you need.

—*Shannon Jones*

IDEA TO NOTE: To make the pockets "pop out," Shannon folded the sides accordion style.

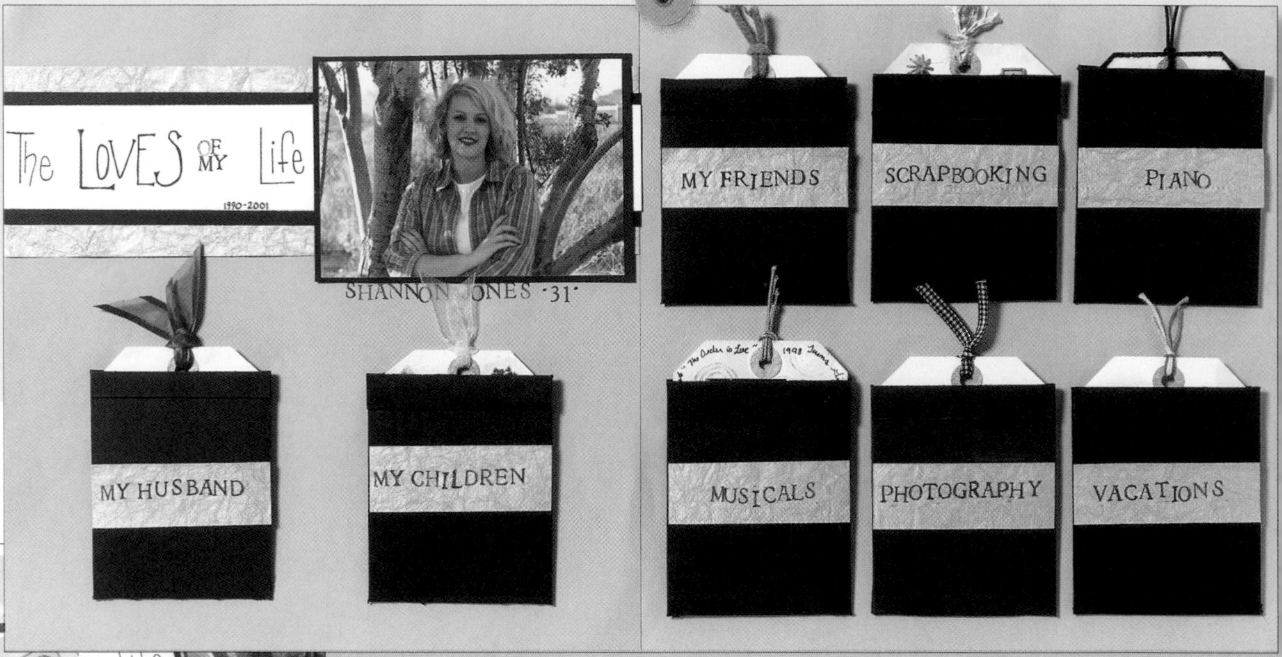

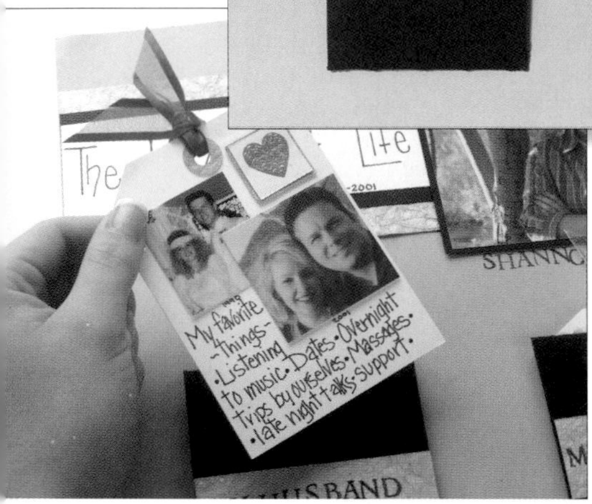

"The Loves of My Life"

Supplies *Textured paper:* Source unknown; *Lettering idea:* Shannon used rubber stamps for the pocket titles. *Rubber stamps:* Pixie Press (letters), Hero Arts (circles); *Punches:* Family Treasures (circle); *Dried flowers:* Nature's Pressed; *Embossing powder:* Emboss It; *Stamping ink:* Ancient Page and VersaColor, Tsukineko; *Fibers:* Rubba Dub Dub; Chenille Wrights, Inc.; *Embroidery floss:* DMC; *Chalk:* Craf-T Products; *Pen:* Zig Millennium, EK Success; *Pockets and tags:* Shannon's own designs; *Other:* Ribbon and studs.

ACCORDION-STYLE MEMORABILIA POCKET

Some mementos are just too thick or bulky to fit in a pre-made memory pocket, but they can still be included in your scrapbook. Here's how to create an accordion-style envelope that expands to hold memorabilia:

1. Transfer the pattern onto cardstock and score each of the fold lines with a bone folder or scoring blade (Figures 1a and 1b).
2. Sew any accents to the front of the envelope before you adhere it to your page.
3. Adhere the bottom fold only to the page, making sure not to adhere the accordion folds together. Let the glue dry completely (Figure 2).
4. Insert the page into a page protector and trace around the pocket where you want to cut a slit to make the pocket accessible.
5. Cut the page protector with a craft knife to create the slit, and insert the page back into the page protector.

—Shannon Jones

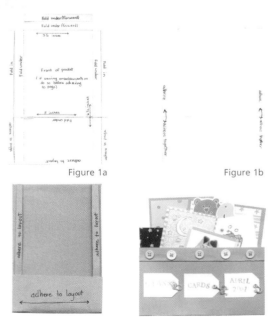

Figure 1a

Figure 1b

Figure 2

"Our Annual Trip"

Supplies *Specialty paper:* Source unknown; *Computer fonts:* Comic Sans, Curlz MT, Lucida Consoles, Lucida Handwriting and Tempus Sans, Microsoft ; *Pen:* Zig Millennium, EK Success; *Rubber stamp:* Hero Arts; *Embossing powder:* Suze Weinberg; *Chalk:* Craf-T Products; *Embroidery floss:* DMC; *Regtangle accents around photo and journaling blocks:* Shannon's own designs.

IDEA TO NOTE: To ensure all of the flowers were the same size and proportion, Shannon made a template using a small circle punch.

"The Jones Girls"

Supplies *Lettering:* Shannon's own design; *Rubber stamp:* Hero Arts
Stamping ink: VersaColor, Tsukineko; *Hand-sewn flowers:* Shannon's own designs; *Pen:* Zig Millennium, EK Success; *Circle punch:* Source unknown; *Paper clips:* Clipiola; *Embroidery floss:* DMC.

IDEA TO NOTE: Erin took photos of her favorite books and silhouetted the images to include on her layout.

"Pages from My Past"

Supplies *Patterned paper:* Rocky Mountain Scrapbook Company; *Embossed paper:* Lasting Impressions for Paper; *Lettering template:* Fun, Chatterbox for EK Success; *Computer fonts:* CK Journaling, "The Best of Creative Lettering" CD Vol. 2, *Creating Keepsakes*; Alternative Gothic, downloaded from the Internet; *Punches:* EK Success (rectangle, tri leaf), All Night Media (squiggle); *Rubber stamp:* Impress Rubber Stamps; *Stamping ink:* VersaMark, Tsukineko; *Embroidery floss:* DMC; *Eyelets:* Doodlebug Design; *Chalk:* Craf-T Products; *Pen:* Zig Writer, EK Success.

"Don't be shy about scrapping your hopes, dreams and interests. Future generations will thank you for it."

ERIN LINCOLN • FREDERICK, MD

Erin's stash of scrapbook supplies could last her for the next 50 years, she jokes, and it proves to be inspirational when she need a little creative boost. "More often than not, I find something I forgot I had. The creative juices start flowing when I think of the possibilities each item holds." Erin doesn't scrapbook without her computer, which she says organizes her journaling into a small, organized space and adds variety with a huge selection of fonts and clip art.

"One Fall Day"

Supplies *Computer fonts:* Atlantic Inline, downloaded from the Internet; CK Journaling, "The Best of Creative Lettering" CD Vol. 2, *Creating Keepsakes; Leaf accent:* Source unknown; sFibers: Rubba Dub Dub; *Pen:* The Ultimate Gel Pen, American Crafts; *Pop dots:* All Night Media.

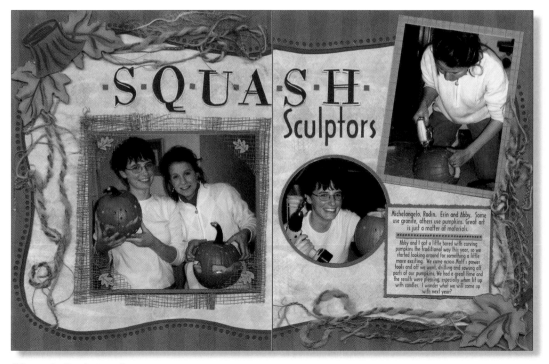

"Squash Sculptors"

Supplies *Patterned papers:* Lasting Impressions for Paper (orange striped), Colorbök ; *Computer fonts:* Bottled Fart ("Squash"), downloaded from the Internet; CK Journaling, "The Best of Creative Lettering" CD Vol. 2, *Creating Keepsakes; Stamp and stamping ink:* Stampin' Up!; *Leaf template:* Provo Craft; *Fiber:* Rubba Dub Dub; *Punches:* Lasting Impressions for Paper (hole), EK Success (leaf); *Chalk:* Craf-T Products; *Pens:* Zig Writer and Zig Scroll and Brush, EK Success; *Scissors:* Deckle edge, Provo Craft; *Other:* Ribbon.

"Trust"

Supplies *Patterned papers:* Karen Foster Design (solid), Sweetwater (dark dot), Making Memories (all remaining); *Computer fonts:* Eurostile T (title) and President (subtitle), downloaded from the Internet; CK Journaling (journaling), "The Best of Creative Lettering" CD Vol. 2, *Creating Keepsakes; Eyelets:* Doodlebug Design; *Circle punch:* Emagination Crafts.

"Just as with a wardrobe, the basics are essential. Black, white and khaki/kraft-colored cardstock can go a long way when paired with patterned paper."

"You Glow Girl"

Supplies *Patterned paper:* Scrapbook Sally; *Lettering template:* Funky, ABC Tracers, Pebbles for EK Success; *Computer fonts:* Encino (title), downloaded from the Internet; CK Journaling (journaling), "The Best of Creative Lettering" CD Vol. 2, *Creating Keepsakes; Craft wire:* Artistic Wire Ltd.; *Other:* Beads.

journaling tips

I'll admit it—I'm selfish when it comes to journaling. I love to work out my feelings, reflect on events and plan for the future, then organize it into text. Talk about cheap therapy! Aside from these motives, I love journaling because I can pass on information I would have loved to have received from my own mother. Here are some ideas to consider writing about:

- What kind of young woman you were before you had children
- What you thought about
- What you saw in your future
- What you dreamed about
- If you acted silly occasionally
- What your struggles were

—Erin Lincoln

"Sweet Stuff"

Supplies *Patterned paper:* Making Memories; *Cross-stitch paper:* Source unknown; *Computer fonts:* Brody (title) and Black Boys on Mopeds (journaling), downloaded from the Internet; *Flower punches:* EK Success (small), Emagination Crafts (large); *Embroidery floss:* DMC; *Pen:* Zig Scroll and Brush, EK Success; *Chalk:* Craf-T Products; *Other:* Buttons.

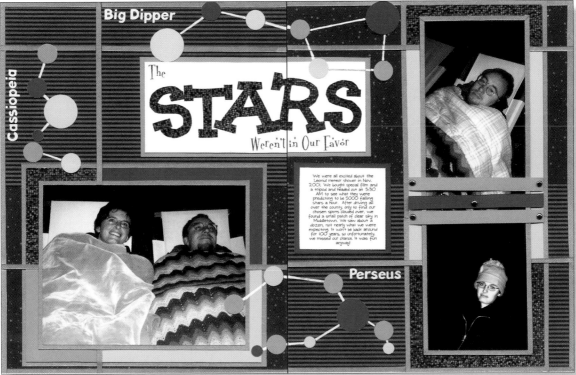

"Stars Weren't in Our Favor"

Supplies *Patterned papers:* Scrapbook Wizard (black spot), Pixie Press (striped); *Sparkle paper:* Funky Films, Graphix; *Metallic paper:* Envelopments; *Computer fonts:* Fontdiner, downloaded from the Internet; CK Journaling, "The Best of Creative Lettering" CD Vol. 2, *Creating Keepsakes*; *Lettering template:* Scrapbook, Provo Craft; *Brads:* American Pin & Fastener; *Punches:* Emagination Crafts; *Letter stickers:* Making Memories; *Pen:* Pigma Micron, Sakura.

there was a

Little Girl

that had a

Little Curl

Right in the middle of her forehead.
And when she was good,
she was very, very good.
But when she was bad,
she was horrid.

When you were about three, I started reciting this little poem to you because of all your curls and your attitude. Of course, you usually were very, very, very good more than horrid, but you had your moments! Now you have it memorized and finish it for me when I start it.

– November 2001 –

"Little Girl That Had a Little Curl"

Supplies *Computer fonts:* Spring and Maiandra GD, downloaded from the Internet; *Paper clips:* Source unknown; *Fibers:* On the Fringe; *Embossing powder:* Source unknown; *Embossing ink:* ColorBox, Clearsnap, Inc.

"I love embellishments because they add a little 'oomph' and texture to my pages, but I make sure they fit the style and feel of my pages and aren't overdone."

ANITA MATEJKA • LINCOLN, NE

Anita loves embellishments, and she'll use everything from fibers to anything she deems "small enough" to fit in her scrapbook. A web designer, Anita incorporates many principles of design into her layouts. "Quite often I find myself using elements of scrapbooking in my web design also," Anita shares. She also draws inspiration from ads, whether on billboards, in magazines or at stores, and she'll never be found without her little notepad for jotting down ideas.

IDEA TO NOTE: Anita placed pebbles over the word "Fishy" in her title to create the look of a fish bowl.

"Little Fishy"

Supplies *Computer fonts:* CK Cursive, "The Best of Creative Lettering" CD Vol. 2, *Creating Keepsakes*; Boulder, downloaded from the Internet; *Fibers:* Rubba Dub Dub; *Pebbles:* Source unknown.

"Honeybun, I Love You"

Supplies *Mulberry paper:* Paper Palette; *Computer font:* Brady Bunch, downloaded from the Internet; *Tags:* Avery ; *Eyelets:* Impress Rubber Stamps; *Fibers:* Rubba Dub Dub.

MAKE YOUR OWN PHOTO TAGS

Metal-rimmed tags are fun and functional accents that can be used for title lettering or mini photos, as in my "Honeybun" layout shown here. Here's how to create these simple accents:

❶ Use a punch to punch a circle out of the photo that's the same size as the tag. You can also trace around the tag and cut the photo with a craft knife and cutting mat. You'll want to trim the edges slightly so the photo will fit inside the metal rim.

❷ Adhere the photo to the tag and set an eyelet in each side of the tag. (Be sure to line up the eyelets properly.)

❸ Thread the tags onto fibers or string as desired, and glue them onto your page. Also try setting the eyelets in a vertical line and hanging the tags vertically on your page.

You can also punch holes in the top of the tags and hang them from other accents with jute, raffia, embroidery floss and more.

—*Anita Matejka*

"Build-a-Bear Workshop"

Supplies *Computer font:* Carrick Groovy, downloaded from the Internet; *Eyelets:* Impress Rubber Stamps; *Paper yarn:* Twistel, Making Memories; *Pop dots:* All Night Media; *Buttons:* Dress-It-Up, Cut-It-Up.

Figure 1a

Figure 1b

TRY THIS TECHNIQUE

A busy background can detract from the subject of a photo. When bright colors or other items in the background are distracting, I use my computer to help me draw attention back to a specific part of the photo, without having to crop. Here's how:

❶ Change your color photo to black and white using photo-editing software, or ask your local film processor to print the photo in black and white.

❷ Print out a black-and-white and a color version of your photo (Figures 1a and 1b).

❸ Decide which part of the photo is the focal point and cut it from the color photo. I used skewed shapes to give the layout more variety (Figures 2a and 2b).

❹ Mat the cut-out photo with black cardstock. Adhere the color version over the black-and-white version with foam mounting tape for dimension (Figure 3).

—*Anita Matejka*

Figure 2a

Figure 2b

Figure 3

"I try to make each layout its own unique piece of 'artwork.' With scrapbooking,

I know the work I do will be cherished forever by my kids and family."

IDEA TO NOTE: Anita printed her journaling on vellum and placed it over the photo of the park.

"Primary Park"

Supplies *Computer fonts:* Generic Font, Tangerine (title) and Ziggy Zoe (journaling), downloaded from the Internet; *Brads:* American Pin & Fastener; *Pop dots:* All Night Media

IDEA TO NOTE: Anita aged her handmade vellum envelopes with chalks, and sanded the cardstock for a worn look.

"Warm Wishes from the Past"

Supplies *Patterned paper:* Debbie Mumm, Creative Imaginations; *Vellum:* K & Company (patterned), Paper Adventures (tan); *Computer fonts:* Dauphin and Corabel, downloaded from the Internet; *Tags:* Avery; *Chalk:* Craf-T Products; *Fibers:* Rubba Dub Dub; *Other:* Buttons and string.

2002
pascale michaud-finucan

IDEAS TO NOTE: Pascale reversed the font in WordArt and cut it out using a craft knife and fine-tipped scissors.

HOW TO EAT YOUR YOGURT WITHOUT A SPOON.

BLUEBERRY BLAST!

SOPHIE
13 MONTHS OLD
JANUARY 2001

WHO NEEDS UTENSILS?

SOPHIE. Our creative, independent spirit. Watching her find inventive solutions to perplexing problems is always a favorite activity of mine!

On this particular day, I was busy with the dishes while she was enjoying a cup of blueberry yogurt. At some point, Sophie lost her spoon on the floor. No matter – she didn't complain at all and was quite content to get the rest of the yogurt out using a variety of other methods: squeezing the cup; turning it upside down and letting the yogurt run out; digging to the bottom of the cup with her fingers; licking around the rim with her tongue. How could I possibly be upset about the mess when she demonstrated such perseverance and creativity?

"Scrapbooking is the perfect integration of all the things I'm most passionate about: family, writing, art and photography. I'm continually inspired by all of these things, and I love that I can express my passion for them through scrapbooking."

"Blueberry Blast"
Supplies *Computer font:* Futura Med, Microsoft Word; *Blueberries:* Pascale's own designs.

PASCALE MICHAUD-FINUCAN • CARLETON PLACE, ONTARIO, CANADA

Her "easy-on-the-eyes" style is inspired by magazines and advertising, Pascale says, but her best designs and most heartfelt journaling come when she's out running. "The combination of adrenaline and fresh air invariably clears my mind," she explains. Her favorite technique is using reverse lettering for titles—printing the letters on cardstock and cutting them out using a craft knife or fine-tipped scissors. She also loves incorporating her journaling right onto the background of her layouts for a more unified design.

170 Creating Keepsakes • Pascale Michaud-Finucan

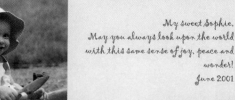

Every Grain of Sand

In the fury of the moment I can see the Master's hand In every leaf that trembles, in every grain of sand.

Bob Dylan

My sweet Sophie, May you always look upon the world with this same sense of joy, peace and wonder! June 2001

"Every Grain of Sand"

Supplies *Computer font:* Gigi, Microsoft Word; *Embossing powder:* Mark Enterprises; *Embossing pen:* EK Success; *Circle template:* Coluzzle, Provo Craft.

"I go through long periods when I just don't feel like scrapbooking. I don't force myself to work through these times. Instead, I just allow myself a 'creative break' while I focus on other things. When I do feel like scrapbooking again, my creativity always comes back with a vengeance."

INSPIRATION FROM THE WORLD AROUND YOU

My scrapbooking process almost always starts with my sketchbook, which is filled with design ideas I've seen in magazines, on television and in advertising. My idea for the layout shown above came from an Oil of Olay ad. I was inspired to create color blocks of the three shades of pink in my daughter's dress to make the background. Here's how to create this look:

❶ Enlarge two photos to 8" x 10", then crop them down to 8" x 8". Crop the smaller photo to 4" x 4". (Be careful when enlarging a photo to 8" x 10". The full frame of the negative is not developed, so you have less background to crop.)

❷ Choose three shades of cardstock and a natural white as your background colors.

❸ Print out the title in reverse on cardstock. Flip the title strip over and tape it to a light box or sunny window. Trace the letters with an embossing pen, and sprinkle the wet design with white embossing powder. Shake off any excess powder and emboss the design with a heating tool, holding it at least 6" away from the paper.

❹ Print the journaling blocks onto cardstock.

❺ Create circles for the polka-dotted strip using a circle template and adhere them to cardstock. Mount the photos and cardstock strips on two pieces of any color cardstock.

—Pascale Michaud-Finucan

HALF MARATHON.

INTENSE HEAT
SHADED TRAILS
OTTAWA RIVER
ACHING BLISTERS
ENERGY GELS
WATER STATIONS
DUSTY PATHS
FRIENDLY RUNNERS
BARE BELLIES
BORROWED SHADES
STICKY GATORADE
SHUFFLING FEET
BLOODY SHOES

GLOUCESTER HALF MARATHON
SEPTEMBER 9th, 2001

Running the Gloucester Half Marathon was an incredible turning point in my life. It changed me in ways that I never anticipated.

BEFORE ➡

Leslie and I had trained for this race together all summer. But at the end of August, I didn't think I would be able to run the race at all. In one heartbreaking week, I learned I was pregnant, then had a miscarriage and then discovered a lump in my breast. Suddenly, I felt like my world was falling apart.

Thankfully, after several medical examinations, my doctor determined that I was healthy. I decided that despite everything I had to continue to run — and even though I was feeling defeated, I decided to attempt the race.

AFTER ➡

The half marathon ended up being such a blessing to me. Somehow, running twenty-one kilometers during that difficult time made me feel strong again. I regained my courage to move forward and found a sense of peace about everything that had happened just a few weeks before. Two long hours running mostly by myself gave me time to reflect and to understand that I had been given a challenge to overcome. I crossed the finish line with a renewed spirit, a happy heart and a strong sense of hope for the future.

FULL ACCOMPLISHMENT.

"Half Marathon, Full Accomplishment"

Supplies *Computer fonts:* Anhedonia (title), downloaded from the Internet; Courier New (journaling), Microsoft Word.

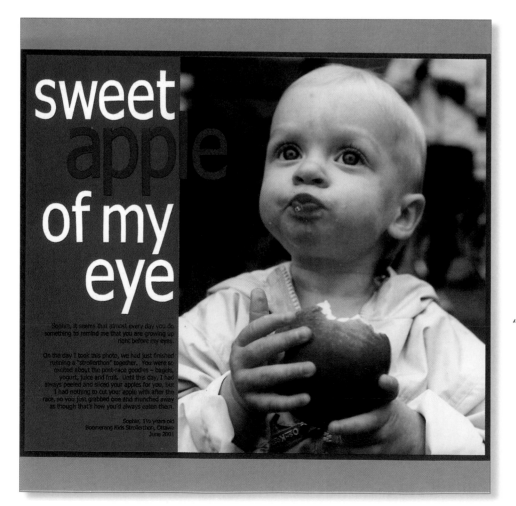

sweet apple of my eye

Sophie, it seems that almost every day you do something to remind me that you are growing up right before my eyes.

On the day I took this photo, we had just finished running a "strollerthon" together. You were so excited about the post-race goodies — bagels, yogurt, juice and fruit. Until this day, I had always peeled and sliced your apples for you, but I had nothing to cut your apple with after the race, so you just grabbed one and munched away as though that's how you'd always eaten them.

Sophie, 1½ years old
Boomerang Kids Strollerthon, Ottawa
June 2001

"Sweet Apple of My Eye"

Supplies *Computer font:* Tahoma, Microsoft Word.

IDEA TO NOTE: Kathy scanned in the photos, enlarged them and printed them in the center of her photo paper. Then she printed the journaling onto vellum and created a vellum overlay, cutting out the center so the photos would show through.

PHOTOS BY CAROL ACCORD

Kolene Marie Anderson Whitworth

The grand essentials to happiness in this life are something to do,

something to love, and something to hope for.
Joseph Addison

"Grand Essentials"

Supplies *Vellum:* Keeping Memories Alive; *Computer font:* Ribbon 131 BT, WordPerfect.

"The real inspiration for my scrapbook style comes from the photos themselves. They help me determine the colors and mood I want to portray, how much I want to embellish, and the style my layout will be—formal, playful, subdued, etc."

KATHY PETERSEN • SPANISH FORK, UT

Kathy's daughters look forward to scrapbook night as much as she does—it's when their dad throws a video party so their mom can have some peaceful scrapping time! Kathy, who loves a creative challenge, seldom uses pre-made products because she loves to see what she'll come up with on her own. "What inspires me to scrapbook is simply my love of design and using different techniques and elements together to create one layout," she shares.

IDEA TO NOTE: Karen enlarged the lighthouse photo to 5" x 7", cut it into a thinner strip, and then cut it into three pieces to create the look of a panoramic photo.

"Cabrillo"

Supplies *Textured paper:* Keeping Memories Alive; *Computer fonts:* CK Script, "The Best of Creative Lettering" CD Combo, *Creating Keepsakes*; Staccato 222 BT, WordPerfect.

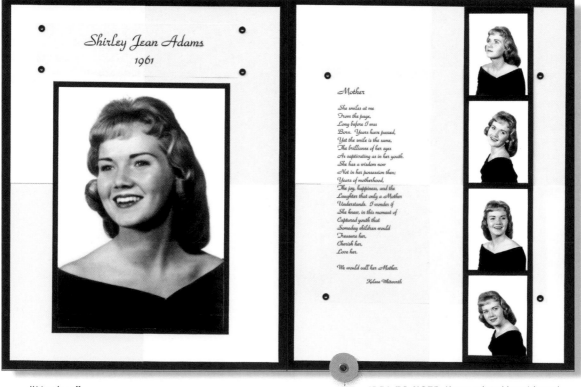

"Mother"

Supplies *Vellum:* Keeping Memories Alive; *Computer font:* Park Avenue BT, WordPerfect; *Eyelets:* Source unknown.

IDEA TO NOTE: Karen printed her title and journaling onto vellum, and attached them to her layout using eyelets.

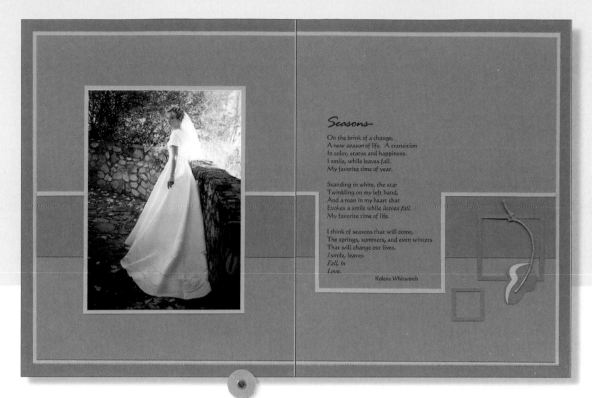

IDEA TO NOTE: Karen chalked over the green cardstock to brighten it, and chalked the hemp to match the cardstock.

"Seasons"

Supplies *Computer fonts:* Page Italic LET and Calligraphy 421 BT, WordPerfect; *Chalk:* Craf-T Products; *Hemp:* Darice; *Leaf accent:* Karen's own design, inspired by a leaf on a Winnie the Pooh comforter.

COLOR-BLOCKING TECHNIQUE

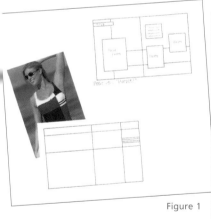

Figure 1

Figure 2

"Positively Purple"

Supplies *Computer fonts*: CK Journaling and CK Toggle, "The Best of Creative Lettering" CD Vol. 2, *Creating Keepsakes*; DJ Squiggle, "Fontastic! 2" CD, D.J. Inkers; *Lettering template:* Spunky, Déjà Views, The C-Thru Ruler Co. *Flower punch:* EK Success; *Mini brads:* Source unknown.

While it may sound technical, color-blocking is simply using different colors in various geometric patterns and shapes. This technique uses blocks of color to fill in the empty spaces of a layout, producing a clean look that requires little embellishing. Here are some tips that have helped me color-block effectively:

◆ Start with a few sketches from magazine ads or clothing designs (Figure 1). Avoid designs that are too symmetrical; the idea is to be abstract.

◆ Keep photo mats around ⅛" so they don't compete with the other color blocks.

◆ Use repositionable adhesive so you can rearrange the design later.

◆ To keep the lines on the layout from running together and making the page look like two instead of one, mat three sides of the background cardstock with a different color (Figure 2).

◆ To print your journaling directly onto the background cardstock, measure with a ruler exactly where you want the journaling to go and use the measurements to format the margins on the computer. Always print a sample sheet on scratch paper first.

—*Kathy Petersen*

"I love my first album for its

'scrap innocence,' because even with the

stickers splashed everywhere and the goofy photo

cropping, I still managed to tell the story.

Three years later, I still enjoy telling the story,

but hopefully I do it with just

a bit more elegance."

"Are You Going to Poke Me with That Knife, Grandpa?"

Supplies *Patterned papers:* Colors By Design (pink and green in title), Doodlebug Design (blue plaid), Making Memories (willow and dark blue), Paper Patch (dark pink), Cut-It-Up (swirl), Scrap-Ease (green flower border), Magenta Rubber Stamps (green circles); *Computer fonts:* Calvin and Hobbes (title and journaling) and First Grader (journaling), downloaded from the Internet; *Rubber stamp:* Planet Rubber; *Stamping ink:* ColorBox, Clearsnap, Inc.; *Iridescent ink:* Stampa Rosa; *Accents:* Roxx, Judi-Kins; *Pen:* Zig Writer, EK Success; *Chalk:* Craf-T Products; *Colored pencils:* Prismacolor, Sanford.

ALLISON STRINE • ATLANTA, GA

Allison's scrapbooking style is inspired by everything from flowers to greeting cards to toy packaging, and she'll never be found without her digital camera for taking photos of interesting designs. A former television editor, Allison says she sees a lot of similarities between editing TV commercials and scrapbooking. "In both cases, you've got a finite amount of 'space' to work with, and you need to tell your story without superfluous information."

IDEA TO NOTE: Allison painted the paper she journaled on with watercolors to create the look of patterned paper.

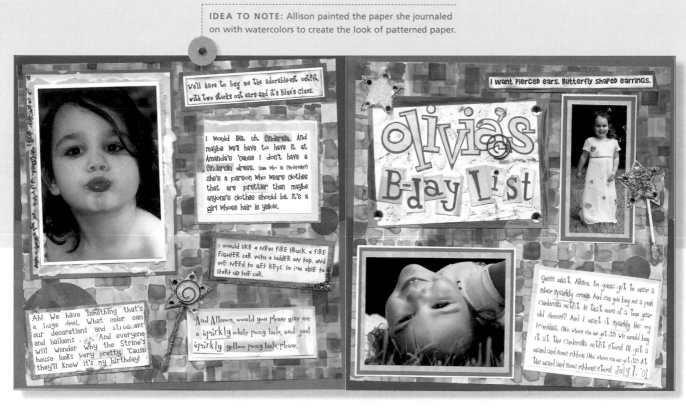

"Olivia's Birthday List"

Supplies *Patterned papers:* Colors By Design (mosaic); Dana Simson, Making Memories; *Patterned vellum:* Over The Moon Press; *Specialty paper:* Paper Al Fresco, Paper Adventures; *Computer fonts:* Mandingo, Brady Bunch, Fontdiner, Robot Teacher, Calvin and Hobbes, Girls Are Weird and Weehah, downloaded from the Internet; *Stamping ink:* ColorBox, Clearsnap, Inc.; *Accents:* Roxx, Judi-Kins; *Wand accents:* The Bee Hive; *Jewels:* Beedz; *Chalks:* Craf-T Products; *Other:* Watercolors and spiral paper clips.

"The Queen of Carpe Diem"

Supplies *Patterned papers:* Paper Adventures (green and yellow), Scrap-Ease (magenta); *Specialty papers for title:* Paper Al Fresco, Paper Adventures; *Computer fonts:* Hey It's Red, Yahoo and Annifont, downloaded from the Internet; CK Journaling, "The Best of Creative Lettering" CD Vol. 2, *Creating Keepsakes*; *Rubber stamp:* Planet Rubber; *Stamping ink:* VersaMark, Tsukineko; *Embossing powder:* Inkadinkadoo; *Chalk:* Craf-T Products; *Crown clip art:* Microsoft Photo Gallery; *Pen:* EZ Gel, Pentel; *Paper cord and mica chips:* Judi-Kins.

"The best advice I could give a scrapbooker is to trust her instincts. Follow the basic principles of color and design, and when it looks good, tape that baby down!"

From Russia With Love

"From Russia with Love"

Supplies *Metallic paper:* Paper Adventures; *Computer fonts:* Brock Script, Witchcraft (title), Kallamar and Architect (journaling), downloaded from the Internet; *Rubber stamps:* Planet Rubber (passport), Stampendous! (crackle background); *Stamping ink:* ColorBox, Clearsnap, Inc.; *Embossing powders:* Inkadinkadoo, All Night Media; *Pen:* Zig Writer, EK Success; *Chalk:* Craf-T Products; *Colored pencils:* Prismacolor, Sanford; *Pop dots:* All Night Media; *Other:* Postage stamps.

IDEAS TO NOTE: To preserve the original stamps, Allison scanned them, printed them out, and aged the scanned copies by rubbing them with cocoa-colored ink. More stamps are displayed under the vellum overlay.

CREATIVE FRAME TECHNIQUE

A creative twist on the traditional frame, this technique is a simple and elegant way to accent your photos. All you need is a background rubber stamp, embossing powder, transparency film and a few basic scrapbooking supplies. Here's how to achieve this look:

❶ Mount the photo on cardstock. With a craft knife and cutting mat, trim the cardstock to make a ⅛" mat, stopping about ⅛" away from each corner.

❷ Trim away the excess cardstock to create a second ⅛" mat. Stop cutting about ⅛" away from each corner to leave four strips that connect the two mats together (Figure 1).

❸ Adhere the transparency film to the back of the matted photo. Attach adhesive pop dots or foam mounting tape to the back of the outer mat (Figure 2).

❹ Stamp the background stamp onto gold metallic paper, and heat-emboss with gold embossing powder. Stamp a second time and emboss with red embossing powder.

❺ Trim the stamped paper and adhere it behind the matted photo (Figure 3).

—*Allison Strine*

Figure 1

Figure 2

Figure 3

"When You Were One"

Supplies *Computer fonts:* Jeff Chris (title) and Pooh (journaling), downloaded from the Internet; *Clock rubber stamp:* Above the Mark; *Stamping ink:* VersaMark, Tsukineko; Dr. Ph. Martin's; *Embossing powders:* Suze Weinberg, Inkadinkadoo; *Fibers:* Rubba Dub Dub; *Mica chips:* Judi-Kins; *Gold paint:* Source unknown; *Chalk:* Craf-T Products; *Hole punch:* Fiskars; *Other:* Brass heart, twig, twine and microbeads.

IDEAS TO NOTE: Allison embossed, impressed and inked the clock rubber stamp onto the brass heart. To add visual interest to the focal-point photo, she sandwiched mica chips between two sheet protectors and adhered them to the photo mat.

"This Is Heaven"

Supplies *Mulberry paper:* Source unknown; *Computer fonts:* Hansa (title and journaling) and Aria Script (nameplate), downloaded from the Internet; CK Cursive, "The Best of Creative Lettering" CD Vol. 2, *Creating Keepsakes; Fibers:* Rubba Dub Dub; *Rubber stamps:* Above the Mark (pattern under "Heaven"), Judi-Kins (texture on background); *Stamping ink:* ColorBox, Clearsnap, Inc.; VersaMark, Tsukineko; *Embossing powder:* All Night Media; *Metallic rub-ons and chalk:* Craf-T Products; *Gold leafing:* Accents Unlimited; *Pen:* Marvy Uchida; *Circle punch:* Family Treasures; *Eyelet:* Impress Rubber Stamps; *Other:* Mesh and brads.

"Where'd All the Dinosaurs Go?"

Supplies *Patterned paper:* Scrap-Ease; *Computer fonts:* Jungle Juice (title), Brady Bunch, Gilligan's Island, Adventure, First Grader, Yikes, Good Dog Plain and Wee Bairn (journaling), downloaded from the Internet; CK Journaling, "The Best of Creative Lettering" CD Vol. 2, *Creating Keepsakes; Textured rubber stamp:* Stampendous!; *Stamping ink:* ColorBox, Clearsnap, Inc.; *Embossing powder:* Inkadinkadoo; *Metallic rub-ons:* Craf-T Products; *Mica:* U.S. Artquest; *Mica chips:* Judi-Kins; *Other:* Mesh and hinges.

IDEAS TO NOTE: Allison sandwiched mica chips between two pieces of mica to create a prehistoric look. The title block flips open to reveal journaling and additional photos.

shelley sullivan 2002

IDEA TO NOTE: Shelley included her own panoramic photos on her layout.

"When I See Clouds"

Supplies *Computer fonts:* Graphic Light, Carpenter ICG, Donny's Hand, Imprint MT Shadow and Scrap Twiggy, downloaded from the Internet; Scrap Rhapsody, downloaded from *www.inspire-graphics.com*.

"My daughter inspires me to scrapbook. I think back to my childhood and wish I had more photos that showed what life was like for me. I would treasure being able to read my mom's thoughts and feelings."

SHELLEY SULLIVAN • ABBEVILLE, SC

"Simple is better when it comes to scrapbooking," shares Shelley, a believer in single-photo layouts. To create the clean look she loves best, Shelley uses bold colors to enhance her photos. "Many scrappers say they're afraid of color, but if you experiment with it, you'll find you can create a striking layout with just a few strong photos and cardstock."

"Autumn Bold"

Supplies *Pen:* Zig Writer, EK Success.

"When I'm really not feeling the creative juices flowing, I concentrate on taking pictures of things and people I love."

IDEA TO NOTE: Shelley used pieces of her daughter's broken bracelet to create the wire and flower accents.

"Only You"

Supplies *Computer fonts:* Scrap Rhapsody and Franks, downloaded from the Internet.

only you

Chandler: I sometimes call you a little heifer because you do things that annoy me and crack me up at the same time. It is a term of endearment bestowed on probably the only person who could get away with sweetly asking me for a kiss, only to plant a big zerbert on my mouth. This is always followed by regales of laughter. Only you could make me laugh by dialing your own phone number then quickly hanging up and waiting for me to answer. You then pick up and have a conversation with me. This is especially heifer worthy when you call just to ask for a glass of water. At least you say I love you before saying goodbye. Only mischievous you could get away with telling me you want to have a race climbing the stairs and you start before I say go. Only you could talk a lot during a really good movie, and have me answer most all of your questions or comments. There are so many things you do that make up the unique girl you are. I love you when you are sweet and even when you are a little heifer.

photos of Chandler: fall 2001; 1/0: 2/2002

Dear Chandler—
    I occasionally find little scraps of paper you've doodled or written on. I always stop and look at them because it's a glimpse at your thoughts. Since I'm a packrat ☺ I usually tuck these scraps away.
    I love these photos! Especially the 2nd shot where your smile has "burst" into laughter.
    The little pocket is from an old pair of jeans. Did I mention I was a pack rat?! ☺ Love You!
                                    Mom ♥

IDEA TO NOTE: Shelley used pop dots underneath the notes to create dimension.

"To-Do List"

Supplies *Pen:* Zig Writer, EK Success; *Pop dots:* All Night Media; *Other:* Blue jean pocket (cut from an old pair of jeans) and a small notebook.

"If I only had three colors of cardstock to work with, I would have to pick a shade of blue, a shade of green and a khaki color. Soft shades of blue and green can complement many different colors. Khaki is a great background color that lets prominent colors in photos shine."

journaling solution If journaling is too personal or if you run out of room to include it on your layout, try Shelley's solution—include it on the back of the layout. Shelley's personal notes to her daughter are sure to be cherished for years to come.

"Glimpse"

Supplies *Patterned paper:* Karen Foster Design;
Pen: Zig Writer, EK Success; *Craft wire:* Artistic Wire Ltd.;
Craft paint: Folk Art; *Other:* Plastic canvas.

*Take time
every day
to do
something
silly.*

*In a daughter you see
a glimpse of yourself,
only better.*

*When I see
the world
through your
young eyes,*

everything

becomes new again.

*The moon is brighter,
the sun warmer,*

*and the stars
even more
mysterious.*

*Yet nothing
is as*

glorious

as you.

- Maya Angelou

"Silly"

Supplies *Chalk:* Craf-T Products; *Metallic colored pencils:*
Pentech; *Pen:* Zig Writer, EK Success.

greeting card accents

Most of us receive so many cards each year, we're not sure what to do with them all! Why not cut them up and use them as accents on your scrapbook pages? The three laser cuts accenting my "Silly" page were trimmed from a greeting card. Save embossed designs, glittery accents, cute pictures, or even poems and sentiments to use in your scrapbook—or use them as inspiration for designing your own embellishments.

—*Shelley Sullivan*

"Glorious"

Supplies *Computer fonts:* Tom's New Roman and Carpenter ICG,
downloaded from the Internet; *Studs:* Bedazzler.

IDEA TO NOTE: Darcee printed her photos onto fabric, and wove fibers together for the title mat and accent.

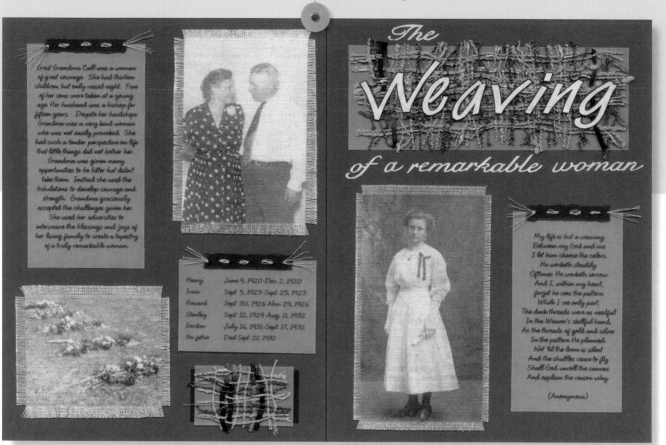

The
Weaving
of a remarkable woman

Great Grandma Call was a woman of great courage. She had thirteen children, but only raised eight. Five of her sons were taken at a young age. Her husband was a bishop for fifteen years. Despite her hardships Grandma was a very kind woman who was not easily provoked. She had such a tender perspective on life that little things did not bother her. Grandma was given many opportunities to be bitter but didn't take them. Instead she used the tribulations to develop courage and strength. Grandma graciously accepted the challenges given her. She used her adversities to interweave the blessings and joys of her living family to create a tapestry of a truly remarkable woman.

Henry	June 9, 1920-Dec. 2, 1920
Irvin	Sept. 5, 1923-Sept. 25, 1923
Howard	Sept. 30, 1926-Nov. 29, 1926
Stanley	Sept. 12, 1929-Aug. 11, 1932
Gordon	July 16, 1931-Sept. 17, 1932
Her father	Died Sept. 22, 1932

*My life is but a weaving
Between my God and me
I let him choose the colors
He worketh steadily
Ofttimes He worketh sorrow
And I, within my heart,
forget he sees the pattern
While I see only part.
The dark threads were as needful
In the Weaver's skillful hand,
As the threads of gold and silver
In the pattern He planned.
Not 'til the loom is silent
And the shuttles cease to fly
Shall God unroll the canvas
And explain the reason why.*

(Anonymous)

"The Weaving of a Remarkable Woman"

Supplies *Vellum:* Paper Adventures; *Computer fonts:* Hand Label and Impressive Bold, Parson's Technology; Marita Script (journaling), package unknown, Hallmark; *Embroidery floss:* DMC; *Fibers:* On the Surface ; *Embossing powder:* Stamp-N Stuff, Mark Enterprises; *Other:* Fabric.

"It wasn't until I discovered scrapbooking and treated it as an art form that my creative energy was successfully channeled."

DARCEE THOMPSON • PRESTON, ID

Darcee's been known to take cardstock and a rolling-ball embosser to the hardware store to glean ideas for creative textures. "I get a lot of inspiration from textures. I'm always looking at carpet mats, ceilings and more to get texture ideas," she explains. Darcee is also passionate about experimenting with her scrapbook supplies to come up with innovative techniques. "I'm constantly asking myself questions like 'What would happen if I tried to write with a wood burner on paper?'"

"Forks"

Supplies *Transparency paper:* Highland; *Computer font:* Marita Medium, package unknown, Hallmark; *Embossing powder:* Stamp-N Stuff, Mark Enterprises; *Other:* Aluminum foil.

"Darcee"

Supplies *Embossing powder:* Stamp-N Stuff, Mark Enterprises; *Embossing tool:* Empressor, Chatterbox; *Chalk:* Craf-T Products.

IDEAS TO NOTE: Darcee cut a mosaic pattern out of a blank stencil to create the background paper. After she embossed it, she chalked the "down" areas and heat-embossed the lettering.

Inner Profile

Cache,
Even your name suggests your incredible potential. A cache is a hiding place for precious items. Within you lies a reservoir of talents and abilities waiting for you to develop and draw upon. What great opportunities you have to bless others' lives. Some nuggets of potential I've seen glimpses of are leadership, sharp intellect, creativity, music, determination and a perceptive spirit. Use them well.
♥ Mom

"Inner Profile"

Supplies *Transparency paper:* Highland
Computer font: Bernard Hand, package unknown; *Eyelets:* Doodlebug Design; *Craft wire:* Artistic Wire Ltd.; *Other:* Bracelet clasps.

IDEAS TO NOTE: Darcee created a torn paper mosaic for the background, then cut Cache's silhouette from a stencil and embossed it onto the mosaic. She also printed her photo onto transparency paper, allowing the actual photo and texture to show through.

IDEA TO NOTE: To create the title and accents, Darcee sketched the strips on a scrap of cardstock and cut them out. After running the strips through a Xyron machine, she laid them onto cardstock, applied a layer of white embossing powder and heated the area with a heat-embossing tool. She repeated the process with blue embossing powder and used a wood burner to texturize and blend the embossing powders together.

Not only are Caleb and Kennedy 2nd cousins, they are also great friends. They seem to find each other at every reunion even though there are so many other kids. When they're together they are the best of friends and they seem to pick up right where they left off.

Dean R. Bingham Family Reunion
June 2001

"Cousins/Friends"

Supplies *Pen:* Zig Writer, EK Success; *Metallic rub-ons:* Craf-T Products; *Embossing powder:* Stamp-N Stuff, Mark Enterprises; *Embossing tool:* Empressor, Chatterbox.

IDEA TO NOTE: Darcee dry-embossed a border on the edges of two photos, and a square on the focal-point photo.

"Originations of Patriotism"

Supplies *Transparency paper:* Highland; *Computer font:* Freehand Script, Hallmark; *Pens:* Zig Writer, EK Success; Galaxy Glitter Gel, American Crafts; *Rub-ons:* Craf-T Products; *Embossing powder:* Stamp-N Stuff, Mark Enterprises.

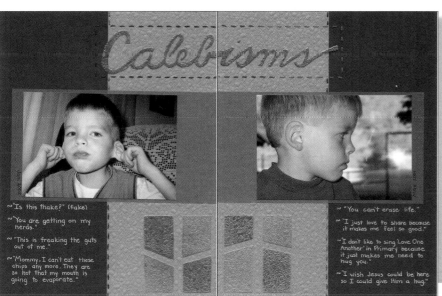

"Calebisms"

Supplies *Title and accents:* Darcee's own designs; *Rub-ons:* Craf-T Products; *Embossing powder:* Stamp-N Stuff, Mark Enterprises; *Embossing tool:* Empressor, Chatterbox; *Embroidery floss:* J & P Coats.

EMBOSSING TECHNIQUE

Dry embossing adds a beautiful textured look to scrapbook pages, and it's easy to do. Here's how to re-create the look on my "Calebisms" layout shown here:

❶ Find an item with texture you like (such as a thick, textured sheet of plastic), lay a piece of cardstock over the item and emboss using a stylus. Set the textured piece of cardstock aside.

❷ Sketch or print your lettering to the desired size and trace it on flexible plastic with a pen. (You'll want to use fairly thick plastic. If the plastic isn't thick enough, you may consider adhering two pieces together.)

❸ To create a template, cut the lettering from the plastic with a craft knife and cutting mat (Figure 1).

❹ Lay the template on the front of the embossed paper where you want the title to be and mark the position with a pencil. Place the template on the back of the paper so the image is backward, lining it up with the pencil marks. Trace around the template to mark where you'll emboss. Secure the template again on the front side with repositionable tape.

❺ Dry-emboss the lines, following the pencil marks you drew. Repeat Steps 1–4 to complete all the embossed designs on this layer of cardstock.

❻ Lay the template on the front of the paper, matching it up with the dry-embossed lines.

Go over the title with an embossing pen and sprinkle embossing powder on it. Carefully remove the template and heat-emboss the design (Figure 2).

—*Darcee Thompson*

Figure 1

Figure 2

I captured him at just the right moment. He was
leaning over our table, talking to our sister
and brother in law when I called his name. He
was laughing and relaxed as he glanced at me,
giving me the perfect
opportunity to steal
this moment back from time.

When I developed this roll of film,
and flipped through it to
this photo, I had to stop.
To compose myself.
I felt a physical and almost
unbearable surge of **love** for him.
It isn't that my feelings of love
had stopped... the love is
always there.
But in our day-to-day existence,
something happens. At odd moments,
I feel myself caught off guard
in my feelings for him.

When he catches a cricket and
imprisons it in the trash.
When he almost cries during the
same commercials I do.
When he surprises me with gifts,
trips, or a clean house and
happily bathed children.
When we share an old inside
joke and a hearty chuckle.
When he settles our arguments
with compromises I could never
come up with.
When he is proud of something
I have done.
When I do something that makes him
roll his eyes and laugh at me.
When he dances like a fool.

He has a smile that heals me...

More often than not, it is even simpler.
He calls my name. He touches my hand.
He makes me feel important.
He tells me I am beautiful-and then
I know that I am.
So many people say this, but
with me it is so true-
He is not just my husband.
He is my laughter, my joy,
my teacher, my support, my fun,
my **life**, and my forever love.

IDEA TO NOTE: The
title was inspired by Billy
Joel's song "She Has a
Smile That Heals Me."

"Smile That Heals Me"

Supplies *Vellum:* Paper
Adventures; *Computer font:*
Courier New, downloaded
from the Internet.

"Sometimes I see a layout idea or think of a word, and that gets me hunting for a picture that goes with it. Journaling is super important to me, so I often think of something I just need to record in my scrapbook, then I hunt for a picture and design the layout."

TARA WHITNEY • MISSION VIEJO, CA

"I feel like I've finally found my niche," says Tara, who once looked at other scrapbookers'
pages and thought, "I could never scrap like that." Tara says the little moments in life are
the most important to her—and she tries to capture them on film. A photographer at
heart, Tara lives her life in pictures. "I have to have them out so people can see them—so
I can see them. They consume me."

moment
by
moment

Ventura beach

we create
our
LIFE'S
adventure.

-unknown

"Moment by Moment"

Supplies *Patterned paper:* Colors By Design; *Vellum:* Paper Adventures; *Pen:* Zig Writer, EK Success.

"Play in the Clouds"

Supplies *Stickers:* Kathy Davis, Colorbök; *Computer font:* CK Sketch, "The Best of Creative Lettering" CD Vol. 2, *Creating Keepsakes.*

Drew, you just amaze me every day with all that you are taking in about the world around you. You come up with these comments about things that just make everyone start laughing! Today, my friend Tina had come out to visit with Mattea and Aidan. It had rained the night and day before, and the sky was a BEAUTIFUL shade of blue...splattered with huge, white cotton candy clouds. We were in the car, driving home from Wal-Mart. Tina and I were talking in the front seat, and you and Tea were babbling in the back, when you said,

"Mom, I want to play in the clouds."

Tina and I looked at each other, and cracked up! It amazed me that you came up with that all on your own—and I loved hearing you say something so full of childhood innocence. I remember being your age and wanting SO badly to just JUMP into a fluffy pillow of clouds... and I am glad that I have you to constantly remind me to think like that child. I hope you never lose the ability to stop me in my tracks and make me think and laugh with you.
I love you, Momma.

1·31·02

IDEA TO NOTE: Tara converted the color photo to black and white.

Innocent
simple
classic
small
Buckles
tights
Sashes
straps
Dressed up

These precious feet

Buttons
Sweet

"These Precious Feet"

Supplies *Computer font:* Lovitz, downloaded from the Internet; *Fibers:* Rubba Dub Dub; *Pop dots:* All Night Media.

IDEA TO NOTE: Tara hand-colored her black-and-white photos.

"Quirky Kenna"

Supplies *Computer font:* Mammagamma, downloaded from the Internet; *Photo-tinting pens:* Zig Photo Twin, EK Success.

quirky kenna's

ears and feet...

mckenna is full of unique and special surprises. her third little toes curl underneath her feet. her right ear is pointed like an elf. she has a hairy little monkey back. and a strawberry mark above her left breast.

her personality is full of quirks as well. she must speak about certain things in a rigid routine. hold her food for a certain period of time before she takes a bite. watch every movie from the very beginning with no fast forwarding involved. tap the pages of her books three times as she turns them. carry around different items as she deems them worthy. (a movie in its case, a toy figurine, a stuffed animal or, at times, even an oreo) sneak around like a cat in order to find any candy or soda in the house. climb, climb, climb. memorize her books and movies in astonishing speed. and shake with laughter and love when overwhelmed by how she feels about us.

for most of her life, we have worried about her. thankfully, we see growth in her every day-just at her own pace. now we know that she is our quirky little kenner's, and we love her so.

weaving technique In the mood for a weave? This simple weaved pattern makes a beautiful background, and it's easy. Here's how to create this fun design:

❶ Measure the strips of paper with a ruler and mark them with a pencil.

❷ Use a craft knife and cutting mat to cut the slits.

❸ Cut a strip of paper the same width as the slits and slide it through.

—*Tara Whitney*

"My children have the ability to take my breath away. I have to record those moments."

"Shine"

Supplies *Computer font:* Foxjump, downloaded from the Internet; *Pen:* Zig Writer, EK Success.

"D.J.W."

Supplies *Letter stickers:* David Walker, Colorbök; *Other:* Twine.

simple accents Accents are meant to enhance your photos, not overwhelm them. I'm such a minimalist that the fewer the accents and the simpler they are, the better. Try these tips for keeping your embellishments simple:

• Wait to select your accents until after you've decided on photos and journaling.

• Make sure the accents aren't just cute, but that they complement the theme and feel of your photos.

• Don't make the embellishments the focal point of the layout. Photos should be the first thing viewers see.

• Use a monochromatic color scheme when it comes to accents. You want them to blend into the paper.

—*Tara Whitney*

jennifer wohlenberg 2002

IDEAS TO NOTE: Jennifer scanned the smaller photos, converted them to black and white, re-sized them and increased the contrast. Then she printed them on vellum and overlapped them onto the enlarged picture.

These Hands

Change Diapers

Fold Clothes

Make Meals

Tie Shoes

Fill Bottles

Hold Hands

Love Our Family

"I've always wanted to be a writer for as long as I can remember. I wrote poems as a very young child, and I started writing short stories in grade school. One of the reasons I love scrapbooking is that I get to indulge my love of writing on every single page."

"These Hands"

Supplies *Patterned paper:* Making Memories; *Vellum:* Pebbles in my Pocket; *Computer font:* Swenson, package unknown.

JENNIFER WOHLENBERG • STEVENSON RANCH, CA

Scrapbooking is "illustrated journaling" for Jennifer, who begins planning each page with writing. "Since I use a lot of symbolism in my layouts, it's important for me to know exactly what story I'm telling so I can repeat certain things symbolically," she explains. Jennifer's friends even tease her about the number of rules she has to guide her through the scrapbooking process. "I just want to be inspired all the way through, and to be happy with the outcome," she says.

IDEA TO NOTE: Jennifer stamped the stamp pad in a random pattern on the cardstock to add texture without overwhelming the photos.

"Always Wonder, Never Wonder"

Supplies *Patterned paper:* Making Memories; *Vellum:* Bazzill Basics; *Stamping ink:* Colorbök; *Computer font:* Scrap Calligraphy, downloaded from *www.letteringdelights.com*; *Poem:* Jennifer's own work.

IDEA TO NOTE: Jennifer created a layered torn-vellum mat for the photo and over-lapped the journaling onto it.

title trimming hints

What's my secret to perfectly cut letters? Read on to find out:

◆ I use patterned-weight paper instead of cardstock for letters—it's much more forgiving. The lighter weight lets you smooth out any wrinkles you make while cutting, unlike cardstock, which bends and creases, leaving little nicks and mess-ups.

◆ I begin by cutting around the outside of the let-ter, and I leave a small border outside the line just in case I goof.

— Jennifer Wohlenberg

"My Forever Mom"

Supplies *Specialty paper:* Stained Glass, Roylco; *Vellum:* Bazzill Basics; *Computer font:* Amaze, downloaded from the Internet.

"Love Is the Little Things"

Supplies *Patterned paper:* Making Memories; *Computer fonts:* Amaze (title) and Jikharev (journaling), packages unknown; *Heart:* Jennifer's own design.

IDEA TO NOTE: To continue the symbolism of the title, Jennifer printed out the things she and her husband do for each other, then ripped them into little bits and placed them inside the heart.

journaling the little things So many adults look back on their childhood with only a vague idea of what they were really like. You may know the pertinent facts—what age you got chicken pox, when you wrecked your bike and broke your arm, or that you hated peas from the moment you tasted them—but do you know the things you did that bugged your mother the most? Or the strange foods you loved when you were a baby? Record these simple facts about your children for them to treasure forever:

◆ What your kids want to be when they grow up

◆ The nighttime rituals they can't go to bed without

◆ Why they love a certain item, such as a book, a song or a stuffed animal

◆ Their favorites during various stages in life

In addition to scrapbooking these memories, start a journal for each of your children when they're born. I started a journal for each of my daughters when I found out I was expecting. I wrote my impressions about them, their sleeping patterns (or lack thereof), and how we got acquainted with each other. Most importantly, I included my feelings of love for them.

—Jennifer Wohlenberg

"Trepidation"

Supplies *Patterned paper*: Scrap-Ease; *Computer fonts:* Gradl (title), package unknown; CK Penman, "The Best of Creative Lettering" CD Vol. 3, *Creating Keepsakes.*

"Archival Mistmas"

Supplies *Patterned paper:* Making Memories; *Computer fonts:* Verdana ("Archival"), Arial Black ("Mistmas") and Abodi MT Condensed Light (journaling), packages unknown; *Fibers:* Rubba Dub Dub.

IDEAS TO NOTE: Jennifer based the idea for her layout on the packaging for Archival Mist. She used fibers to re-create the circles on the packaging and used WordArt to impose the circles on the journaling text.

STITCHING GUIDE

Incorporating stitched designs into your layouts is an ideal way to add variety and a homespun look to your scrapbook—and you don't have to be a master seamstress to do it. Experiment with sewing by hand and by machine to see which works best for you. Here's what you'll need to stitch by hand:

- Tapestry needle
- Needle threader (optional)
- Embroidery floss, thread, fibers, yarn, jute, or raffia

Then, follow these steps:

1 Lightly sketch the design you want to stitch onto paper with a pencil.

2 Select the desired stitch (see below). Then poke holes with a sharp needle or needle tool along the pencil marks, making them ¼" to ⅛" apart depending on how long you want your stitches to be.

3 Stitch the design.

Stitching with a machine will produce much steadier and straighter stitches in less time. Here's how:

1 Drop or cover the feed on the sewing machine as you would for free machine embroidery.

2 Loosen the top tension a fraction so the bottom thread won't show through, and thread the bobbin with ordinary machine thread.

3 Lightly sketch the design you want to stitch directly onto paper and sew over it.

Remember, sewing on paper will make the needle blunt easily, so you'll have to replace it more often.

Use stitches to create titles; attach photo mats or other embellishments to your layout; dress up stickers, die cuts and page cutouts; or create unique borders for pages and mats. You can even sew your own pockets. Experiment with the stitches below to find what best suits your style.

—Jennifer Wohlenberg

"Beautiful Mind"

Supplies *Patterned paper:* Making Memories; *Handmade paper:* Jennifer Collection, Thompson Paper Company; *Computer font:* Rage Italic, package unknown.

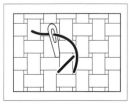

Cross Stitch

Satin Stitch

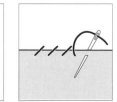

Straight Stitch

Whipstitch

cathryn zielske 2002

"My Little Man"

Supplies *Computer font:* American Typewriter Condensed, Adobe Systems; *Fibers:* Rubba Dub Dub; *Scrabble letters:* Limited Edition ; Rubber Stamps; *Chalk:* Craf-T Products; *Pop dots:* All Night Media.

IDEAS TO NOTE: Cathryn used a paper crimper for texture, and printed her journaling directly onto the cardstock.

I saw something in this picture I had not yet seen before in your two-plus years on this earth. a glimpse of my little boy growing up. You are always running and yelling and singing and yammering, and I rarely see this side of you. I imagine that you will be one wondrous surprise after another, showing me things I never thought possible, or even thought of, period. If you let me come along for the ride, I'll try my very best not to crowd you along the way, and let you just be the glorious little man you are...

"Black and white is as truthful as it gets for me. That's why I shoot in black and white so often, and incorporate those colors into my layouts."

CATHRYN ZIELSKE • SAINT PAUL, MN

"I want people to truly see my family, my kids and themselves when they look at my scrapbook pages," says Cathryn, a graphic designer who loves black-and-white photos and simple, single-photo layouts. "Black-and-white photos are timeless and beautiful, and truly capture the essence of the subjects." Cathryn loves finding innovative and unique layouts on the web, and says that's where she realized there are no rules to scrapbooking—just freedom to "explore and develop a style that fits who you are."

"Inquisitive"

Supplies *Vellum:* Glama, CTI; *Corrugated paper:* DMD Industries; *Computer fonts:* Carpenter, Image Club; Gill Sans Light, Adobe Systems; *Eyelets:* Doodlebug Design; *Mini-brads:* Stamp This; *Jute:* Darice.

IDEA TO NOTE: Cathryn incorporated her title into the journaling.

Mom, there had better be color film in there!

"Mom, There Had Better Be Color Film in There!"

Supplies *Computer font:* American Typewriter, Adobe Systems; *Punches:* EK Success.

Could you be more beautiful?

Aidan Isabella at 5

"Could You Be More Beautiful?"

Supplies *Computer font:* Marydale, downloaded from the Internet; *Flower punch:* Marvy Uchida; *Craft wire:* Artistic Wire Ltd.; *Eyelets:* Doodlebug Design; *Mini pop dots:* All Night Media.

IDEA TO NOTE: Cathryn placed the punches on pop dots to add depth to her layout.

my first **true** love

If ever I'm asked, "When was the first time you ever fell in love?" I'm sure the obvious answer would be when I met Daniel. But the truth of the matter is, my first love was not of the human kind.

Bandit came into my life when I was 17. I was too concerned with impending acne outbreaks and whether or not I would ever get asked to the Junior Prom to concern myself with the little ball of fur tearing around our house. Looking back, those were wasted efforts compared to the companionship and joy I would eventually grow to experience with that sweet, sweet doggie boy of mine.

I called him Biggs McGlennis (and it always sounded much better when spoken with a hint of an Irish accent) and he was my sweet, sweet lover boy. Bandit was mostly Siberian Husky, with an eighth wolf in him, or so the breeder claimed. He was as skittish as the day was long with the outside world, often cowering under our pool table when strangers or friends would drop by. But with us, he was a lovable marshmallow.

Whenever Bandit saw me, he would lay down and bury his nose in the carpet, with his tail wagging furiously, and peek up at me coyishly. One of my dog expert friends thought this overtly submissive behavior was a signal that something wasn't right with the dog's head. Me, I just thought it was the most endearing thing on planet Earth.

After college, I met and fell in love with my "human" soul mate. I was living in Texas at the time, and I made a decision to move to Minnesota to be with him. Bandit wouldn't be coming. I simply wouldn't have the means to care for another being other than myself. He was better off staying with my parents. The night before I hit the road, I sat in my bedroom with Bandit on my bed, crying my eyes out because there was no way to explain that I wouldn't be coming home the next day. It seemed so unfair to just ditch him like that. So very unfair, after all he'd given me.

Life moved on. I got married. I even got a Siberian Husky of my own to replace the void I felt in my life. But it was never quite the same as Bandit.

Years later, when I was seven months pregnant with my first child, the phone rang. It was my Mom. Biggs McGlennis had fulfilled his time on this Earth, and he left it with all the grace and dignity and innocence he came into it with.

I miss that furry lover boy. The tears in my eyes remind me just how much.

He was such a good dog.

"My First True Love"
Supplies *Computer fonts:* Bell Gothic and American Typewriter, Adobe Systems; *Mesh:* Magic Mesh, Avant Card; *Paw print:* Cathryn's own design; *Other:* Milkbone I.D. tag .

"Paparazzi"
Supplies *Computer font:* Unknown; *Stickers:* Jolee's Boutique, Stickopotamus; *Photo corners:* Stickopotamus.

"I usually look at the photo, think of a title and then decide if the layout should have journaling or not. The journaling is almost always driven by the photo."

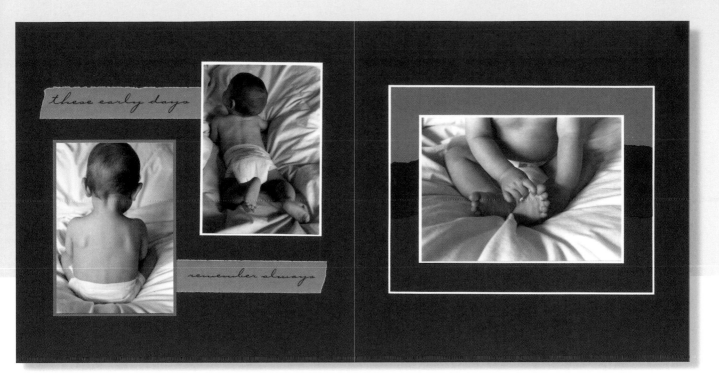

"These Early Days"

Supplies *Vellum:* Glama, CTI; *Computer font:* Carpenter, Image Club.

TAKING TERRIFIC BLACK-AND-WHITE PHOTOGRAPHS

Anyone can take beautiful black-and-white portraits with a little practice, a little patience and a willing subject. While I'm not a professional photographer, I do have some tried-and-true methods that consistently give me the results I'm looking for. These hints will help:

❶ **Find a place to shoot.** Your first step is to find a well-lit area of your home—a place that lets in natural light. The more light you let in, the better the shot will be. I always set up my shots within a couple of feet of a large window in my home; however, I avoid setting up the shot in direct sunlight, which can lead to harsh shadows on my subject.

❷ **Create a backdrop.** I use an old, cream-colored sheet as a backdrop (the more wrinkled the better). I tack it up on the wall, or even throw it over the back of a chair, and have my subject sit in front

of it. A plain wall will also do fine. Just be sure there isn't anything on the wall that will detract from your subject.

❸ **Turn off your flash.** While flash photography is useful in many instances, your goal is to capture the subtle nuances of the gray spectrum by using the available light. A flash will cause your subject to be too uniformly lit. Rely on Mother Nature to give you the natural highs and lows that make black and white so appealing.

❹ **Use 400-speed film or higher.** I always shoot with 400-speed film. Anything slower will result in underexposed, blurry photos. I use both true black-and-white film, such as Kodak T-Max, as well as color-processed (C-41) black-and-white film, such as Kodak Black and White.

❺ **Shoot on program mode.** Today's cameras are so sophisticated, especially in the SLR realm. I always shoot in pro-

gram mode. While it's fun to experiment with different settings, I'm always impressed at how well my shots turn out when I let the camera do all the work.

❻ **Get in close.** When looking through the viewfinder, you should see your subject and very little else. Don't be afraid to get in close for the shot. If you learn to crop as you shoot, you'll end up with more usable shots.

❼ **Have fun and practice—a lot!** Don't be afraid to burn through a few rolls in a sitting, especially if you're just starting out. Go to different parts of your house and find what works for you. Remember, a little practice and patience will give you beautiful black-and-whites that make stunning additions to your scrapbook.

—Cathryn Zielske

easy ideas for text and texture

Figure 1. To add texture without adding bulk, stamp a texture pattern on your cardstock. *Pages by Ashley Gull.* **Supplies** *Texture stamps:* Raindrops on Roses; *Compass stamp:* Stampabilities; *Stamping ink:* Clearsnap, Ink Xpressions and Tsukineko; *Tags, snaps and page pebbles:* Making Memories; *Clips:* Boxer Scrapbook Productions; *Fiber:* On the Surface; *Beads:* Magic Scraps; *Coin:* Impress Rubber Stamps; *Chalk:* Stampin' Up!; *Pen:* Zig Writer, EK Success; *Computer font:* CK Newsprint, "Fresh Fonts" CD, *Creating Keepsakes.*

Adding Texture with Stamps

I own a scrapbook store and many of my customers are interested in a textured look without the bulk (Figure 1). Texture stamps offer an easy (and flat) way to add dimension and visual interest to background paper, journaling blocks, tag accents and more.

Simply stamp the images, then sponge a little ink or chalk over them to enhance the aged look. You can create a neat effect by stamping from the edge of the paper and coming in from the sides. Sponge the ink or chalk darker on the edges, going lighter as you approach the center of the page.

—*Sherril Watts, Raindrops on Roses*

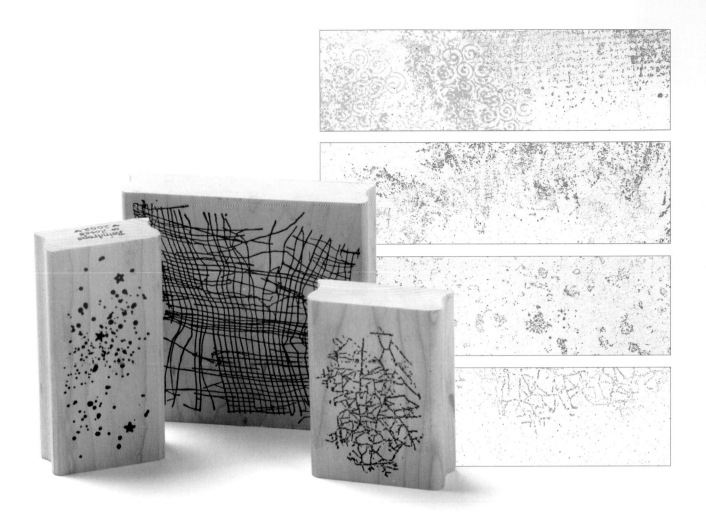

Easy Scanning for 12" x 12" Pages

I love sharing my pages online, but since I scrapbook in a 12" x 12" format, scanning my pages is a dilemma. Most reasonably priced scanners aren't large enough to scan an entire 12" x 12" page. This means I have to scan a 12" x 12" page in two separate images, then "stitch" them together electronically. This can be both frustrating and time-consuming.

I've found a good solution. The Ulead COOL 360 software package creates both 360° and wide-angle panoramic images in just three steps. The panoramic image feature is perfect for the wide 12" x 12" format that I like to use.

The "blending" feature allows stitching without noticeable variances between the two images—just be sure to disable the "warp" feature so your completed image doesn't appear curved. I've found that the JPEG file format takes up the least amount of space on my hard drive. Because the TIFF file format is the default setting, you'll need to select the JPEG format before scanning your images.

In my experience, saving the completed image takes the most time. Your time may vary, but I found that after I learned the software package, I could scan and save a 12" x 12" page in about 10 minutes.

The Ulead COOL 360 software package is available for Windows. Check the software system requirements to make sure your computer can support this software. While the program retails for around $40, a trial version of the software is available at *www.ulead.com/cool360/*.

—*Robyn McKay, Eudora, KS*

Editor's note: For additional help with stitching, see "Scanner Stitching Made Easy" in the April 2003 issue.

Figure 2. Use your journaling as a creative accent. *Page by Heather Lancaster.* **Supplies** *Patterned paper:* SEI, Inc.; *Die cuts:* Sizzix; *Brads:* Provo Craft; *Computer font:* Times New Roman, Microsoft Word; *Title letters:* Heather's own design.

Text as Embellishments

I love collage art's torn text and layered effects, so I used them to create an updated style on my layout. Here's how to create these fresh accents:

❶ Print out a journaling block on your computer. For the layout in Figure 2, I copied an Olympic swimming article from the Internet, but you can also use the journaling from your page. If you plan to tear several text pieces to use on your page, copy and paste the same text block several times before you print. No one will read the torn portions closely enough

to know they're duplicated. Choose a color that suits your layout.

❷ Cut your die-cut shapes from the printed text. For each dolphin on my page, I cut two dolphins—one from paper that coordinated with my layout and the other from printed text.

❸ Rip the text die cut and layer it over the colored die cut.

❹ Rip small pieces of printed text to serve as page highlights. I combined straight and ripped edges of text to emphasize the vertical lines of my pat-

terned paper. Your text will make a subtle statement without cluttering or overwhelming the rest of your layout.

After you're done, if you look closely at your page you can even read whole words that reflect the feel of your page. My layouts feature fun words like "Olympics," "competition," "improved" and "international swimming."

—Heather Lancaster
Calgary, AB, Canada

OPEN ROAD

WHEN IT COMES TO TRAVELING I AM DEFINITELY MY FATHER'S DAUGHTER. WE BOTH LOVE TO JUST GET ON THE ROAD AND GO. WE DON'T PLAN TOO MUCH AND WE HAVE FUN STOPPING AT RANDOM PLACES. WE ALSO CAN DRIVE FOR LONG PERIODS SO DAD JOKES AROUND AND CALLS US 'ROAD WARRIORS'. ONE OF MY FAVORITE TIMES WITH DAD WAS WHEN WE DROVE MY BELONGINGS OUT WEST RIGHT BEFORE I STARTED GRADUATE SCHOOL. WE HAD A FEW MISHAPS LIKE BREAKING DOWN IN STURGES, S.D. DURING THE BIG MOTORCYCLE RALLY AND COWS IN THE MIDDLE OF THE ROAD IN THE LITTLE BIGHORN MOUNTAINS. WE LAUGHED THEM OFF AND ENJOYED SEEING THE SIGHTS AND BEING IN GOOD COMPANY. IT WAS A TRIP I WILL ALWAYS REMEMBER.

AUGUST 1999

"Open Road"

Supplies *Pens:* Pigma Micron, Sakura; Zig Writer, EK Success; *Chalk:* Craf-T Products; *Map and compass:* Lisa's own designs.

"Since I crop my pictures a lot, I only scrapbook pictures I have negatives for. If I don't have the negatives or reprints to use, I use the Kodak Picture Maker. I especially love enlarging photos to 8" x 10". Using a large picture really makes the photograph the focal point of the layout."

LISA BROWN • BERKELEY, CA

"I've been keeping photo albums since I was a child, but I found out about 'scrapbooking' while I was in college," shares Lisa. "As an electrical engineer, I need a creative outlet, and scrapbooking is perfect! I mostly scrapbook travel pictures and photos from my everyday life, but my most recent scrapbooking project was an album for my grandparents' fiftieth wedding anniversary. I learned so many things about them and their lives together, and loved having the opportunity to show them how special they are to me." In addition to scrapbooking, Lisa loves watching old movies, reading, traveling, baking and listening to NPR.

"Coffee and Doughnuts"

Supplies *Title, coffee beans and steam:* Lisa's own designs; *Watercolor pencils:* Derwent; *Pen:* Zig Writer, EK Success; *Hand with coffee:* Lisa adapted the idea from a coffee mug.

"Sisters Are …"

Supplies *Vellum and handmade paper:* Paper Cuts ; *Patterned paper:* Provo Craft; *Lettering template:* Perfect Letter, The C-Thru Ruler Co.; *Pen:* Zig Writer, EK Success; *Craft wire:* Colour Craft.

"The Magic of Snow"

Supplies *Vellum:* The Robin's Nest Press; *Pen:* Zig Writer, EK Success; *Embroidery floss:* DMC; *Grommets:* Stamp Studio.

IDEA TO NOTE: To give her photos an old-fashioned look, Lisa used the Kodak Picture Maker to change the photos' coloring to sepia.

"By the Light of the Silvery Moon"

Supplies *Specialty papers:* DMD Industries (corrugated), Paper Adventures (velveteen), Solum World Paper (handmade); *Grommets:* Stamp Studio.

"The Badlands"

Supplies *Patterned paper:* Frances Meyer ; *Handmade paper:* Solum World Pape ; *Pen:* Zig Writer, EK Success.

"Sisters by the Sea"

Supplies *Pen:* Zig Writer, EK Success; *Title:* Lisa's own design.

Recipe in image:
- Combine a family of loving hearts.
- Melt together.
- Add a lot of love.
- Mix well with respect and trust.
- Add gentleness, laughter, faith, hope and joy.
- Pour in much understanding.
- Sprinkle with kisses and a dash of hugs.
- Bake for a lifetime.

YEILD: One happy family!

In the garden. Calgary. September. 2000.

The Recipe For a Happy Home

"The Recipe for a Happy Home"

Supplies *Patterned papers:* Provo Craft, Scrapbook Wizard; *Vellum:* Write Stock; *Computer font:* Gilligan's Island, downloaded from the Internet; *Pen:* Zig Millennium, EK Success; *Paper piecing:* Christina's own design.

"Before I start any scrapbook page, I do a rough sketch of the design so I can 'see' the layout while I'm working on it."

CHRISTINA COLE • SALT LAKE CITY, UT

Christina has been scrapbooking for four years and loves it more with each page she creates. "My kids really enjoy looking through the pages I've made, and my two oldest children have even started creating their own scrapbook pages," says Christina. "I love seeing their creativity develop through scrapbooking." Christina has been working on her photography skills since age 12 and loves taking pictures of her four children and her wonderful husband.

"Favorite Things"

Supplies *Patterned papers:* Provo Craft, Making Memories; *Pen:* Zig Millennium, EK Success; *Computer font:* Gilligan's Island, downloaded from the Internet; *Leaves, butterflies and rope:* Christina's own designs.

"Each of Elise's Piggies"

Supplies *Patterned paper:* Provo Craft; *Vellum:* Paper Adventures; *Pen:* Zig Millennium, EK Success; *Computer font:* PC Leere, "Family Frenzy" HugWare CD, Provo Craft; *Piggies:* Christina's own design.

"Ninja Turtles"

Supplies *Patterned paper:* Making Memories, Provo Craft; *Vellum:* Write Stock; *Pen:* Zig Millennium, EK Success; *Computer fonts:* Fatty and Babelfish, downloaded from the Internet; *Squares:* Christina's own designs.

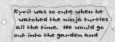

"Fairy"

Supplies *Patterned paper:* Provo Craft; *Vellum:* Write Stock; *Computer fonts:* Desyrel and Baby Kruffy, downloaded from the Internet; *Pen:* Zig Millennium, EK Success; *Ribbon and dots:* Christina's own designs.

"Stop and Smell the Flowers"

Supplies *Patterned paper:* Provo Craft; *Vellum:* Write Stock; *Pen:* Zig Millennium, EK Success; *Computer font:* Flowerchild, downloaded from the Internet; *Bees, hearts and flowers:* Christina's own designs.

"Lots of Love"

Supplies *Patterned paper:* Karen Foster Design (red plaid), Provo Craft; *Vellum:* Write Stock; *Pen:* Zig Millennium, EK Success; *Computer font:* Whatevur, downloaded from the Internet; *Blocks, hearts and flowers:* Christina's own designs

"Dreamin' "

Supplies *Patterned papers:* The Robin's Nest Press; Debbie Mumm, Creative Imaginations; *Star punch:* Emagination Crafts; *Die cuts:* Pebbles in my Pocket *Computer font:* CK Handprint, "The Best of Creative Lettering" CD Combo, *Creating Keepsakes; Chalk:* Craf-T Products; *Other:* Twine.

.cade is on the go all the time. He is such a busy little boy! If he takes the time to sit and relax it does not take long for him to fall asleep! (Nov. 19, 2000)

"Always remember to add journaling to your pages. It will help retell memories more completely."

BRENDA COSGROVE • OREM, UT

"Scrapbooking has definitely affected my family. Looking at our scrapbooks reminds us of our past, our good memories and the future to come," shares Brenda. "My goal is to pass on the love of preserving memories to my children so they'll continue this tradition." Brenda loves the constant challenge of coming up with brand-new ideas. She is the mother of four children and is thankful for a wonderful, supportive husband.

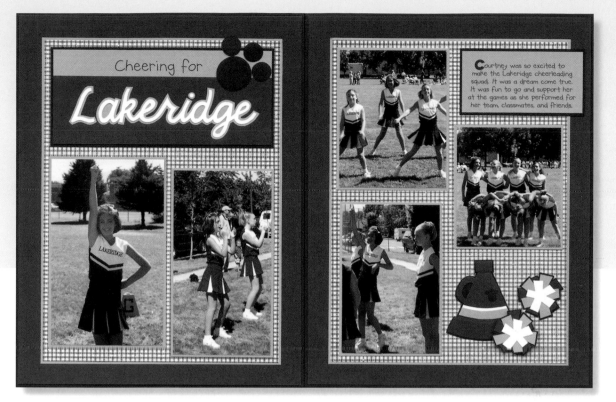

"Cheering for Lakeridge"

Supplies *Patterned paper:* Loves Me; *Circle punch:* EK Success; *Die cuts:* Funky Shape, Pebbles in my Pocket; *Letter stickers:* Little Letters, Making Memories; *Computer fonts:* CK Toggle, "The Best of Creative Lettering" CD Vol. 2, *Creating Keepsakes*; Doodle Cursive, "PagePrintables" CD Vol.1, Cock-A-Doodle Design, Inc.; *Megaphone:* Brenda's own design; *Pop dots:* All Night Media.

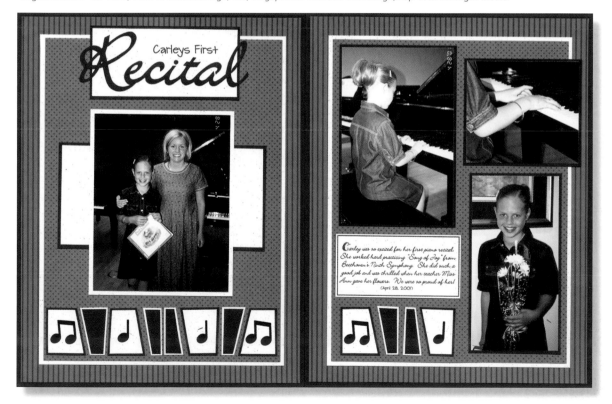

"Carley's First Recital"

Supplies *Patterned paper:* O'Scrap!, Imaginations!; *Music note stickers:* Mrs. Grossman's; *Computer fonts:* CK Journaling, "The Best of Creative Lettering" CD Vol. 2, *Creating Keepsakes*; Scrap Calligraphy, "Lettering Delights 2" CD, Inspire Graphics; *Border:* Brenda's own design.

"Our Cute Critter"

Supplies *Patterned paper:* Doodlebug Design; *Stickers:* Doodlebug Design; *Computer font:* CK Toggle, "The Best of Creative Lettering" CD Vol. 2, *Creating Keepsakes; Pop dots:* All Night Media; *Alphabet stickers:* Schooldays, EK Success.

"Hangin' Out at the Pool"

Supplies *Patterned paper:* Making Memories; *Punches:* EK Success (teardrop and splashes); *Letter stickers:* Little Letters, Making Memories; *Computer font:* CK Toggle, "The Best of Creative Lettering" CD Vol. 2, *Creating Keepsakes; Templates:* Tracerkins, EK Success (ball and sun); *Pool:* Brenda's own design; *Pop dots:* All Night Media.

"Scootin' Around"

Supplies *Patterned papers:* Loves Me, Doodlebug Design; *Scooter:* Friends, My Mind's Eye; *Computer font:* CK Handprint, "The Best of Creative Lettering" CD Combo, *Creating Keepsakes; Alphabet stickers:* Schooldays, EK Success.

"Cade & Dad"

Supplies *Patterned paper:* Making Memories; *Paper doll:* Paperkins, EK Success; *Die cuts:* Pebbles in my Pocket (clouds and sun); *Computer font:* CK Handprint, "The Best of Creative Lettering" CD Combo, *Creating Keepsakes; Embossed clouds:* Dimension.

"Caitlyn Learns to Swim"

Supplies *Patterned paper:* Loves Me; *Paper doll:* Pebbles in my Pocket; *Splash punch:* EK Success; *Computer font:* CK Journaling, "The Best of Creative Lettering" CD Vol. 2, *Creating Keepsakes; Lettering template:* Block, ABC Tracers, Pebbles for EK Success.

"2 Youth"

Supplies *Patterned paper:* Doodlebug Design; *Fish punch:* EK Success; *Pop dots:* All Night Media; *Glitter:* Creative Beginnings.

"A Christmas Toy Story 2 Remember"

Supplies *Vellum:* Paper Adventures; *Computer font:* CK Journaling, "The Best of Creative Lettering" CD Vol. 2, *Creating Keepsakes; Stickers:* Déjà Views; *Lettering template:* Blocky, Provo Craft; *Punches:* Emagination Crafts; (Christmas light), EK Success (small holly and small Christmas light); *Pop dots:* All Night Media; *Holly:* Caroline's own design.

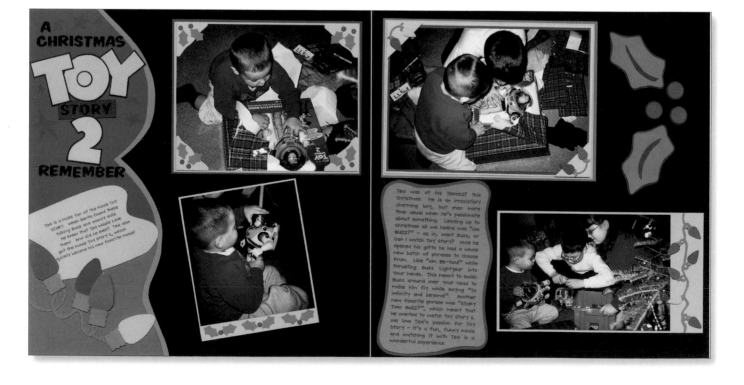

Courtney
1½
Ashley
3½
October '99

"Autumn Time"

Supplies *Chalk:* Craf-T Products; *Pen:* Zig Opaque Writer, EK Success; *Leaves and flowers:* Amy's own designs; *Lettering template:* Block, ABC Tracers, Pebbles for EK Success.

"If the colors in your photos are distracting or don't go with the mood you want to portray, change them to black and white. Check to see if your photo processor offers this service, or use the Kodak Picture Maker."

AMY EDINGTON • LAS VEGAS, NV

Amy has had an eye on the scrapbooking industry since she started scrapbooking in high school. "It's been fun to watch 'creative scrapbooking' evolve over the last few years," she says. "In some ways I envy the scrapbookers who are just getting started because there are so many good sources of information and ideas available now." Amy is the mother of two girls and a baby boy. An additional reward of scrapbooking? "My five-year-old already likes to 'make scrapbooks' with me. Her latest game is playing scrapbooking class—she's the teacher, and she gives me 'great, new ideas'."

October 1999
This is my
favorite
picture of
you! (3½ yrs.)

"Ashley"

Supplies *Pens:* Zig Writer and Zig Millennium, EK Success; *Punches:* McGill (hole and circle); *Flowers:* Amy's own designs.

"Sold"

Supplies *Computer fonts:* CK Chunky, "The Best of Creative Lettering" CD Vol. 2, *Creating Keepsakes*; CK Handprint, "The Best of Creative Lettering" CD Combo, *Creating Keepsakes; Pen:* Zig Writer, EK Success.

Things we'll miss

- Friends in the Hacienda ward
- Heated pool just a few steps away
- Blossoming "popcorn" trees in the spring
- Walking distance to walmart, Paradise Park, $2 Movies, Michaels, Sam's Club & more
- "Yardwork" done for us

Things we won't

- Speed bumps
- The walk to & from our parking spot
- Bringing groceries upstairs
- Trying to keep kids quiet so we won't bother the neighbors
- Silly newsletters & rules from the homeowners association
- Gated entry
- Pigeons
- "Taco smell" that permeates building when the downstairs neighbor cooks
- Being so CROWDED! (No place to store our stuff)
- Having a balcony as our "backyard"

3061 Key Largo Dr. #204 Las Vegas, Nevada

We were amazed at how fast our condo sold, especially since there were several of our model for sale at the same time (they were all vacant so I felt they had the advantage of always having their condos spotless) & sales had been very slow. Only 2 people came to look at ours but we had a buyer in three weeks! (I thought our realtor was joking when she called with the news. The buyer had only spent about 5 minutes looking.) Not only did it sell fast, but the buyer offered exactly what we were asking and he was willing to rent it back to us as long as we needed to stay since our new home was not built yet. He didn't even charge us more for rent than we had been paying on our mortgage or require a cleaning deposit. It was an amazing blessing—we never had expected things to work out so perfect! It took off so much stress and allowed us to save the money we needed for our new home. The condo has been a great place for our family to spend the last 5 years, but we've outgrown it and feel really ready to "move on!"

This is Ashley at 5 years old. She is growing up way too fast! Tom & I think she is becoming more beautiful all the time. I asked her about some of her favorites at 5 and this is how she answered:

Favorite things to do: Play with Courtney, art, make scrapbooks, get my picture taken, go to the Disney store at get catalogs
When I asked which things she liked to play with Courtney she elaborated: play "little girl" (like playing "house"-one is the little girl and one is the mom), "Safari" (packing their backpacks with "hunting" gear and searching the house for stuffed animals), and "Vet."

Favorite Foods: macaroni & cheese, bagels with cream cheese, half bananas, apples

Favorite Desserts: "OK, that's gonna be easy...ice cream, cake, & cookies."

Favorite Places to go: "The place we went last night because we get candies on the receipt" (we had gone to Macayo's, a Mexican restaurant for the first time), McDonalds-you know that, Play-Plus, and the park."

Favorite Toys: stuffed animals & dress-ups

Favorite Songs: "Somewhere Over the Rainbow," "Once Upon a Dream" (from Sleeping Beauty), & "Beautiful Savior"

What Ashley wants to be when she grows up: an artist & a fingernail polish painter

"Adorable"

Supplies *Patterned paper:* Lasting Impressions for Paper; *Paw print punch:* EK Success; *Computer fonts:* Doodle Cursive, "PagePrintables" CD Vol.1, Cock-A-Doodle Design, Inc.; CK Script, "The Best of Creative Lettering" CD Vol. 1, *Creating Keepsakes; Ribbon:* Offray.

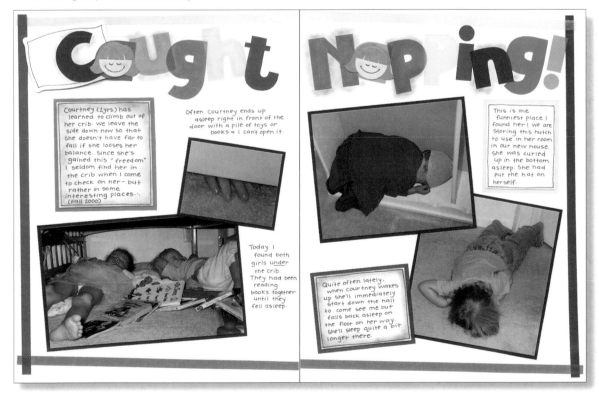

Courtney (2yrs) has learned to climb out of her crib. We leave the side down now so that she doesn't have far to fall if she looses her balance. Since she's gained this "freedom" I seldom find her in the crib when I come to check on her- but rather in some interesting places... (Fall 2000)

Often Courtney ends up asleep right in front of the door with a pile of toys or books & I can't open it.

Today I found both girls under the crib. They had been reading books together until they fell asleep.

Quite often lately, when Courtney wakes up she'll immediately start down the hall to come see me but falls back asleep on the floor on her way. She'll sleep quite a bit longer there.

This is the funniest place I found her! We are storing this hutch to use in her room in our new house. She was curled up in the bottom asleep. She had put the hat on herself.

"Caught Napping"

Supplies *Pillow template:* Pebbles in my Pocket; *Chalk:* Craf-T Products; *Circle punch:* Family Treasures; *Lettering template:* Blocky, Provo Craft; *Pen:* Zig Millennium, EK Success.

Hawaiian

Whodunit?!?

- August second 2000 -
So who killed our Hawaiian Host? That's what we found out when we gathered at a Hawaiian paradise..a.k.a. Kaycee's dining room. Was it I, Holly, a rich heiress? Or was it BoJo (Jason)-world class surfer? Maybe chief Wiki-Wiki who chased the Hawaiian Princess Leilani? (Jenny & KC) Possible suspects were the bumbling tourist Les Baggs (Kevin) or the tempting swim suit model Nadia? (Kaycee)

BO JO BOARDS

"Hawaiian Whodunit"

Supplies *Patterned paper:* Doodlebug Design; *Punches:* EK Success (flower and lotus), Family Treasures (daisy, snowflake, sun and large flower), Fiskars (circle), Marvy Uchida (star and small sun), All Night Media (small star); *Pens:* Zig Writer and Zig Millennium, EK Success *Palm tree and speared fish:* Paperkins, EK Success; *Title, pineapple and surfboard:* Annie's own designs.

"Don't be afraid to be bold. Sometimes putting bright, attention-getting colors together seems intimidating, but you'll be surprised at how they'll make your layouts 'glow'!"

ANNIE GUBLER • OREM, UT

Annie has been scrapbooking since she was 10, and loves to be surrounded by her scrapbook supplies. "I am not a clean scrapbooker!" she laughs. Her goal is to get completely caught up on her own scrapbooks, so when she has her own family she can jump right into theirs.

"Mr. Orem"

Supplies *Specialty papers:* Paper Adventures (Diamond Dust), Making Memories (sparkly paper); *Folk star punch:* EK Success; *Pen:* Zig Writer, EK Success; *Flower stencils:* Fun Flowers, Provo Craft; *Pirate ship, rocks and waterfall:* Annie's own designs.

IDEA TO NOTE: Annie adapted the idea for the title from the Harry Potter book series, published by Scholastic.

"Harry Potter"

Supplies *Patterned paper:* Provo Craft; *Specialty paper:* Diamond Dust, Paper Adventures; *Vellum:* Paper Cuts; *Punches:* EK Success (circles), Marvy Uchida (small star and small swirl), McGill (circle); *Die cuts:* Ellison (jellybeans), Pebbles in my Pocket (paper doll hair); *Paper doll:* Paperkins, EK Success; *Pen:* Zig Writer, EK Success; *Snitch wings, wand, ribbon, stem, Harry's clothes, glasses and thought bubbles:* Annie's own designs.

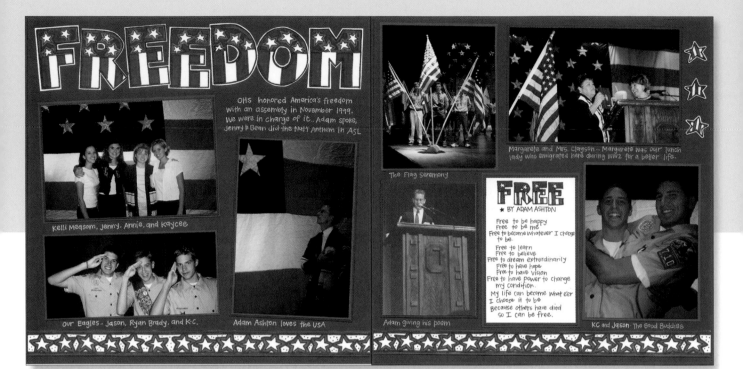

FREEDOM

OHS honored America's freedom with an assembly in November 1999. We were in charge of it.. Adam spoke, Jenny & Bean did the Nat'l Anthem in ASL

Kelli Meqsom, Jenny, Annie, and Kaycee.

Our Eagles- Jason, Ryan Brady, and K.C.

Adam Ashton loves the USA

The Flag Ceremony

Margarete and Mrs. Clayson.. Margarete was our lunch lady who emigrated here during WW2 for a better life.

Adam giving his poem

FREE
★ BY ADAM ASHTON

Free to be happy
Free to be me
Free to become whatever I choose to be.
Free to learn
Free to believe
Free to dream extraordinarily
Free to have hope
Free to have vision
Free to have power to change my condition.
My life can become whatever I choose it to be
Because others have died so I can be free.

KC and Jason. The Good Buddies

"Freedom"

Supplies *Lettering template:* Block, ABC Tracers, Pebbles for EK Success; *Pens:* Zig Writer, EK Success; The Ultimate Gel Pen, American Crafts; *Borders and stars:* Annie's own designs.

$100 Pie

November 1999. Adam and I donned our aprons and made three apple pies one Sunday for our Operation Smile bake sale. We then sold them to our parents for $100 a pie! (Their contribution to Op☺) We had so much fun making pies with eachother. So yummy!

$100

"$100 Pie"

Supplies *Patterned papers:* The Robin's Nest Press, Pixie Press; *Vellum:* Paper Cuts; *Apple punch:* EK Success; *Lettering template:* Block, ABC Tracers, Pebbles for EK Success; *Apple die cuts:* Pebbles in my Pocket; *Pen:* Zig Writer, EK Success; *Pie and tag:* Annie's own designs.

lori houk

"Son-flowers"

Supplies *Punches:* Family Treasures (daisy and square); *Pens:* Zig Writer, EK Success; *Colored pencils:* Prismacolor, Sanford; *Computer font:* Girls Are Weird, downloaded from the Internet; *Chalk:* Craf-T Products.

"I love matting my actual scrapbook pages.

Layouts look more complete with a 'frame' around

the entire layout. Without a mat, I feel like my

pictures are going to slide off the page."

LORI HOUK • LAWRENCE, KS

What started as a simple task of recording major events in her first son's life has evolved into a passionate endeavor to capture everyday moments that will bring back good memories in the years to come. "As my boys got older, I could see the pride and joy in their eyes as they looked at their albums," smiles Lori. "It made me want to do more. I want to convey fun and humor in my work—I want the boys to remember all the fun times we've had together."

"CD Repairman"

Supplies *Patterned paper:* Scrap in a Snap; *Computer font:* Bradley Hand, Corel Draw; *Lettering template:* Blocky, Provo Craft; *Miniature tools:* Small Town Treasures; *Grommets:* Dritz.

"Figure out which colors of cardstock you use the most and make sure you have every shade of that color on hand. You never know when you'll need them, and there's nothing worse than having to set aside a layout because you don't have the right shade!"

ALANNAH JURGENSMEYER • ROGERS, AR

When Alannah decided she was fed up with the poor-quality photographs she was taking of her then three-month-old son, she bought a new camera and read up on photography techniques. Soon after, she had a stack of beautiful photographs of her son. The need to organize and display these photos led Alannah to create her first scrapbook page. "I started out very simple," she explains, "but my style has definitely evolved over time." Alannah and her husband, Steven, are the proud parents of two sons.

"Go Jump in a Lake"

Supplies *Computer font:* CK Handprint, "The Best of Creative Lettering" CD Combo, *Creating Keepsakes; Lettering templates:* Kids and Blocky, Provo Craft; *Flag designs:* Inspired by bedding in an Exposures catalog.

"Playground Antics"

Supplies *Leaf punch:* Family Treasures; *Pen:* Zig Writer, EK Success; *Computer font:* Boink, Corel Draw; *Chalk:* Stampin' Up!; *Slide:* Alannah's own design.

"Carter"

Supplies *Punches:* Hyglo (snowflake), Family Treasures (cloud); *Computer font:* Jungle Juice, downloaded from the Internet; *Punch art and greenery:* Alannah's own designs.

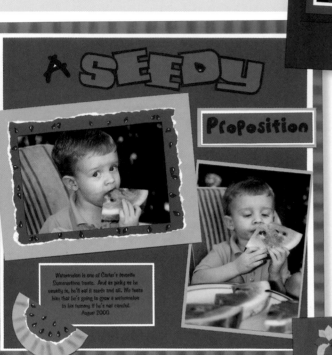

"A Seedy Proposition"

Supplies *Patterned paper:* Close To My Heart; *Pens:* Zig Millennium, EK Success; Gel Roller, Staedtler; *Computer fonts:* Benguat Frisky, Corel Draw; Before Attack, downloaded from the Internet; *Lettering templates:* Kids, Provo Craft; Big Fat Font, ScrapPagerz; *Chalk:* Stampin' Up!; *Watermelon slice:* Alannah's own design.

"Hanging Out at the Park"

Supplies *Leaf punch:* All Night Media; *Stickers:* me & my BIG ideas; *Computer fonts:* Tag and Enviro (journaling), Corel Draw; CK Journaling ("at the Park"), "The Best of Creative Lettering" CD Vol. 2, *Creating Keepsakes* ; *Chalk:* Stampin' Up!; *Tree branches:* Alannah's own design.

"You Give Me the Creeps"

Supplies *Computer fonts:* Chiller (journaling), Corel Draw, WordPerfect; Crooked Classic, "The Art of Creative Lettering" CD, *Creating Keepsakes; Plastic screen:* Magic Mesh, Picture Perfect Scrapbooks; *Embroidery floss:* DMC.

"Waiting for Daddy"

Supplies *Handmade paper:* DMD Industries; *Patterned paper:* Solum World Paper; *Computer font:* Fine Hand, Corel Draw, WordPerfect.

"Searching for Our Tree"

Supplies *Computer fonts:* Lucida Handwriting ("Searching") and Graphite Light (journaling), Corel Draw, WordPerfect; *Raffia:* Raffia Accents, Plaid Enterprises; *Chalk:* Stampin' Up!

"I like to complete all the elements of my page layout before I attach them to the background paper. This allows me to move them around and find the best placement for all of the elements."

"Love You No Matter What"

Supplies *Computer font:* 42, Macromedia Fontographer; *Chalk:* Craf-T Products; *Pop dots:* All Night Media; *Buttons:* Dress It Up, Country Hearts; *Hemp:* Darice.

NICOLE KELLER • RIO HONDO, TX

Nicole got hooked on scrapbooking when she "innocently" ordered a scrapbooking kit from a mail-order catalog. Although she's always loved arts and crafts, Nicole says scrapbooking is the perfect hobby: "It's a medium that fulfills my need to create, and it's also a practical use of my crafting time and money." Nicole's main goal in scrapbooking is to create albums that will be a legacy for the generations to come. She often motivates herself to scrapbook by thinking what a treasure it would be if she had a completed album from a grandmother, or an album of her childhood created by her mother.

"Marvelous Are Thy Works"

Supplies *Vellum:* Source unknown *Computer font:* CK Script, "The Best of Creative Lettering" CD Vol. 1, *Creating Keepsakes; Circle punch:* CARL Mfg.; *Pen:* LePlume, Marvy Uchida; *Leaf:* Nicole adapted the idea for the leaf from the leaves on the vellum paper.

IDEA TO NOTE: Nicole printed her journaling on cardstock, then crumpled it to create an aged look.

Marvelous are Thy works, that my soul knoweth right well. — Psalms 132:14

nicole 1974

I have always been amazed by the wonders of God's creation.

LORRAINE ELIZABETH SMITH
February 12, 1919 – January 12, 1998
My Grandmother

ARTHUR EDWARD TILLEY, SR.
April 28, 1917 – January 5, 1971
My Grandfather

"My Grandmother and Grandfather"

Supplies *Handmade paper:* Black Ink; *Computer fonts:* Bookman Old Style and Black Adder II, Microsoft Word; *Craft wire:* Wild Wire, Natural Science Industries; *Leaves:* Black Ink; *Other:* Wooden beads.

"Always and Forever

Supplies *Vellum:* The Paper Company; *Computer fonts:* Ramona Regular, WSI-Font Collection, Weatherly System; CK Script, "The Best of Creative Lettering" CD Vol. 1, *Creating Keepsakes; Embossing powder:* Stamp-n Stuff; *Pen:* Zig Writer, EK Success; *Vellum die cuts:* Paper Reflections, DMD Industries; *Pop dots:* All Night Media; *Craft wire:* Wild Wire, Natural Science Industries.

"Nicole"

Supplies *Patterned paper:* Provo Craft; *Computer font:* Courier New, Microsoft Word; *Chalk:* Craf-T Products; *Flower punch:* CARL Mfg. *Scissors:* Corkscrew edge, Fiskars; *Flowers:* Nicole color-copied the flowers from a newspaper ad from Target.; *Seed beads and pop dots:* All Night Media.

"Jane and Ann"

Supplies *Vellum:* The Paper Company; *Computer fonts:* Stylograph, ParaGraph, Intl.; Priority, package unknown; *Flower punch:* CARL Mfg.; *Embossing powder:* Stamp-n Stuff; *Pop dots:* All Night Media; *Seed beads:* Westrim Crafts; *Flowers:* Nicole's own design.

IDEA TO NOTE: Nicole created the photo mat with two sheets of vellum. She tore one in strips lengthwise, and the other in strips widthwise. Then she wove the strips together to create a basket look.

"Arthur"

Supplies *Vellum:* The Paper Company; *Computer fonts:* DweeboGothic, Omega Fontlabs; Jazzposter Heavy, Fontographer.

"I carry a small spiral notebook in my purse to record inspirational quotes, scrapbook-page ideas, title ideas, great things my kids say and a list of scrapbooking supplies I already have. I also carry a disposable camera in my purse. Now I don't miss those spontaneous 'I wish I had a camera' moments."

"Taryn has 'Purse'sonality"

Supplies *Patterned paper:* Current, Inc.; *Die cuts:* Making Memories (paper purses), My Mind's Eye (jean pocket), Fibre Craft (black velvet purse); *Pens:* Zig Writer, EK Success; Pigma Micron, Sakura; *Colored pencils:* Prismacolor, Sanford; *Stickers:* Making Memories; *Computer fonts:* CK Journaling, "The Best of Creative Lettering" CD Vol. 2,; *Creating Keepsakes*; Andy and ITC Bradley Hand, Microsoft Works; First Grader, Print Artist; *Embroidery floss:* DMC; *Velcro and buttons:* LaMode; *Chalk:* Craf-T Products.

CINDY KNOWLES • MILWAUKIE, OR

"Some of my favorite times are sitting with my kids, looking at our scrapbooks and remembering family stories," shares Cindy. "I try to scrapbook every day—mostly in the middle of the night when everyone else is in bed!" Cindy has been keeping scrapbooks for years and loves every aspect of scrapbooking: paper, photography, stickers, writing and designing. She is the mother of four children and enjoys drawing, reading, organizing, bargain shopping, eating M & M's, playing on the computer and volunteering at her children's school.

"Don't Feed the Duck!"

Supplies *Patterned paper:* Colors By Design (ducks); *Vellum:* Paper Accents; *Punches:* Fiskars ; *Stickers:* Mrs. Grossman's (ice cream, pop, lollipop and candy); Cock-A-Doodle Design, Inc. (sun); *Computer fonts:* CK Print, "The Best of Creative Lettering" CD Vol. 1 and CK Primary, "The Art of Creative Lettering" CD, *Creating Keepsakes*; PC Wingdings, "Color Me Kids" HugWare CD, Provo Craft; Blades, Macintosh Fonts; *Pop dots:* All Night Media; *Chalk:* Craf-T Products; *Twine:* Saint Louis Trimming; *Feathers:* Zucker Feather Products; *Foam:* Darice Foamies

"We Love to Hear You Laugh"

Supplies *Patterned paper:* Bo-Bunny Press ; *Vellum:* Frances Meyer ; *Punches:* Emagination Crafts (primitive heart), McGill (heart), Fiskars (circle); *Rubber stamps:* Hero Arts; *Pen:* Zig Writer, EK Success; *Colored pencils:* Memory Pencils, EK Success; *Ribbon:* Offray; *Pop dots:* All Night Media; *Chalk:* Craf-T Products; *Voice box:* Voice Express ; *Other:* Raffia.

"Who Can Resist This Face?"

Supplies *Confetti vellum:* Paper Accents, Peterson-Arne; *Stickers:* me & my BIG ideas; *Computer font:* Scrap Rhapsody, "Lettering Delights" CD, Inspire Graphics; *Mosaic glass tiles:* Mosaic Mercantile; *Mini brass fasteners:* Hyglo Deco Fasteners; *Pop dots:* All Night Media.

IDEA TO NOTE: To evoke the feeling of Cindy's girls dancing down the dunes, Cindy created a lever from cardstock and attached it to the back of her photo. She also created the word "Down" from other photos she had taken of the dunes.

"Dancing Down the Dunes"

Supplies *Computer fonts:* CK Cursive and CK Toggle, "The Best of Creative Lettering" CD Vol. 2, *Creating Keepsakes; Pen:* Zig Writer, EK Success; *Colored pencils:* Memory Pencils, EK Success; *Lettering template:* Blocky, Provo Craft; *Craft wire:* Westrim; *Circle punch:* Fiskars; *Torn paper seagull and sandals:* Cindy's own designs.

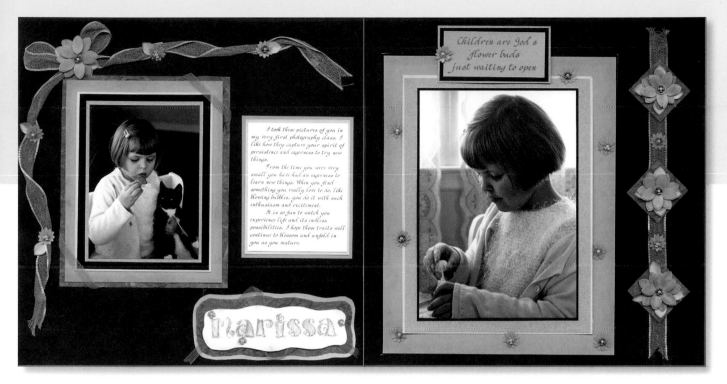

"Marissa"

Supplies *Mulberry paper*: PrintWorks ; *Chalk:* Stamping Station; *Punches:* Family Treasures (daisy), EK Success (leaf and circle); *Computer fonts:* CK Voluptuous, "The Art of Creative Lettering" CD and CK Calligraphy, "The Best of Creative Lettering" CD Vol. 1, *Creating Keepsakes; Ribbon:* Offray (sheer), MSI (weaved); *Glitter:* Prismacolor; *Other:* Beads.

"Use your computer to enhance your scrapbooking. It's great for printing titles and journaling, and the Internet is a fantastic resource for creative, new page ideas and fun, innovative techniques."

TAMMY KRUMMEL • HANCOCK, IA

"Scrapbooking has opened many doors for me since I started over four years ago," explains Tammy. "I've become a teacher and employee at my local scrapbook store, and I've gone back to college at the age of 40 to become a photographer. It's also brought so many new friends into my life. Scrapbooking isn't just about creating memorable pages—it's also about the relationships that grow because of it." Tammy and her husband, Denny, live on a farm with their two children.

"Flowers We Love"

Supplies *Patterned paper:* Bo-Bunny Press ; *Punches:* Family Treasures (medium daisy, large daisy and butterfly); *Computer fonts:* CK Bella, "The Best of Creative Lettering" CD Vol. 3, *Creating Keepsakes*; Duchess, downloaded from the Internet; *Other:* Beads.

"The Baby Bunnies"

Supplies *Patterned paper:* Making Memories (blue checked), Doodlebug Design (green plaid), The Paper Patch (green dot), Mary Engelbreit (flowered), Keeping Memories Alive (green checked); *Vellum:* Paper Adventures; *Computer font:* Package unknown; *Craft wire:* Darice; *Grommets:* Impress Rubber Stamps; *Punches:* All Night Media (medium circle and mini spiral), Family Treasures (small bunny, small oval, mini circle and birch leaf).

"Splish Splash"

Supplies *Computer fonts:* Blacksmith Delight, package unknown; CK Journaling, "The Best of Creative Lettering" CD Vol. 2, *Creating Keepsakes; Circle punches:* Family Treasures ; *Grommets:* Impress Rubber Stamps; *Craft wire:* Darice; *Other:* Beads and seashells.

"Yellow"

Supplies *Patterned papers:* Keeping Memories Alive (plaid); Making Memories (yellow checked); O'Scrap!, Imaginations! (yellow dots); Doodlebug Design (yellow flowered and yellow striped); source unknown (light yellow); *Computer fonts:* CK Calligraphy, "The Best of Creative Lettering" CD Vol. 1, *Creating Keepsakes;* Edwardian Script, downloaded from the Internet; *Other:* Beads; *Bee, flowers, sun, peach and mitten:* Tammy's own designs.

"Sometimes when I have 'scrapbooker's block', I like to scrapbook someone else's photographs. Working with another's photos encourages me to try something new. Then I can approach my own photos with a new outlook."

"London in Black and White"

Supplies *Computer font:* CK Concave, "The Art of Creative Lettering" CD, *Creating Keepsakes; Pop dots:* All Night Media.

SHIMELLE LAINE •
STANFORD-LE-HOPE, ESSEX, ENGLAND

Shimelle began scrapbooking a few years ago when she had a role in a play that featured a family scrapbook filled only with horrible events. "On closing night, it's a tradition for the cast to present the director with a gift," says Shimelle. "We decided a scrapbook would be a perfect reminder of our makeshift family." After completing that small gift album, Shimelle was ready to get started on the boxes of photos she had at home. Shimelle also teaches English in secondary school.

"Moving Day Again"

Supplies *Lettering template:* ScrapPagerz; *Computer font:* CK Toggle, "The Best of Creative Lettering" CD Vol. 2, *Creating Keepsakes; Embroidery floss:* DMC; *Punch:* Fiskars.

"Brighton Beach"

Supplies *Scissors:* Wavy edge, Big Cuts, Provo Craft; *Computer font:* Fontdinerdotcom, Font Diner Designs *Accents:* Cut from photos.

"Confessions of a Cricket Groupie"

Supplies *Computer font:* Seriffic Grunge, E. Perlin Designs; *Lettering template:* Hand Drawn, Pebbles in my Pocket.

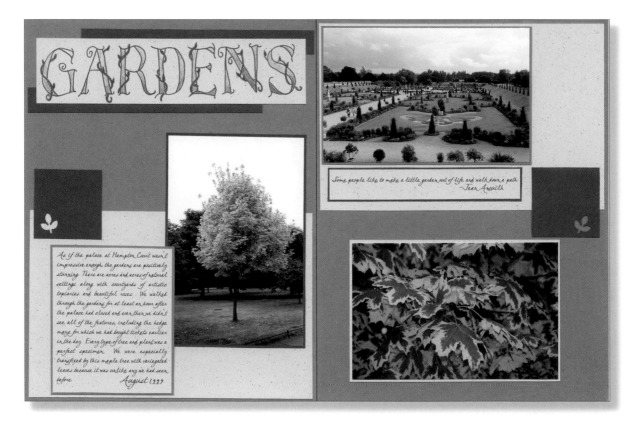

"Gardens"

Supplies *Leaf punch:* EK Success; *Pens:* Zig Writer and Zig Scroll & Brush, EK Success; *Colored pencils:* Prismacolor, Sanford; *Computer font:* CK Bella, "The Best of Creative Lettering" CD Vol. 3, *Creating Keepsakes; Lettering idea:* Leafy Capitals, *The Art of Creative Lettering,* Creating Keepsakes Books.

"It's a Beautiful Day"

Supplies *Patterned papers:* Crafter's Workshop (blue), Pixie Press (black); *Vellum:* Paper Adventures; *Computer font:* CK Script, "The Best of Creative Lettering" CD Vol. 1, *Creating Keepsakes; Lettering template:* Blocky, Provo Craft.

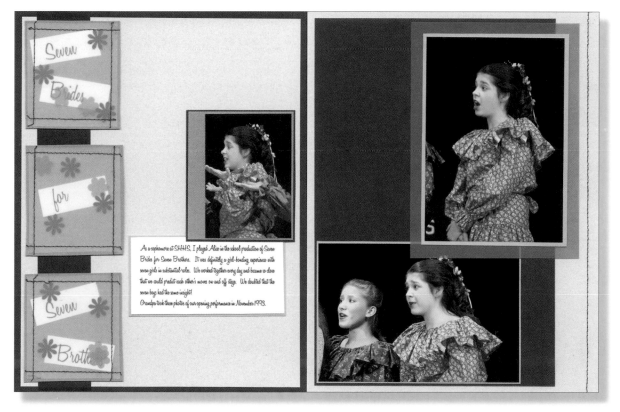

"Seven Brides for Seven Brothers"

Supplies *Vellum:* Judikins; *Punches:* McGill (daisy and flower); *Computer font:* Suzanne Quill, package unknown.

mary larson
2001

"Crocodile Hunters"

"All the endless catalogs I get in the mail have become some of my favorite scrapbooking resources. Before throwing them out, I look through them and cut out ideas for colors, frames, designs, paper-piecing patterns, borders and more. I organize and browse through them when I'm looking for something fresh and new for my pages."

Supplies *Patterned paper:* Making Memories; *Computer font:* CK Penman, "The Best of Creative Lettering" CD Vol. 3, *Creating Keepsakes; Chalk:* Craf-T Products; *Frame and crocodile tail:* Mary's own designs; *Title:* Mary adapted the idea for her title from the TV series "The Crocodile Hunter."

MARY LARSON • CHANDLER, AZ

In May 1999, Mary bought *Creating Keepsakes' The 1999 Scrapbook Idea Book* from QVC. "After graduating from college with an accounting degree and working 15 years in a technical field as a computer analyst, I was ready to explore my creative side," explains Mary. "Buying that book was the beginning of what has become a very rewarding hobby for me!" Mary and her husband have four young sons, including a set of twins. "I never want to be caught up with my albums. I hope that when my sons have grown and left the house, I'll still have a few of their baby pictures left to scrapbook so I can relive those precious moments again."

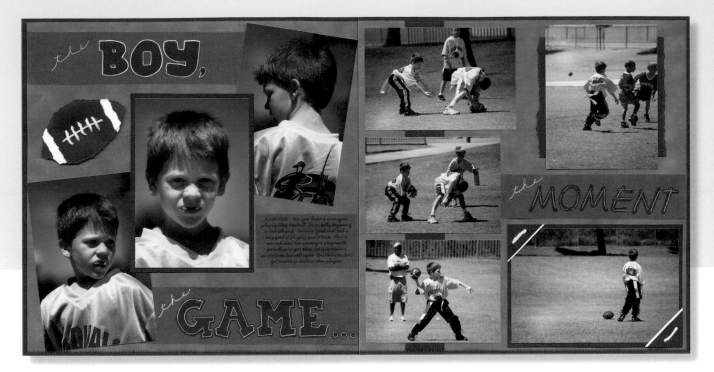

"The Boy, the Game, the Moment"

Supplies *Patterned paper:* Making Memories; *Vellum:* Paper Adventures; *Computer fonts:* Scrap Color Me 2, "Lettering Delights" CD, Inspire Graphics; DJ Cheer, package unknown, D.J. Inkers; CluffHmk, Hallmark Card Studio; *Circle punch:* Punchline; *Pen:* Staedtler; *Football:* Mary's own design.

"Six"

Supplies *Vellum:* Paper Adventures; *Computer font:* CK Handprint, "The Best of Creative Lettering" CD Combo, *Creating Keepsakes; Leaf and fern punches:* Martha by Mail; *Embossing powder:* Mark Enterprises.

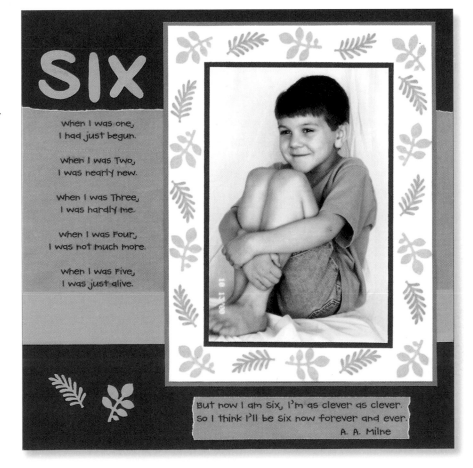

when I was one,
I had just begun.

when I was Two,
I was nearly new.

when I was Three,
I was hardly me.

when I was Four,
I was not much more.

when I was Five,
I was just alive.

But now I am Six, I'm as clever as clever.
So I think I'll be six now forever and ever.
A. A. Milne

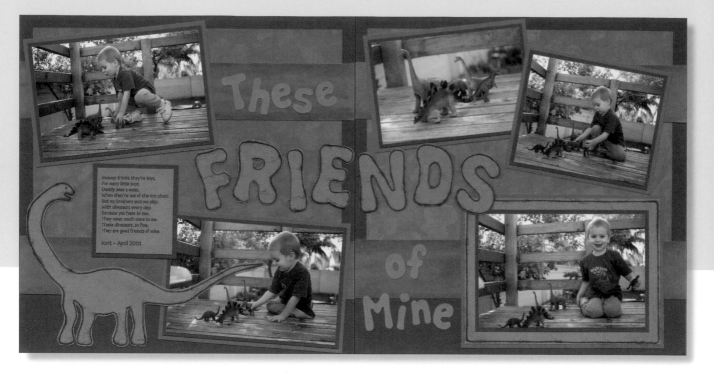

"These Friends of Mine"

Supplies *Vellum:* Autumn Leaves; *Computer font:* BaaBookHMK Bold, Hallmark Card Studio; *Lettering template:* Pillow Talk, ScrapPagerz; *Dinosaur template:* ScrapPagerz; *Poem:* By Mary Larson.

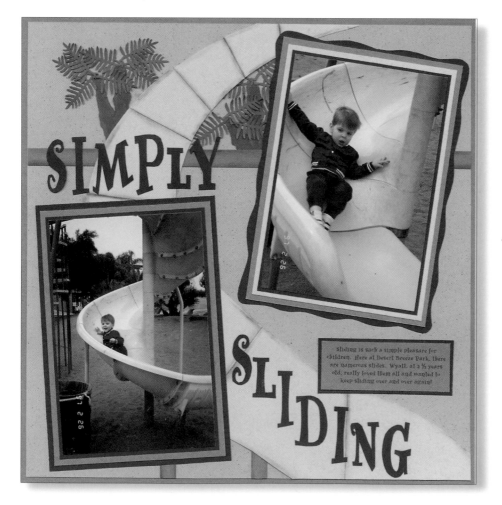

"Simply Sliding"

Supplies *Computer font:* Whimsey Heavy, package unknown; *Chalk:* Craf-T Products; *Fern punch:* Martha by Mail ; *Slide:* Mary's own design.

"Lake Powell"

Supplies *Pen:* Zig Writer, EK Success; *Accents:* Megan cut out the accents from a shopping bag she got at Lake Powell; *Lettering:* Megan's own design.

"Try to keep your pages as simple as possible. I don't like my pages to have so much going on that you have to hunt for the photos."

MEGAN STAKER MCMURDIE • SHELBY TOWNSHIP, MI

Megan began scrapbooking about nine years ago, but her passion was fueled when she moved to Denver to help her aunt open an All My Memories scrapbook store. "Right then, I fell in love with the whole scrapbooking industry," says Megan. "I just knew I had to be involved." She also works for her local store teaching classes and creating displays.

"Working with a Vengeance"
Supplies *Pens:* Zig Writer and Zig Scroll & Brush, EK Success.

"Dream Cruise"
Supplies *Pens:* Zig Writer, EK Success; Milky Gel Roller, Pentel; *Metallic paper:* Paper Adventures; *Wheel:* Megan adapted the idea for the wheel from a picture she took of a Cadillac wheel.

"Donut"

Supplies *Pens:* Zig Writer, Zig Scroll & Brush and Zig Calligraphy, EK Success; *Chalk:* Craf-T Products; *Donuts:* Megan's own designs.

"Just Can't Wait"

Supplies *Pens:* Zig Scroll & Brush, EK Success; Scrapright; Gelly Roll, Sakura; *Tree die cut:* All My Memories ; *Metallic paper:* Paper Adventures; *Stars:* Megan's own design.

2001
lynne montgomery

Every child is a different kind of little flower,
and all together,
they make this world a garden

emily 5/01

"Take advantage of the scrapbooking classes

your local stores offer. You can always learn from

others, and every little bit helps!"

"Every Child Is Different"

Supplies *Computer font:* Technical, Microsoft Word; *Dried flowers:* Nature's Pressed; *Ribbon and jute:* May Arts; *Grommets:* Memory Lane; *Window screen:* Home Depot; *Hole punches:* Fiskars; *Metallic rub-ons:* Craft-T Products.

LYNNE MONTGOMERY • GILBERT, AZ

Lynne and her husband, Mark, like to scrapbook together on Sunday evenings after their three children are in bed. "I'm so lucky my husband and I share the same hobby. I was jealous at first because Mark's pages were so much better than mine—it came so naturally for him," remembers Lynne. "But it's inspired me to work harder and find my own style." Lynne started teaching workshops at her local store, Memory Lane, about six months ago and loves how much the experience has helped her stop copying other scrapbookers and start creating things based on her own personality. "I was so excited to enter the Hall of Fame contest because it drew creativity out of me I didn't know I had!"

"My Sunshine"

Supplies *Patterned paper:* Memory Lane; *Embossing powder:* Suze Weinberg; *Embossing ink:* VersaColor, Tsukineko; *Computer font:* Brush Script, Microsoft Word; *Grommets:* Dritz; *Dried flowers:* Nature's Pressed; *Other:* Twine, studs and a sun charm.

"Little Girls"

Supplies *Patterned paper:* Memory Lane; *Computer font:* Curlz, Microsoft Word; *Rubber stamps:* Bunch of Fun; *Stamp ink:* Dauber Duos, Tsukineko; *Pen:* Zig Writer, EK Success.; *Metallic rub-ons:* Craf-T Products; *Twine:* May Arts; *Craft wire:* Artistic Wire Ltd.; *Beads:* Memory Lane; *Grommets and Fun Fiber:* Ink It Up

"Armour of God"

Supplies *Patterned paper:* Memory Lane ; *Embossing powder:* Suze Weinberg; *Embossing pad:* Emboss It; *Stamping ink:* VersaColor, Tsukineko; *Computer font:* Lucida Handwriting, Microsoft Word; *Ribbon:* Memory Lane; *Embroidery floss:* DMC; *Square punch:* Family Treasures; *Pop dots:* Pop-it-Up, Cut-it-Up; *Tags:* Lynne's own design.

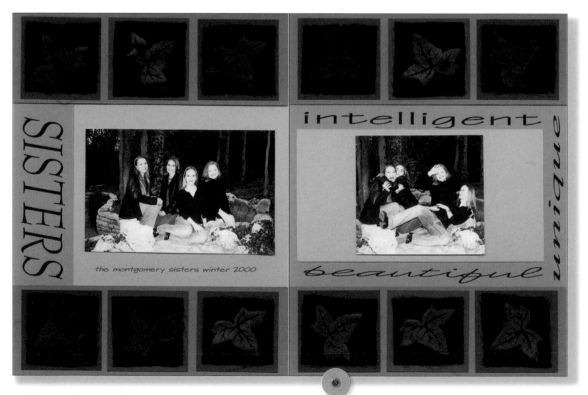

"Sisters"

Supplies *Computer fonts:* Bernhard Modern Roman and Technical, Microsoft Word; CK Print and CK Script, "The Best of Creative Lettering" CD Vol. 1, *Creating Keepsakes; Ivy rubber stamp:* Personal Stamp Exchange; *Other:* Velvet

IDEA TO NOTE: To get the ivy impression in the velvet, Lynne pressed the velvet against the rubber stamp with an iron.

"Baiting Is the Hardest Part"

Supplies *Computer fonts:* CK Script, "The Best of Creative Lettering" CD Vol. 1, *Creating Keepsakes;* Bernhard Fashion BT, Microsoft Word; CK Flair, "The Art of Creative Lettering" CD, *Creating Keepsakes; Other:* Chicken wire and fishing lures.

"Tour of Duty"

Supplies *Patterned paper:* Memory Lane; *Background paper:* Lynne's own design (created from old passport pages); *Computer fonts:* CK Script and CK Fill In, "The Best of Creative Lettering" CD Vol. 1, *Creating Keepsakes; Embossing pad:* VersaColor, Tsukineko; *Embossing powder:* Suze Weinberg; *Marble:* Mega Accent Marbles; *Craft wire:* Artistic Wire Ltd.; *Beads:* Memory Lane; *Pop dots:* Pop-it-Up, Cut-it-Up; *Embroidery floss:* DMC; *Metallic rub-ons:* Craf-T Products.

2001
denise pauley

holding
Stars
in a net

Erin's childhood slips through my fingers like sand... keeping the memories in my heart is like holding stars in a net – some slip away, others break free. So I am blessed to capture a timeless moment such as this, one that I can preserve forever...even as her youth streaks out of sight.

January 2001

"Use cardstock and vellum to add texture, depth and dimension to your layouts. Whether you tear, chalk, cut, crumple or layer it, you'll find endless creative possibilities that will complement your layouts."

"Holding Stars in a Net"

Supplies *Computer font:* Papyrus, Microsoft Word; *Magic mesh:* Avant'CARD; *Embossing powder:* Mark Enterprises; *Chalk:* Craf-T Products; *Stars:* Rusty Shapes, Provo Craft; *Beads:* Darice; *Craft wire:* Darice; *Pop dots:* All Night Media; *Pen:* Zig Millennium, EK Success.

DENISE PAULEY • LA PALMA, CA

Denise doesn't complain about losing a few hours of sleep so she can scrapbook at night when her two children are in bed. "Scrapbooking is my way to unwind, relax and spend some quality 'me' time while doing something extremely constructive in the process—creating a lasting legacy of my family's cherished times together," she shares. What started about two years ago as a pastime has become a part of Denise's everyday life. Whether she's shopping for supplies, taking photos, journaling or sketching layouts, scrapbooking is never far from her thoughts.

"Keys to My Heart"

Supplies *Lettering idea:* Classic, *The Art of Creative Lettering* Creating Keepsakes Books; *Computer font:* CK Journaling, "The Best of Creative Lettering" CD Vol. 2, *Creating Keepsakes; Quilling paper:* Lake City Craft Company; *Gold key charms:* Source unknown; *Other:* Twine.

IDEA TO NOTE: To create the title, Denise traced the printed font with an embossing pen and sprinkled it with embossing powder.

The two of you are everything I ever dreamed of, but never knew existed...being your mommy has brought me more joy, pride and laughs (and, yes, exhaustion and frustration at times!) than I could have imagined. Thank you for teaching me to see the world through your eyes and for rejuvenating my sense of wonder. But especially, thank you for filling my heart with so much love. Even if I had all the children of the world to choose from...I'd still pick you!

Youth fades; love droops; leaves of friendship fall; a mother's secret wish outlives them all...
—Oliver Wendell Holmes

January 2001

Erin and I stop at every fountain we see... she loves to stare into the glassy water and pat the cool tile, while I never miss a chance to toss in a coin and wish for her happiness, safety and health. I hope she will do the same with her child someday!

"Fountain of Youth"

Supplies *Computer fonts:* CK Journaling, "The Best of Creative Lettering" CD Vol. 2, *Creating Keepsakes;* Mistral, Microsoft Word; CaflischScript, package unknown; *Vellum:* Paper Adventures; *Embossing pen:* EK Success; *Embossing powder:* Mark Enterprises; *Square punch:* Fiskars; *Pen:* Zig Millennium, EK Success; *Fountain:* Denise's own design.

"Like a Kid in a Candy Store"

Supplies *Vellum:* Paper Adventures; *Computer fonts:* CK Toggle, "The Best of Creative Lettering" CD Vol. 2, *Creating Keepsakes*; Curlz, Microsoft Word; *Pearlescent powder:* Jacquard Products; *Embossing pen:* EK Success; *Plastic swirls:* Darice; *Ribbon:* Offray.

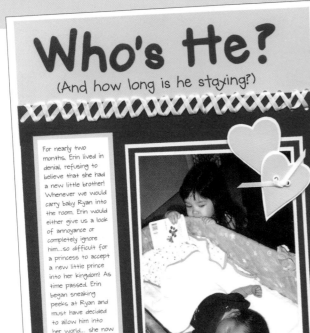

For nearly two months, Erin lived in denial, refusing to believe that she had a new little brother! Whenever we would carry baby Ryan into the room, Erin would either give us a look of annoyance or completely ignore him...so difficult for a princess to accept a new little prince into her kingdom! As time passed, Erin began sneaking peeks at Ryan and must have decided to allow him into her world... she now calls him "My Beebee Eye-an" and even bestows the occasional kiss upon him!

"Who's He?"

Supplies *Grommets:* Impress Rubber Stamps; *Computer fonts:* CK Toggle and CK Journaling, "The Best of Creative Lettering" CD Vol. 2, *Creating Keepsakes; Circle punch:* Fiskars; *Ribbon:* Offray; *Hearts:* Denise's own design.

"Pieces"

Supplies *Computer font:* CaflischScript, package unknown; *Colored pencils:* Prismacolor, Sanford; *Grommets:* Impress Rubber Stamps; *Embroidery floss:* DMC; *Heart:* Denise's own design; *Poem:* By Denise.

"Palm Springs Aerial Tramway"

Supplies *Lettering template:* Blocky, Provo Craft; *Computer fonts:* CK Script, "The Best of Creative Lettering" CD Vol. 1 and CK Journaling, "The Best of Creative Lettering" CD Vol. 2, *Creating Keepsakes; Silver metal sheeting:* American Art Clay Co.; *Pen:* Zig Writer, EK Success; *Chalk:* Craf-T Products; *Trees:* Denise's own design.

"Dream Dust"

Supplies *Computer fonts:* Sixty Seven, downloaded from the Internet; font unknown, downloaded from the Internet ; *Craft wire and beads:* Darice; *Vellum:* Paper Cuts ; *Metallic paper:* Stampin' Up!

"Baby, You're a Star"

Supplies *Lettering template:* Party, ScrapPagerz; *Computer fonts:* CK Journaling, "The Best of Creative Lettering" CD Vol. 2, *Creating Keepsakes;* Willow, package unknown; *Alphabet beads:* Darice; *Grommets:* Impress Rubber Stamps; *Embroidery floss:* DMC; *Other:* Sequins.

"Garden of the Gods"

Supplies *Patterned paper:* Scrap-Ease; *Vellum:* Paper Adventures; *Computer font:* Bud Easy, Freeware; *Chalk:* Craf-T Products.

"I don't live by the 'scrapbooking standards.' If I decide that I need five pages of pictures to capture a memory, I create a five-page spread. I'm excessive when I want to be, verbose when it warrants, and short on journaling when it's appropriate for me. I don't scrapbook to make others happy—I scrapbook for my family and me."

ERICA PIEROVICH • LONGMONT, CO

"It's often said that pictures turn moments into memories. I feel that just having the pictures isn't enough," explains Erica. "You need to capture the who, what, when, where, why and how behind the pictures. That's what scrapbooking does—it turns memories into lifelong treasures." Erica began scrapbooking four years ago when she attended a crop with some friends from work. Her family is the focus of her photos and the inspiration behind her scrapbooking. "My husband, David, is very supportive of my hobby and often serves as my design consultant. He's loaded with great ideas." Erica and David have two children, Alexandra and Maxwell.

Max and Mommy decided to welcome in the New Year, 2001, with a visit to one of Max's favorite places in Boulder, Colorado. Alexandra and Daddy were watching a special movie together, so we headed out for a little road trip. Between Denver and Boulder, with a spectacular view of the Flatiron Mountains, there is a scenic lookout that Max calls "Boulder rocks." He is so thrilled to climb, lay on, and to leap from the many boulders. His routine involves running through the meadow, climbing and leaping off of every boulder at least three times, jumping off of the giant boulders into Mommy's arms, and gathering little rocks to stuff in his pockets. On New Year's Day, we enjoyed a sunny, but windy visit to the lookout. We had so much fun playing together and Max agreed with Mommy that, "Boulder rocks!"

"Boulder Rocks"

Supplies *Patterned paper:* Provo Craft (bark), Solum World Paper (title paper); *Computer font:* Rockwell, Freeware; *Lettering template:* Whimsey, Déjà Views; *Frogs:* Source unknown.

"The Great Hopper Caper"

Supplies *Patterned paper:* Karen Foster Design (yellow and green), Making Memories (speckled green), Paper Adventures (white terry cloth); *Computer font:* Monkey Chunks, Freeware; *Chalk:* Craft-T Products; *Pen:* Zig Writer, EK Success; *Grasshopper stickers:* Suzy's Zoo; *Letter stickers:* Provo Craft; *Sun and rocks:* Sources unknown; *Pewter metal:* Art Emboss; *Butterflies, net and dragonfly:* From craft store.

"The Villani Whinery"

Supplies *Patterned paper:* Paper Adventures (wood), Solum World Paper (light purple); *Vellum:* Paper Adventures; *Computer font:* Amazon BT, Freeware; *Chalk:* Craft-T Products; *Grape accents:* Wallies, McCall's; *Pewter metal:* Art Emboss; *Metal grape leaves:* Heartland Crafts.

"An Apple a Day"

Supplies *Computer font:* Accent Dot Writer, Freeware; *Lettering template:* Dicey, ScrapPagerz; *Apple accents:* Wallies, McCall's.

- - - - - - - - - - - - - - - - - -
IDEAS TO NOTE: Erica incorporated the book onto her layout.

"My Favorite Book"

Supplies *Vellum:* Paper Adventures; *Computer font:* CK Journaling, "The Best of Creative Lettering" CD Vol. 2, Creating Keepsakes; *Dragonfly punch:* Emagination Crafts; *Alphabet stickers:* Kid, Provo Craft.

A bud...
A bloom...
A blossom
Isn't nature
Awesome...
Shirley O. Pilkington

The flowers in my garden...make my heart happy. The blooms and blossoms spill all over my yard and I give thanks to Heavenly Father for His creations.

"Always make sure your layout has a focus. A layout with a focal point gives order to the composition and makes it easier to take in all of the information on the layout."

"A Bud, a Bloom, a Blossom"

Supplies *Patterned paper:* Daisy D's; *Die cuts:* Cock-A-Doodle Design, Inc.; *Pen:* Zig Writer, EK Success; *Computer font:* CK Handprint, "The Best of Creative Lettering" CD Combo, *Creating Keepsakes; House:* PageProps, Cock-A-Doodle Design, Inc.

SHIRLEY PILKINGTON • EDEN, UT

Shirley started scrapbooking to record all the things she loves about her life: family, friends, traveling, country living and much more. She especially loves scrapbooking her seven grandchildren, who give her endless opportunities to take pictures and scrapbook. "Scrapbooking has given me a creative avenue and a way to return to the delightful times in my life," smiles Shirley. "I wanted others to have the chance to experience this as well, so I opened my own retail store so others can discover the joys of scrapbooking." Shirley is grateful for a good husband, three great children, her life, and a business and hobby in scrapbooking.

"Mack at McDonald's"

Supplies *Patterned paper:* Daisy D's; *Die cuts:* Cock-A-Doodle Design, Inc.; *Computer font:* CK Shadowed Block, "The Best of Creative Lettering" CD Vol. 3, *Creating Keepsakes.*

"Farm Girls"

Supplies *Patterned paper:* Daisy D's; *Die cuts:* Frame-Ups, My Mind's Eye; Cock-A-Doodle Design, Inc.; *Pen:* Zig Writer, EK Success; *Top of barn and weather vane:* Shirley's own designs.

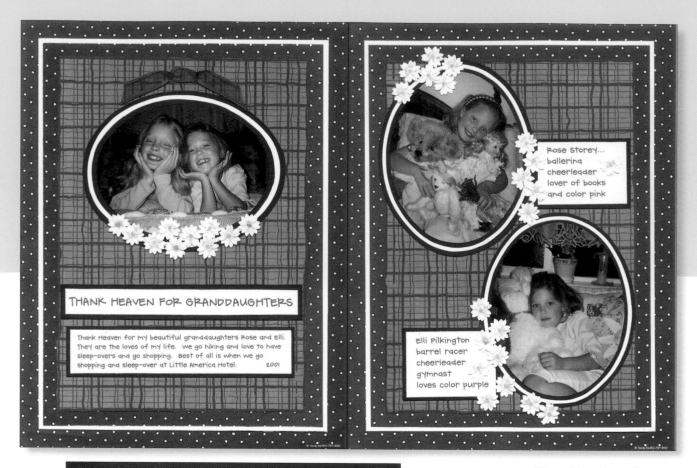

THANK HEAVEN FOR GRANDDAUGHTERS

Thank Heaven for my beautiful granddaughters Rose and Elli. They are the loves of my life. we go hiking and love to have sleep-overs and go shopping. Best of all is when we go shopping and sleep-over at Little America Hotel. 2001

Rose Storey...
ballerina
cheerleader
lover of books
and color pink

Elli Pilkington
barrel racer
cheerleader
gymnast
loves color purple

Man is that he might have Joy. Suilia, our hostess, teaching Gary, Rod and Mike to hula.

"Granddaughters"

Supplies *Patterned paper:* Daisy D's; *Punches:* EK Success (daisy and dot), Fiskars (rectangle); *Computer font:* CK Handprint, "The Best of Creative Lettering" CD Combo, *Creating Keepsakes; Chalk:* Craf-T Products.

"Man Is ..."

Supplies *Patterned papers:* Daisy D's; Hilo Hatties, Island Heritage (shirt paper); *Computer font:* CK Handprint, "The Best of Creative Lettering" CD Combo, *Creating Keepsakes.*

"Growing Up 50's Style"

Supplies *Poodle skirt paper piecing:* Lana's own design *Poodle:* Custom Chenille; *Patterned paper:* The Paper Patch (plaid), PrintWorks (black polka dot); *Punches:* Learn to Play (flower), Memories Forever (circle); *Scissors:* Seagull edge, Fiskars; *Computer font:* CAC Pinafore, downloaded from the Internet; *Pop dots:* All Night Media; *Lettering template:* Blocky, Provo Craft.

"If I could recommend one product to any scrapbooker, it would have to be chalk. I love how you can take a two-dimensional object and give it depth with nothing more than a bit of chalk."

LANA RICKABAUGH • MARYSVILLE, MO

Lana grew up in a creative home and studied art in high school. After graduation, she designed newspaper layouts and advertisements, and she now works as a teddy bear artist and web designer. "I started scrapbooking last year after taking a trip with a friend," shares Lana. "I wanted something to help me remember the fun times we had. It was an easy progression from design to scrapbooking." She and her husband, Phil, are the parents of two adorable boys.

"Hand Prints on the Heart"

Supplies *Patterned paper:* Keeping Memories Alive; *Computer fonts:* Arbuckle Fat, downloaded from the Internet; CK Script, "The Best of Creative Lettering" CD Vol. 1, *Creating Keepsakes; Chalk:* Craf-T Products; *Heart punch:* Learn to Play.

"Autumn's Palette"

Supplies *Computer font:* CK Script, "The Best of Creative Lettering" CD Vol. 1, *Creating Keepsakes; Pop dots:* All Night Media.

"Fly Away Home"

Supplies *Patterned paper:* Scrap Happy; *Vellum:* Memories Forever ; *Chalk:* Craf-T Products; *Computer fonts:* Baby Kruffy, downloaded from the Internet; DJ Eightball and DJ Goo, Fontastic! 2, D.J. Inkers; *Pop dots:* All Night Media.

IDEA TO NOTE: Lana used freezer paper to iron on the muslin, then cut it to the correct size and printed her journaling on it with her computer.

"Hey, Sailor"

Supplies *Patterned paper:* Northern Spy; *Sailboat paper piecing:* Lana's own design; *Computer fonts:* Americana BT and Frosty, downloaded from the Internet; *Pop dots:* All Night Media; *Scissors:* Seagull edge, Fiskars.

"Best Friends Stick Together"

Supplies *Patterned paper:* Freckle Press; *Sandwich:* Lana's own design; *Computer fonts:* CK Journaling, "The Best of Creative Lettering" CD Vol. 2, *Creating Keepsakes*; AlDancing Egypt, package unknown; *Lettering template:* Chunky, Provo Craft; *Pop dots:* All Night Media; *Chalk:* Craf-T Products; *Vellum:* Memories Forever; *Pen:* Gel Pen, Marvy Uchida.

IDEA TO NOTE: Lana created the sandwich by cutting cardstock and layering the pieces in the shape of a sandwich.

"Cats"

Supplies *Vellum:* Memories Forever; *Patterned paper:* Keeping Memories Alive; *Computer font:* CK Journaling, "The Best of Creative Lettering" CD Vol. 2, *Creating Keepsakes*; *Street lamp die cuts:* Ellison.

"Be bold about trying new techniques. Two of my favorites are quilling and beading, because they're so versatile. Explore options so you'll find techniques that help you create pages you can be proud of."

"Adelaide"

Supplies *Computer font:* Script MT Bold, Microsoft Word; *Flowers, hearts and other embellishments:* Lee Anne's own designs; *Other:* For her journaling, Lee Anne used the lyrics from the song "I Hope You Dance" by Lee Ann Womack.

LEE ANNE RUSSELL • BROWNSVILLE, TN

Not only did adoption bring a beautiful daughter, Adelaide, into Lee Anne's family, it also brought scrapbooking. "Before I was introduced to scrapbooking," remembers Lee Anne, "I had promised myself that my children would never lack for knowledge about their lives. When an adoptive mother brought her scrapbook about her experience with international adoption to a class we were attending, I knew scrapbooking was something I would love to do." Lee Anne and her husband, Robbie, also have a son, Haynes.

"One Hail of a Storm"

Supplies *Lettering template:* Dicey, ScrapPagerz; *Computer fonts:* CK Journaling, "The Best of Creative Lettering" CD Vol. 2 and CK Primary, "The Art of Creative Lettering" CD, *Creating Keepsakes*.

"Pool Sharks"

Supplies *Computer fonts:* CK Contemporary Capitals, "The Art of Creative Lettering" CD and CK Journaling, "The Best of Creative Lettering" CD Vol. 2, *Creating Keepsakes*; *Colored pencils:* Prismacolor, Sanford; *Chalk:* Craft-T Products; *Pop dots:* All Night Media; *Pens:* Zig Writer, EK Success; Pigma Micron, Sakura.

"It's a Boy"

Supplies *Patterned paper:* Making Memories; *Vivelle paper:* Wintech; *Lettering template:* Grade School, ScrapPagerz; *Punches:* McGill, Posh Impressions; *Grommets:* Impress Rubber Stamps; *Other:* Ribbon.

"Bottom Dwellers"

Supplies *Lettering template:* Dicey, ScrapPagerz; *Computer font:* Doodle Basic, "PagePrintables" CD Vol. 1, Cock-A-Doodle Design, Inc.; *Other:* Beads, stones and craft eyes.

vivian smith **2001**

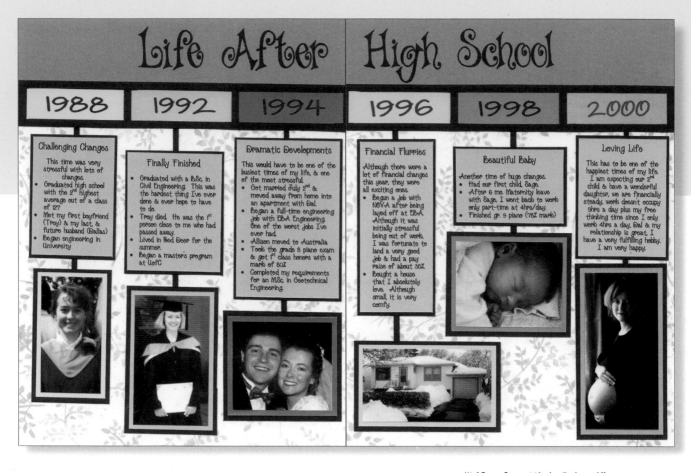

Life After High School

1988 · 1992 · 1994 · 1996 · 1998 · 2000

Challenging Changes

This time was very stressful with lots of changes.
- Graduated high school with the 2nd highest average out of a class of 127
- Met my first boyfriend (Troy) & my last & future husband (Dallas)
- Began engineering in University

Finally Finished

- Graduated with a BSc. in Civil Engineering. This was the hardest thing I've ever done & ever hope to have to do.
- Troy died. He was the 1st person close to me who had passed away.
- Lived in Red Deer for the summer.
- Began a master's program at UofC

Dramatic Developments

This would have to be one of the busiest times of my life, & one of the most stressful.
- Got married July 2nd & moved away from home into an apartment with Dal.
- Began a full-time engineering job with EBA Engineering. One of the worst jobs I've ever had.
- Allison moved to Australia.
- Took the grade 8 piano exam & got 1st class honors with a mark of 80%
- Completed my requirements for an MSc. in Geotechnical Engineering

Financial Flurries

Although there were a lot of financial changes this year, they were all exciting ones.
- Began a job with NOVA after being layed off at EBA. Although it was initially stressful being out of work, I was fortunate to land a very good job & had a pay raise of about 35%.
- Bought a house that I absolutely love. Although small, it is very comfy.

Beautiful Baby

Another time of huge changes.
- Had our first child, Sage.
- After 6 mo. Maternity leave with Sage, I went back to work only part-time at 4hrs/day.
- Finished gr. 9 piano (78% marks)

Loving Life

This has to be one of the happiest times of my life. I am expecting our 2nd child & have a wonderful daughter, we are financially steady, work doesn't occupy this a day plus my free thinking time since I only work 4hrs a day, Dal & my relationship is great, I have a very fulfilling hobby. I am very happy.

"Life after High School"

Supplies *Patterned paper:* Provo Craft; *Computer fonts:* PC Beach Front, "Little Images" HugWare CD, Provo Craft; PC Pizzazz, "For Fonts Sake" HugWare CD, Provo Craft.

"As a scrapbooker who uses the 8½" x 11" format, I've found that if I develop my pictures in the 3½" x 5" size, they require less cropping and fit better on my pages. This size also leaves more room for journaling and embellishments."

VIVIAN SMITH • CALGARY, AB, CANADA

Vivian started scrapbooking in 1999 because she thought it would be a good way to capture the events in her daughter's life. "I've since realized it's wonderful for recording *all* of our family life," says Vivian. "One of the best things about scrapbooking is that it's an excellent creative outlet, and it's so much fun to meet others who share my scrapbooking enthusiasm." Vivian is an engineer for a gas transportation company. She's currently on a one-year maternity leave after the birth of her second daughter.

"The 12 Days of Christmas"

Supplies *Patterned papers:* Carolee's Creations, Provo Craft; *Computer fonts:* PC Old English, "The Font Factory" HugWare CD, Provo Craft; Bradley Hand ITC, Galapagos; *Hole punch:* Marvy Uchida; *Circle cutter:* Fiskars; *Moon, building and star:* Vivian's own designs; *Christmas lights:* Source unknown.

IDEA TO NOTE: Vivian created the snow using Heather Lancaster's crumpled tissue paper tip on page 137. She also used bowls to create the larger-sized circles.

"Christmas Brunch"

Supplies *Patterned papers:* K & Company, Carolee's Creations; *Computer fonts:* Beannie, downloaded from the Internet; Papyrus, Esselte Corporation; Times New Roman and Arial, Monotype Corporation.

"Party Girl"

Supplies *Patterned papers:* Provo Craft, Solum World Paper; *Gold paper:* Canford; *Computer fonts:* PC Line, "Color Me Kids" HugWare CD, Provo Craft; PC Pizzazz, "For Font Sake" HugWare CD, Provo Craft; PC Stone Script, "Little Messages" HugWare CD, Provo Craft; *Scissors:* Wave edge, Provo Craft; *Grommets:* Impress Rubber Stamps.

"Winter Festival"

Supplies *Patterned paper:* Provo Craft; *Computer fonts:* CK Freestyle, "The Best of Creative Lettering" CD Vol 2, *Creating Keepsakes*; Space Woozies, Omega Fontlabs.

IDEA TO NOTE: Sharon created her title and journaling blocks by tearing out leaves from a second piece of patterned paper.

"One Generation Plants the Trees ..."
Supplies *Specialty paper:* Solum World Paper; *Pen:* Zig Millennium, EK Success; *Colored pencils:* Prismacolor, Sanford; *Title and journaling:* Sharon's own designs.

"Experiment with different photo sizes. Reducing photos to wallet size or enlarging them to 8" x 10" can help create dynamic design on your pages."

SHARON SONEFF • SAN CLEMENTE, CA

Sharon has been scrapbooking for 13 years and loves that it synthesizes all of her creative favorites: photography, writing, calligraphy, sketching and watercolors. Her husband, Gerry, is a musician who understands and wholeheartedly supports her need to express herself creatively. She is the full-time mother of two children: eight-year-old Ian, a "remarkably bright and sensitive child" with Asperger's syndrome, and five-year-old Victoria, who has an exuberant love for life and others.

"Little Flower"

Supplies *Patterned paper:* Mara-Mi; *Vellum:* Making Memories; *Pen:* Zig Millennium, EK Success; *Colored pencils:* Prismacolor, Sanford; *Other:* Silk flowers, voile fabric and daisy trim.

IDEA TO NOTE: Sharon sketched and watercolored small whimsical images on the photo mats and in and around the journaling.

"Sweet Age of Innocence"

Supplies *Patterned mulberry paper:* Nature's Handmade Paper; *Vellum:* Paper Cuts; *Pen:* Zig Millennium, EK Success; *Watercolor pencils:* Derwent; *Picket fence:* Provo Craft.

"The Fruit"

Supplies *Mulberry paper:* Black Ink (printed), Personal Stamp Exchange (solid); *Vellum:* Paper Cuts; *Watercolor paper:* Strathmore; *Pen:* Zig Millennium, EK Success; *Colored pencils:* Derwent; *Pop dots:* All Night Media; *Title blocks and fruit:* Sharon's own designs.

IDEA TO NOTE: Sharon created the shade of blue to match the sky in the photo by layering blue vellum and cardstock.

"Sitting on Top of the World"

Supplies *Watercolor paper:* Strathmore; *Vellum:* Paper Reflections; *Pen:* Pigma Micron, Sakura; *Pop dots:* All Night Media; *Watercolor pencils:* Derwent.

"Keeping Cool at the Country Club"

Supplies *Vellum:* Papers by Catherine; *Beads:* Roberts Crafts; *Die cuts:* Papers By Design; *Pop dots:* All Night Media; *Pen:* Zig Writer, EK Success; *Lettering template:* Source unknown.

"Try looking at the process of creating layouts as decorating, just like you would decorate a home or a wall. This will help you choose an appropriate color scheme and create a layout that's pleasing to the eye."

KRIS STANGER • ST. GEORGE, UT

Kris has been scrapbooking since the birth of her daughter in 1995. She's a stay-at-home mom to Kennedy, age five, and Kinkade, age three. Kris and her husband, Corey, have been married for 11 years and love "living in the desert." In addition to scrapbooking, Kris loves the outdoors, hiking and swimming.

"Sassy and Classy"

Supplies *Patterned paper:* Source unknown; *Lettering idea:* Contemporary Capitals, *The Art of Creative Lettering*, Creating Keepsakes Books; *Colored pencils:* Memory Pencils, EK Success; *Beads:* Mini Hill; *Stickers:* me & my BIG ideas; *Ribbon:* Harvest Crafts; *Pen:* Zig Writer, EK Success *Pop dots:* All Night Media.

"Kinkade"

Supplies *Mulberry paper:* Personal Stamp Exchange; *Lettering template:* Source unknown; *Computer font:* Dauphin, WordPerfect; *Stickers:* me & my BIG ideas.

"Nature"

Supplies *Handmade paper:* Papers by Catherine; *Vellum:* Paper Adventures; *Greeting card and quote:* Marjolein Bastin; *Computer font:* Girls Are Weird, downloaded from the Internet.

"Dance, Dream, Make Believe"

Supplies *Vellum:* Paper Cuts; *Mulberry paper:* Personal Stamp Exchange; *Computer fonts:* CK Cursive "The Best of Creative Lettering" CD Vol 2 and CK Handprint, "The Best of Creative Lettering" CD Combo, *Creating Keepsakes; Beads:* Mini Hill; *Flowers:* Kris's own design; *Pop dots:* All Night Media.

"Sooner or Later"

Supplies *Paper:* Scrap-Ease ; *Computer fonts:* Girls Are Weird, downloaded from the Internet; CK Fun, "The Art of Creative Lettering" CD, *Creating Keepsakes; Grommets:* Dritz; *Photo-editing software:* Microsoft Picture It!; *Transparency:* IBM; *Other:* Raffia and beads.

"My favorite tip is a mental one: Don't let anyone

make you feel like you're scrapbooking the 'wrong' way.

Scrapbooking is a purely personal thing. Scrapbooking is all

about what's important to you."

PAM TALLUTO • ROCHESTER HILLS, MI

Pam has always had a love for art and design. "I went to interior design school and could happily decorate and redecorate my home for the rest of my life, but that can be a little expensive!" laughs Pam. In 1997, while wandering the aisles of a craft store in search of a less expensive hobby, she stumbled upon an issue of *Creating Keepsakes* magazine. More than four years later, Pam is hooked. "Oddly enough, scrapbooking is very similar to interior design," says Pam. "Both use the same principles of design: balance, rhythm, emphasis, scale and harmony." Pam loves to scrapbook photos of her two children, Marc and Sara; their pets, Abby the Golden Retriever and Nathan the cat; and her husband Denny.

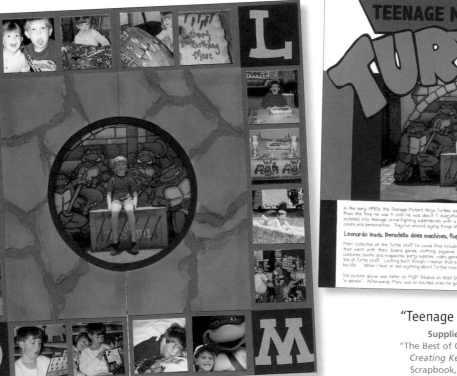

"When?"

Supplies *Leather paper:* Provo Craft; *Lettering template:* Fancy Block, Provo Craft; *Brad fasteners:* Stockwell; *Computer fonts:* CK Pretty and CK Italic, "The Art of Creative Lettering" CD, *Creating Keepsakes.*

Pam 'n Denny · Spring 2000

"Teenage Mutant Ninja Turtles"

Supplies *Computer font:* CK Toggle, "The Best of Creative Lettering" CD Vol. 2, *Creating Keepsakes; Lettering template:* Scrapbook, Provo Craft; *Circle template:* Coluzzle, Provo Craft; *Inside title and turtle shell:* Pam's own designs.

"The More Things Change"

Supplies *Wood paper:* Provo Craft; *Computer font:* CK Toggle, "The Best of Creative Lettering" CD Vol. 2, *Creating Keepsakes; Beads:* Michael's Arts and Crafts; *Index tabs:* Avery Dennison; *Circle template:* Coluzzle, Provo Craft; *Basketball floor:* Pam's own design.

"Cedar Point"

Supplies *Patterned paper:* Provo Craft ; *Title:* From a brochure; *Computer font:* CK Toggle, "The Best of Creative Lettering" CD Vol. 2, *Creating Keepsakes; Pop dots:* All Night Media; *Circle cutter:* Coluzzle, Provo Craft; *Star punch:* Family Treasures.

julie turner 2001

"Shoot your photographs closer, and snap a lot of photos! When you get closer to your subject, it's easier to capture emotion and it helps cut out distracting backgrounds. It's so much easier to create striking layouts when you have great photos to scrapbook."

"Our Home Page"

Supplies *Stamp ink:* VersaColor, Tsukineko; *Embossing powders:* Gary M. Burlin and Company, Suze Weinberg; *Rubber stamps:* PrintWorks; *Rectangle punch:* NanKong; *Ribbon:* Midori; *Pop dots:* All Night Media.

JULIE TURNER • GILBERT, AZ

One of Julie's earliest memories is sitting on the floor of her parents' bedroom sorting through piles of old photos in their bottom dresser drawer. Although she began putting photos in albums as a young girl, Julie didn't start "creative" scrapbooking until she started a home-school yearbook for her children. Scrapbooking quickly became more than a way to record her children's progress. "I never thought I would forget all the little things they did, but as life continues on and memories keep building, you forget," explains Julie. "Scrapbooking is my way of journaling our lives so we won't forget all those precious times." Julie and her husband, Joel, are the parents of three great kids. In her spare time, she enjoys teaching classes at her local scrapbook store.

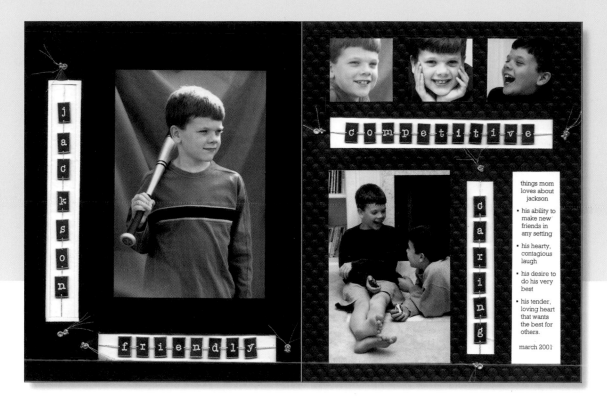

"Jackson"

Supplies *Patterned paper:* Memory Lane ; *Computer font:* Rockwell Light, WordPro; *Rectangle punch:* NanKong; *Grommets:* Coffee Break Design; *Silver beads:* Westrim; *Embroidery floss:* DMC.

"Our Valley Forge"

Supplies *Handmade paper:* Memory Lane; *Hot Foil Pen:* Staedtler; *Computer font:* Tempus Sans, WordPro; *Embossing powder:* Gary M. Burlin and Company; *Star studs:* Memory Lane; *Other:* Little Classic Sealing Wax, Hampton Art Stamps; jute and hemp.

IDEA TO NOTE: Julie created a small book and attached it to her layout so she could add more photos and journaling.

johnathan daniel turner

creative
musical
kind
big brother
inquisitive John
funny
generous

When we toured Gettysburg, Jillian was too young to comprehend the sacrifices made on the battlefield. She danced down the trails, picking flowers at every stop. 5/00

"John"

Supplies *Patterned paper:* Savior Faire (green and cream), Memory Lane (blue handmade); *Computer font:* Rockwell Light, WordPro; *Pen:* Zig Writer, EK Success; *Other:* Slide file page, Print File; *Embroidery floss:* DMC.

"Jillian at Gettysburg"

Supplies *Vellum:* Provo Craft; *Pen:* Zig Writer, EK Success; *Grommets:* Coffee Break Design; *Craft wire:* Artistic Wire Ltd.; *Star studs:* Memory Lane.

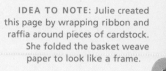

IDEA TO NOTE: Julie created this page by wrapping ribbon and raffia around pieces of cardstock. She folded the basket weave paper to look like a frame.

"Jillian's Hat"

Supplies *Handmade paper:* Memory Lane; *Pen:* Zig Writer, EK Success; *Ribbon:* Offray.

"Jillian Claire"

Supplies *Patterned paper:* Memory Lane; *Computer font:* CK Script, "The Best of Creative Lettering" CD Vol. 1, *Creating Keepsakes; Embossing powder:* Ink It!; *Ribbon:* Midori; *Pop dots:* All Night Media.

IDEA TO NOTE: Julie printed the words on vellum then embossed them with gold embossing powder.